FESTIVALS
of the
WORLD

FESTIVALS of the WORLD
was produced for Transedition Limited
by Bender Richardson White

Project Manager: Lionel Bender
Designer and Art Editor: Ben White
Text Editor: Michael March
Picture Research: Cathy Stastny & Lionel Bender

Production: Kim Richardson and Richard Johnson
Cover Design and Make-up: Ben White

This edition first published in Great Britain in 2002 by Hodder Wayland,
an imprint of Hodder Children's Books.

10 9 8 7 6 5 4 3 2 1

A catalogue record for this book is available from the British Library.

ISBN 0 7502 3934 4

Printed and bound by Mondadori, Italy

Hodder Children's Books
A division of Hodder Headline Ltd,
338 Euston Road, London NW1 3BH

Picture Credits

The producers and publishers are grateful to the following for permission to reproduce copyright material:
t = top, b = bottom, c = centre, l = left, r = right . COR = Corbis Images, Circa = Circa Photo Library.
Page 3: Circa/Zbigniew Kosc. 5: Circa/William Holtby. 6: COR/John Heseltine. 7t: COR/O'Brien Productions/Kevin Cozad. 7b: Circa/John Smith. 8: Circa/Bipin J. Mistry. 9: COR/Vittoriano Rastelli. 11: COR/Enzo & Paolo Ragazzini. 12: PhotoDisc Inc.. 13t: PhotoDisc Inc.. 13b: TRIP/H. Rogers. 14–15: COR/Lindsay Hebberd. 15t: COR/Penny Tweedie. 18–19, 20: Circa/Barrie Searle. 21: Wayland Publishes Limited. 22: Circa/Barrie Searle. 22–23: TRIP/H. Rogers. 23: COR/Nathan Benn. 26: COR/Ted Spiegal. 27, 28, 28–29, 29, 30, 32: Circa/Barrie Searle. 33: TRIP/S. Shapiro. 34: Wayland Publishers Limited. 36: COR/Richard T. Nowitz. 37l, 38r: Circa/Barrie Searle. 38: Christine Osborne Pictures. 39: COR/David Rubinger. 40–41: Circa. 42: Fernleigh Books/Transedition/Steve Gorton. 43: Circa. 45t: COR/Craig Lovell. 46: Circa/John Fryer. 48: Stockholm Information Service. 49: Hutchison Library/N. Michalowsky. 50 Fernleigh Books/Transedition/Steve Gorton. 51tr: COR/Sandy Felsenthal. 51b: COR/Becky Luigart–Stayner. 53: COR/Craig Aurness. 54: Circa/Zbigniew Kosc. 55: Circa/John Smith. 56l: Circa/John Fryer. 56r: COR/Dean Conger. 57: Circa. 58: Circa/Zbigniew Kosc. 59l: Circa/John Fryer. 59b: Christine Osborne Pictures. 60: Circa. 62: Wayland Publishers Ltd./Ville de Nice. 63: Wayland Publishers Ltd. 64tr: COR/Hulton–Deutsch Collection. 64bl: COR/Steve Chenn. 65: COR/ChromoSohm Inc./Joseph Sohm. 66–67: Circa/Zbigniew Kosc. 68: COR/Earl & Nazima Kowali. 69, 71t: Circa/William Holtby. 71b: The Hutchison Library/I. Tree. 72: COR/Jeffrey L. Retman. 74, 74–75: Circa/William Holtby. 76: TRIP. 78: PhotoDisc Inc. 79: COR/Chris Hellier. 80–81, 82tl: Circa/Bipin J. Mistry. 82b: Circa/John Smith. 83, 85t: Circa/William Holtby. 85b: Circa/John Smith. 86, 88, 89: Circa/William Holtby. 90l: Circa/Bipin J. Mistry. 90r: Circa/William Holtby. 91: Circa. 92–93: Circa/Robin Beeche. 93tr, 94: TRIP/Dinodia. 95t, 95b: Circa/Bipin J. Mistry. 96: Circa. 97l: Circa/William Holtby. 97r: Circa/John Smith. 98: Circa/William Holtby. 98–99, 101t, 101b, 102, 103: Circa/John Smith. 104–105, 107tl, 107br, 108, 109tr: Circa/William Holtby. 109bl: Circa. 110, 111, 112, 112–113: Circa/William Holtby. 115t: COR/Adam Woolfitt. 115b, 117l, 117r: Circa/William Holtby. 118: Circa. 119: Circa/John Smith. 120: Wayland Publishers Limited. 121: Circa/Rebecca Thompson. 122: Circa. 123: Eye Ubiquitous/John Dakers. 124, 125, 126l, 126r: Circa/William Holtby. 129: Circa/T. Halbertsma. 130, 131: Circa/John Smith. 132: Circa/Bipin J. Mistry. 133: Circa/William Holtby. 134, 136: Circa/John Smith. 137l: Circa/Twin Studio. 137r: Circa/John Smith. 138: Circa. 139: Circa/T. Halbertsma. 140: Circa/Martin Palmer. 142, 143: Circa. 144, 145: Circa/William Holtby. 146: Hutchison Photo Library. 147: COR/Tony Arruza. 148: Circa/Martin Palmer. 150: Circa/William Holtby. 152: Circa/Barrie Searle. 153: Wayland Publishers Limited/Jimmy Holmes. 154: Circa.

Every effort has been made to contact copyright holders of any material reproduced in this book. Omissions or errors will be rectified in subsequent printings if notice is given in writing to Transedition Limited.

Cover credits: (top row, left to right) Fernleigh Books/Transedition/Steve Gorton; Stockholm Information Service; Fernleigh Books/Transedition/Steve Gorton. (centre left) Fernleigh Books/Transedition/Steve Gorton. (centre right) Circa. (bottom left) Circa. (bottom right) Zefa/Stockmarket. (back) Circa/William Holtby.

Artwork (book and cover) Reconstruction illustrations by John James. Maps by Stefan Chabluk.

FESTIVALS *of the* WORLD

The Illustrated Guide to Celebrations, Customs, Events and Holidays

Elizabeth Breuilly • Joanne O'Brien • Martin Palmer
Consultant Editor • Professor Martin E. Marty

an imprint of Hodder Children's Books

FOREWORD

Are we humans 'hard-wired' to have festivals? Does celebrating them appeal to deep needs in our nature? Whether or not we can answer those questions with a clear scientific 'yes,' it is clear that observing festivals is nearly universal in the human story.

Being imaginative, people everywhere put energy into repeating festivals or inventing new ones. These may be secular, which means they take note of things that everyone can check out easily in experience: football matches, historical pageants, local fairs, parades or anniversaries.

More often, however, the festivals are sacred. They observe that which we picture being behind the scenes. They recognize gods, angels or ghostly characters who act beyond our observation. But people believe that what we do and what they do somehow connect, as through God-pleasing actions, private prayers or deep thinking.

Most religions relate to groups, so religious festivals lead to engagement through rites and practices that bring them together and, they feel, ennoble otherwise ordinary life.

Anyone who has ever looked forward to big events such as weddings or has looked back fondly to others, such as having won a prize, will know how valuable people find it to deal with the really Big Events that they believe have gone on 'behind the scenes', beyond the senses.

So we have festivals. This book carefully, almost lovingly, deals with the tastes of festivals that are rich with foods; with smells, as with incense; with sights designed to produce awe; and with sounds, often rhythmic, to promote dance.

Festivals of the World celebrates the celebrations of the major religions of the world and takes some looks at some smaller ones. It is urgent that we citizens of the globe, crowded ever closer to people who observe festivals other than our own, or are aware of such, thanks to mass media, learn to appreciate what the others are doing. That task is never easy.

The philosopher Spinoza once said that in dealing with complex realities he found it necessary not to laugh, not to cry, not to denounce, but to understand. Misunderstandings can be lethal. We often hear of occasions where celebrators of festivals use them against others, or where two sets of celebrators and their interests collide, particularly over the use of sacred space. (One need only mention the word, 'Jerusalem,' to show how rites and ceremonies, sacred places and festivals, can induce clashes.) We hope that projects like this one will help promote understanding and help lessen conflict over festivals and faiths.

What this book cannot do is provide directories of the places and leaders attractive to people of those other faiths. Most who read and use this book will know that often one telephone call, one letter, one personal request is likely to lead to an invitation to look in on people and festivals that are different. The fortunate visitors might even be asked to march or eat or dance with the festive ones. Readers of this book will know more of what to do when an invitation comes. So, read and celebrate.

Martin E. Marty
Professor of Religion, Chicago University, USA.

AUTHORS

Elizabeth Breuilly holds a BA degree in Language from the Universtiy of York, and has written extensively on religion for an educational and general readership.

Joanne O'Brien studied Comparative Religion and Ancient Near Eastern Religions at the University of Manchester, and holds an MA degree in Theology. She has written a wide range of books that explore both relationships between faiths and between religion and secular society. Joanne O'Brien also runs Circa Photo Library, a commercial agency specializing in photographs of worship in the community and at home, festivals, religious buildings, religious art and artefacts from all over the world. Many of Circa's picture are used in this book.

Martin Palmer studied Theology at the University of Cambridge, specializing in Chinse and Japanese studies, and holds an MA. He founded ICOREC (International Consultancy on Religion, Education & Culture) in 1983.

Consultant Editor

Professor Martin E. Marty is a Professor of the History of Modern Christianity at the University of Chicago. He has written over 30 books and is a respected authority and writer on religion today.

The Authors and Consultant Editor also worked collaboratively to produce *Religions of the World*, a companion volume to *Festivals of the World* and *Mythologies of the World* also published by Hodder Wayland.

Contents

Feasting, Fasting and Fun

SYMBOLS AND FOOD
It is not just stories that are experienced at festival time; the themes and teachings of the festival being celebrated are also given expression. Very many faiths have a festival in which the lighting of lamps or candles symbolizes the new light brought to the world, whether by the birth of Jesus, by the enlightenment of the Buddha, by the just and rightful rule of Rama and Sita or according to some other core teaching. Food, too – the centre-piece of most human celebrations – carries an extra function. Many festival foods symbolize the sweetness of some aspect of the faith, or the bitterness of some experience, such as the bitter herbs eaten by Jews at the Seder meal to symbolize the bitterness of the slavery of their ancestors. There are also 'picture foods' like the mince pies of Christmas, which were originally made in the shape of the manger where the baby Jesus was laid. This book includes a few recipes for festival food, but these can give no more than an indication of its celebratory and symbolic value.

It is no accident that the English word 'holiday' derives from 'holy day'. Down the ages, across all the great faiths of the world, people have celebrated the major days of their faiths as times for fun, feasting, travel, reunion and general enjoyment. As far back as we can discover, people have recognized the need to relieve the monotony of the ordinary working life with special days – days when the normal pattern of work is broken and everyone is permitted, even required, to stop work and enjoy themselves instead.

We have no idea what prehistoric people might have celebrated, but we do know that they had festivals. For example, the long barrows of the Neolithic period – some 5–6,000 years' old – show strong evidence of food preparation and celebration.

An overview

This book looks at the ways in which major religious traditions celebrate the events and teachings of their faiths. These vary enormously between religions and across the world, and many have also changed over time. Of course, by no means all the religious festivals have been covered here, and there are many other ways of celebrating the ones that have been included.

Festivals are the concrete expression of the religious life from which they spring, and the most fascinating windows into a faith. As well as being times of relaxation, times set aside from the ordinary working year, festivals are living reminders to the faithful of what their religion teaches, and an assertion to the rest of humanity about the value of those teachings.

Putting on a show

In all the major faiths, the yearly cycle of festivals not only recounts a story, but reflects on the meaning of that story in relation to the pattern of the universe, the nature of God and the hopes, fears, frail-

The tradition of dancing round a Maypole in springtime, found in different forms in many parts of Europe, is probably a pre-Christian celebration of fertility.

ties and potential of human beings. Through drama, ritual, liturgy or dance, festivals repeat key stories of the faith; they involve symbolic foods and activities that encapsulate core concepts in a way that can be grasped and witnessed by outsiders.

For much of the year, religions are practised in quieter, often enclosed ways. But at festival time, it is as if the faith is putting on a show, offering everyone the chance to see and hear what is of greatest importance and held most dear to its adherents. Festivals such as saints' days, Divali or Chinese New Year are public events, celebrated with street processions through towns and cities when everyone and anyone is invited to come and join in the fun.

Storytelling and faith

Although faiths develop principles, creeds, formulations and explanatory writing to help them pass on their teachings without distortion, they are rooted in lived experience, the experiences of ordinary people, without which they would die. Few believers are theologians. Most people understand their faith not through great philosophical and theological teachings but through the embodiment of these teachings in stories, myths, legends and symbols.

Storytelling is crucial to most festivals. However, the stories are not just told; they are acted, re-enacted, sung, danced and represented in visual arts ranging from stone-carving to embroidery. Whether it be a Nativity play for Christmas in the United States or a performance of Chinese opera telling the story of Kuan Ti, the god of war, in China, the purpose of such festivals is to remind people regularly of the key stories of the faith.

Sometimes those present are simply observers of the drama or listeners to the story, but often they are participants. At the festival of Sukkot, a Jewish family does not just hear or see how their ancestors once lived in shelters during their wanderings; they themselves move into a temporary shelter, experiencing the precarious feeling of a roof partly open to the sky.

These cookies, cut to represent stars, bells, trees and a stable, illustrate parts of the Christmas story and traditions.

At any Sikh festival, five committed Sikhs take the part of five men in Sikh history who were prepared to die in defence of their faith.

The Themes of Life

COMMON THEMES
Although the number of festivals held throughout the world can seem overwhelming, and their variety confusing, most can be categorized in terms of a few major themes that help build up a picture of the faith in question.

Nearly all faiths have a cycle of festivals that reflect a whole range of human emotions and human experiences, as seen from the point of view of a particular religion or faith. People cannot be expected to be mindful of all the teachings and ideas of their faith every day of the week. Instead, through cycles of fasting and festivals, the faithful are asked to put time aside to think more deeply about core beliefs, founder figures, great teachers and fundamental themes of life.

The seasons

Possibly the oldest festivals in the world are those whose roots lie in celebrating the seasons, as in the story from Greek mythology of Demeter, the goddess of the earth and harvests, and her daughter Persephone, who was captured by Hades, the god of the underworld. Demeter's mourning brought winter upon the land, until the other gods intervened. They negotiated an agreement with Hades whereby Persephone would spend six months of every year on earth with her mother, and six months in the underworld with Hades, giving rise to the seasonal cycle of summer and winter.

Major or minor themes of many festivals include springtime and the renewal of life, as in the Christian Easter (whose English name derives from Eostre, the pagan deity of spring); the harvest and thanksgiving, as in the Jewish festival Shavuot; midwinter and fire or light, as in Chinese New Year celebrations.

History

Many festivals celebrate or commemorate key historical events of the faith, such as the founding of the Sikh Khalsa at Baisakhi in 1699; or the escape of the Jewish people from Egypt in prehistoric times, which is remembered, re-enacted and celebrated at Pesach (Passover).

Remembering the past and learning from it is an important aspect of religion. Through special events of the past, the nature of the relationship between the faithful and God can be expressed. The historical and the symbolic are combined, as for example in the Christian celebration of Christmas. No one knows exactly when Jesus was born, but the Church,

The Hindu festival of Divali celebrates the culmination of the great epic story of Ramayana, encouraging reflection on themes of love, loyalty and betrayal, bravery and gentleness.

needing to celebrate the actual, physical birth of Christ, adopted and adapted the traditional Roman festival of the birthday of the sun – 25 December.

Fundamental questions

Festivals also offer an opportunity for focusing on the big issues of life, such as the struggle between good and evil or what happens after death. Buddhists, for example, by reflecting on the birth, enlightenment and passing into nirvana of the historical Buddha, are confronted with the fundamental questions of the meaning of life, the inevitability of suffering and the way to meet it and be released from it. These issues are complex, disturbing and profound, but through the rituals of a festival like Wesak they can be faced.

Festivals such as the Chinese Hungry Ghost festival, or Hallowe'en, with its roots in both Christianity and Celtic religion, allow people to confront the frightening and painful questions of what happens after death, and the demands that the dead make upon the living.

New Year festivals happen at different times of the year in different calendars, but they nearly all give expression to the human need to reflect on the past, to put behind the bad things of the previous year and to make resolutions and good wishes for the year ahead.

Through festivals and the stories enacted around them, faiths illustrate the need to strive for good in the world and the way to undertake that struggle. Festivals offer each individual a model of how to behave in the struggles that we all encounter in our own lives.

LOCAL CELEBRATIONS

Every faith has its universal festivals, but there are also other special events. Often the special character of local communities and local places is celebrated.

In Christianity, for example, many churches have a saint's name. When it is the feast day of that saint, for example, St Andrew on 30 November, churches dedicated to him may hold a local festival. In China, some Taoist temples are dedicated to a deity that is worshipped only in a particular town or village. His or her feast day will involve three or more days of theatre, offerings, partying and rituals intended for local people, though neighbouring communities may also be invited.

In India, the festivals of deities associated with a particular area may attract thousands of pilgrims. In the city of Puri, in Orissa, people come from hundreds of kilometres away to honour the god Jagganath, whose image is taken from his temple and carried around the city on a huge chariot.

At Easter, thousands of pilgrims gather in St.Peter's Square, Rome, to hear the Pope deliver his annual Easter message from the balcony of St. Peter's Basilica. As head of the Catholic Church, the Pope's message is usually broadcast worldwide.

Counting the Days

PHENOMENON CALENDARS
Sometimes a yearly calendar has been founded on the observation of some local, natural phenomenon. For example, the ancient Japanese calendar started the year with the flowering of the peach trees, and many such markers are still used informally. The arrival of migrant birds or animals, the mating behaviour of animals or the coming into leaf or flower of a plant species are often used as indicators that another yearly cycle has begun.

Throughout the world, in many different periods, people of different cultures and faiths have tried to make sure that they celebrate their faith and their festivals at the correct time – at the same time as other communities elsewhere or at the time laid down in their scriptures or by their traditional teachers.

Muslims watch the sky to see the first sliver of the new moon, which will signal the start of a new month, and careful rules govern whose word can be accepted when a sighting is reported. Jews outside Israel traditionally celebrate their festivals for one day longer than those who live there. This arises from the days of slow communications, when they wanted to be sure that at least one of the days would be the right day and would be celebrated by Jews worldwide. Keeping track of the days, and the natural phenomena that mark and measure the passage of time, is no easy business, and different cultures have developed different ways of doing it. The majority of calendars have some connection with religious belief, either current or arising from an earlier culture. In the French Revolution (1789–99) an attempt was made to create a wholly secular calendar, with ten days in a 'week', and non-lunar months that were named according to the state of nature or the weather, such as Pluviôse (rainy month) and Floréal (flowery month).

Cycles within cycles

When does a new day begin? Three points in the day are easy to observe: sunrise, sunset and midday. In most cultures midday would be an awkward time to start a new day. Thus, the Hindu calendar starts the day at sunrise while the Jewish and Islamic calendars start at sunset. The Christian calendar, which arose from earlier Greek and Roman models and has now been adopted as a secular calendar worldwide, starts the day at midnight. Hence, many Christian festivals start with a vigil where worshippers keep awake through the night, or at least until after midnight, so as to be awake and worshipping as the feast day starts. The Chinese calendar also starts a day at midnight.

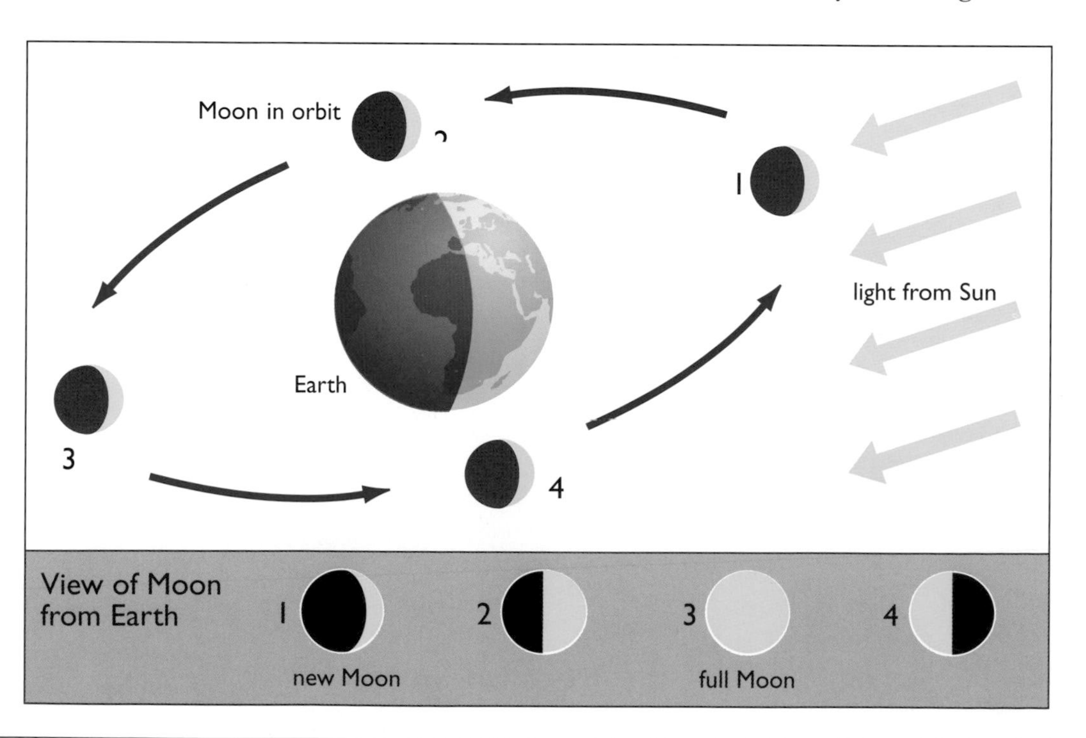

The apparent change in shape of the moon over a month is due to its orbit round the earth. The moon always has one side illuminated by the sun – as does the earth – but most of the time only part of the bright side can be seen from earth. The tilt towards the sun of the earth on its axis of rotation leads to the existence of the seasons.

A week of seven days has no observable marker. The origins of the seven-day week for Jews, Christians and Muslims are derived from scripture, in which God is described as creating the world in six days and resting on the seventh. Each of these faiths takes a different day of the week as the one set aside for worship, and the Jewish and Islamic systems give no names, only numbers, to the other six days. However, a seven-day week also appears in the Chinese and some other ancient calendars, so its origin is not solely scriptural.

The time from one new moon to the next is about 29½ days, and may vary by several hours. Any system of counting days and months needs a complicated alternation of 29- and 30-day months. This is a feature of many traditional calendars, with the length of the months either worked out beforehand in almanacs, as in the Chinese calendar, or regulated by actual sightings of the moon, as in the original Hindu, Jewish and Islamic calendars (some in these faiths now use astronomical calculations). Hindus and Buddhists may use different calendars in different areas, some taking the new moon as the start of the month, others the full moon. Christian and secular calendars have abandoned all connection between the phases of the moon and the calendar months.

SEASONS AND YEARS

From the earliest records, it is clear that people have observed the sun and the stars to predict and measure the seasons, often basing their cycle of festivals on these observations and on the rhythm of the farming year, which spelt prosperity or starvation.

One of the most accurate ways of measuring the passage of a year is by observing the position of the sun when it rises, in relation to the stars, which, from the point of view of the earth, appear to revolve in a steady circle through the year. From very ancient times, astronomers and astrologers have divided this circle into twelve sections, each named after a constellation. In the system derived from Greek astronomy, many of these constellations were named after animals, such as Aries the ram or Taurus the bull, so the whole circle came to be known as the zodiac, meaning 'circle of animals'.

In the Hindu calendar, which is mainly lunar, the twelve signs of the zodiac are used to date certain religious festivals, or determine auspicious days. For example, the Sankranti, or day when the sun passes from one sign of the zodiac to the next, is considered an auspicious day and is a time for ritual bathing in sacred rivers.

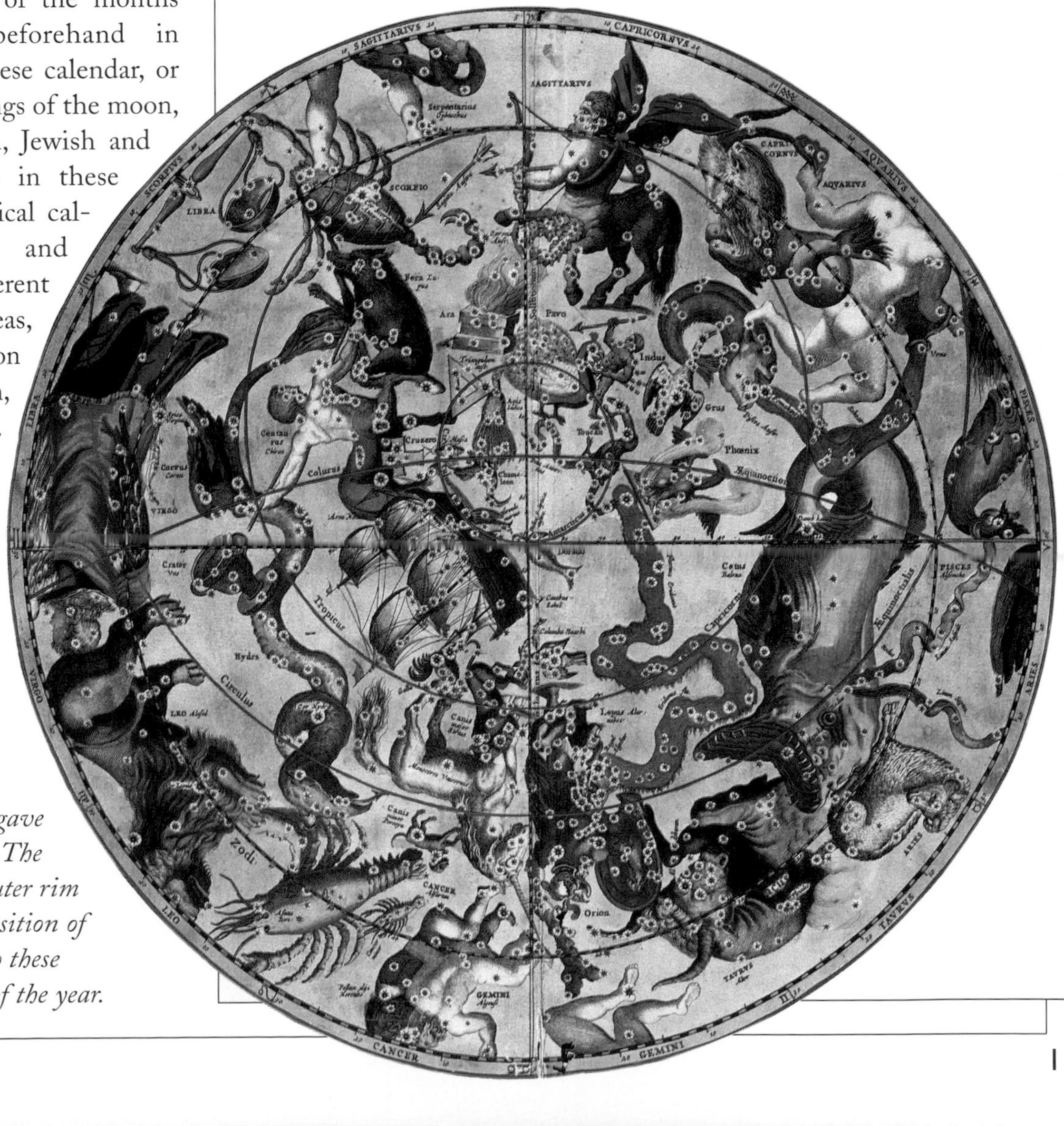

This Renaissance Italian illustration shows how the shapes of the constellations gave rise to their animal names. The constellations around the outer rim form the zodiac, and the position of the rising sun in relation to these gives an accurate measure of the year.

Calendars around the World

To be a usable measure of time, the year must somehow be divided up. The difficulty is that it is neither an exact number of days nor an exact number of months. However, although individual variations in calendars are extremely complex, there have generally been three approaches to the calendar problem namely, solar, lunar and lunisolar.

Reading the Calendar
The diagrams in this book illustrating the calendars used by different faiths can only be an indication of how each calendar works in principle, and how the festivals follow each other through the year. In particular, the relationship shown to the western, secular calendar cannot be used to predict the date of a particular religious festival. Calendars giving accurate dates are published annually by several organizations, some of them listed in the Bibliography.

Solar calendar

The calendar adopted by Christianity, and subsequently by the secular and business world, is based on the year as measured from one equinox to the next. Days are fitted into this in a pattern of ordinary years (365 days) and leap years (366 days). The Baha'is also use a solar calendar, but divide it into 'months' of nineteen days each.

This basic principle of a solar calendar was adopted by the Roman Empire under Julius Caesar. However, because of inaccuracies in measuring the length of the year, adjustments have been needed from time to time to keep the calendar in line with the solar year. The adjustment first authorized by Pope Gregory XIII, in 1582, entailed taking several days out of a year to bring the calendar back in line with the solar year. This change was only gradually adopted in Europe over several centuries, as many people resisted, believing that they were losing days out of their lives.

Lunar and lunisolar calendars

The Islamic calendar as laid down in the Qur'an is a lunar calendar, which bears no consistent relation to the solar year. There are twelve lunar months, which regulate religious observance, and these move in relation to the solar year by ten or eleven days each year.

The Jewish, Chinese and Hindu calendars, among many others, are based on lunar months. However, to keep the yearly cycle of religious observance in line with the solar year, every so often a whole month is added, giving a year of thirteen lunar months instead of the usual twelve. The rules for adding this month vary between calendars.

Counting the years

How to distinguish one year from another? Again, different cultures have developed different ways. Perhaps the most common is to count years from some point that is regarded as epoch-making,

The four corners of the Great Pyramid at Giza, in Egypt, are aligned on the four compass points, and its north passage seems to relate to the movement of the North Star. Other Egyptian pyramids and temples appear to have some astronomical or calendrical significance.

that is, the beginning of a new state of affairs. Jews date years from a calculation about the creation of the world, based on Biblical sources, Christians from the supposed date of the birth of Jesus, and Muslims from the Prophet Muhammad's move to Medina. Other events that have been used as markers include the foundation of a city or the accession of a king. Another system is to name each year according to a unique event in that year.

The Chinese system works by the interaction of two cycles, one of ten years, the other of twelve, so that the combination of both only recurs every sixty years. Markers such as the emperor on the throne at the time, or some other event, were then used to distinguish a year in one cycle from the same year in another cycle.

ANCIENT MARKERS

In many parts of the world there are ancient structures that seem to have a correlation with the position of the sun or planets at particular times of year, and may have been used as markers for a religious or agricultural calendar.

Some of the best-known of these are Stonehenge in southern England, the Egyptian pyramids and the great stone markings known as 'medicine circles' in the Rocky Mountains of North America. Although the exact use and significance of all of these shapes is unknown, the immense trouble taken by early peoples to construct them shows the importance they attached to keeping track of seasonal movements.

The enormous stones of Stonehenge, brought from many kilometres away and erected on Salisbury Plain, UK, around 2000 BC, show evidence of astronomical orientation. On midsummer morning, the sun shines into the centre of the horseshoe shape.

Tonatiuh, the sun god, is depicted at the centre of this Aztec calendar or Sun Stone. The Aztecs believed that the world had already passed through four previous creations or suns that are represented in the ring around the sun god. Their civilization was now in its fifth creation, called the Earthquake Sun.

Evolution, Adaptation and Change

However deeply rooted festivals may be in ancient beliefs and universal themes, they change with the communities that celebrate them. For example, a typical Christmas in the UK or United States is a combination of film, mythology, folk legend, advertising and the Nativity story from the Bible. Over the last century these elements have combined to produce a Christmas that would be almost unrecognizable to someone from an earlier age.

As faiths move beyond their traditional boundaries, their festivals have to adapt. For instance, Wesak, in Buddhism, has become the main festival for Buddhists living in areas that are not culturally Buddhist. It is hard to give proper time to a great festival in a country that does not acknowledge its significance. Thus, for most Muslims in the West, the fasting of Ramadan and the three-day festivities of Eid are celebrated very differently from how they would be in, for example, Jordan or Malaysia. In China, Chinese New Year is a fifteen-day public holiday; in the West it is squeezed into a weekend. Many faith communities have to adapt their festivals to the working week of the country they are living in.

Changes of focus

Traditionally, religion in one form or another has provided the impetus for festivals, but other factors such as national pride or national history are increasingly coming into play. Festivals also change in their focus and in the people involved. For example, Thanksgiving Day in the United States began life as a Christian celebration of the harvest amongst a small community. Today, it has become a much more universal and national festival, when American families of all faiths, or none, get together to dine and to celebrate.

Whereas some pagan festivals from Europe, such as Eostre, were taken over and adopted by the early Christian missionaries, some originally Christian festivals have become far removed from their Christian origins. For example, Carnival and Mardi Gras now have very little connection with the beginning of Lent, while the traditions associated with Hallowe'en owe more to pre-Christian beliefs than to the commemoration of the Christian saints that gives the day its name.

Even more curious traditions have grown up around 1 May –May Day. Long

At this Independence Day celebration in New Delhi, India, a parade marches past a large image of Gandhi, who campaigned tirelessly for Indian independence.

after the coming of Christianity, northern Europe continued to celebrate May Day as a festival of fertility and courtship, with singing and dancing, choosing a May Queen, and sometimes a May King, and various courtship rituals between young men and women.

Such traditions were ignored by the International Socialist congress of 1889, which designated 1 May as International Labour Day. This aspect of May Day was celebrated by the Soviet Union and other communist countries and by workers' organizations outside the communist bloc. The two, totally unrelated, aspects of May Day continue to be celebrated side by side.

Recent history

In the last hundred years, festivals or special days related to historic events have become part of the calendar. Remembrance Day, 11 November, is celebrated in most of the countries that took part in World War I. Despite a decline in its observance in the 1980s, the occasion has recently been revived, and especially the tradition of standing silently at 11.00 am, the time at which, in 1918, the war ended.

Holocaust Day has an obvious importance for Jewish communities, but also for many others. In the United State, it serves as a focus for other issues surrounding the topics of intolerance and racism. Even fifty years after the events of World War II, it strikes a chord with many people and therefore has a contemporary significance.

For Aborginal Australians the Dreamtime songs and stories are a powerful way of maintaining links with their ancestors and traditional lands.

National Festivals

In the Middle Ages, countries such as Scotland, Wales and Ireland had their patron saints: St Andrew for Scotland, St David for Wales, St Patrick for Ireland. The festival day of the patron saint was and still is the national day for those countries. Indeed, St Patrick's Day is one of the world's most widely celebrated saints' days.

The rise of nation states from the sixteenth century onwards has led to the creation of festivals associated with them. Many more recently formed states have adopted secular, rather than religious, national festivals, which often commemorate a crucial event in the country's history

Some of the best-known national festival days are Bastille Day in France, celebrating the outbreak of the French Revolution in 1789, and Independence Day in the United States, which commemorates the signing of the Declaration of Independence from Britain of the original thirteen states on 4 July 1776. Australia Day, 26 January, recalls the landing of a British fleet in 1788 and, in New Zealand, 6 February – Waitangi Day – is the date of a treaty made between the Maori chiefs and the British in 1840. Celebrating an event from more recent history, Germany has set aside 3 October, the date of the reunification of the country in 1990, as a national day, .

How much these secular festivals have found a place in the affections and lifestyles of the people of the countries concerned differs from country to country. Much depends on to what extent they really represent a date of significance for the people. For example, to Australians and New Zealanders, 25 April, Anzac Day – the day that commemorates the terrible losses of the Australian and New Zealand forces in 1916 at Gallipoli – is arguably more significant than either Australia Day or Waitangi Day.

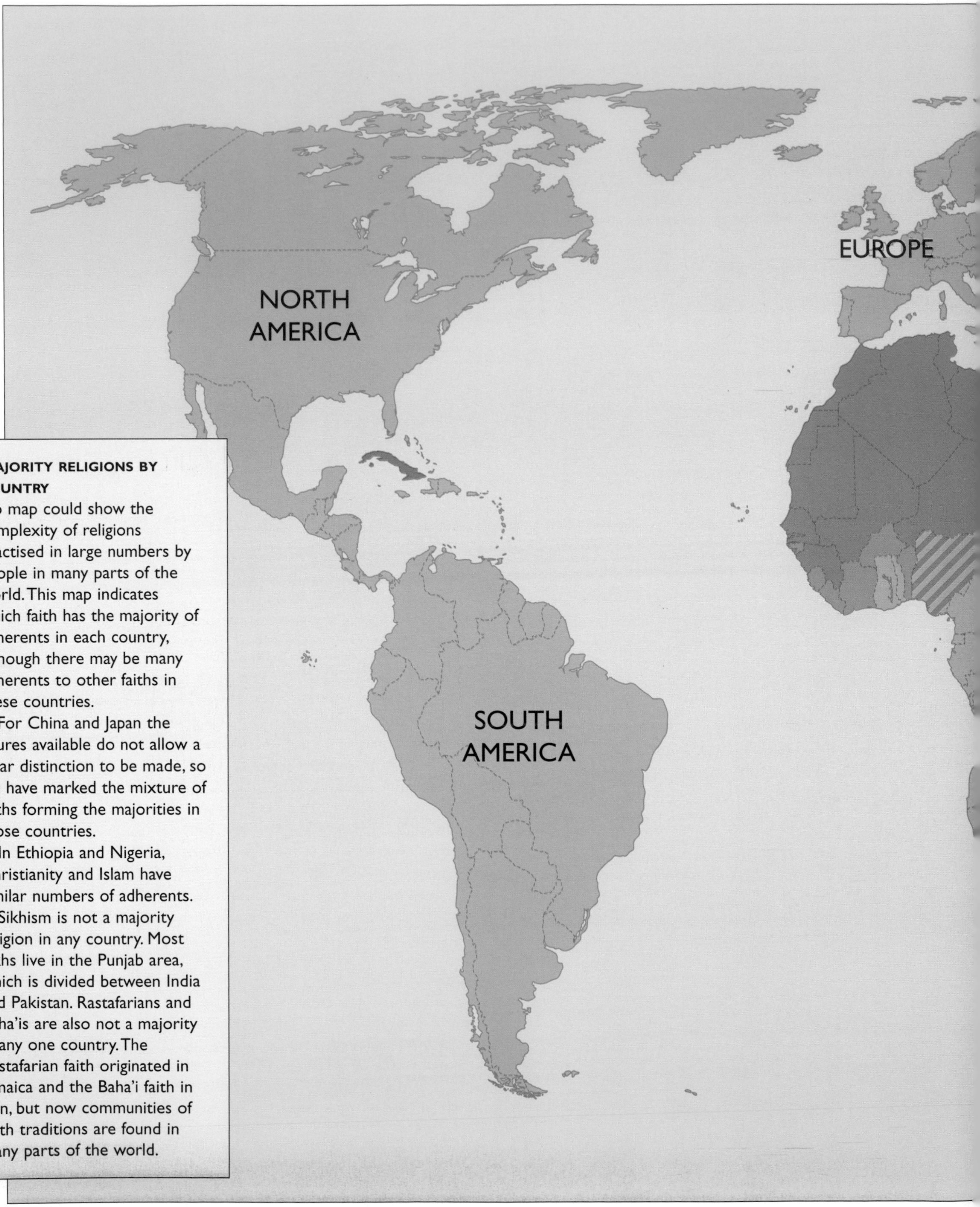

NORTH AMERICA
EUROPE
SOUTH AMERICA

Majority religions by country

No map could show the complexity of religions practised in large numbers by people in many parts of the world. This map indicates which faith has the majority of adherents in each country, although there may be many adherents to other faiths in these countries.

For China and Japan the figures available do not allow a clear distinction to be made, so we have marked the mixture of faiths forming the majorities in those countries.

In Ethiopia and Nigeria, Christianity and Islam have similar numbers of adherents.

Sikhism is not a majority religion in any country. Most Sikhs live in the Punjab area, which is divided between India and Pakistan. Rastafarians and Baha'is are also not a majority in any one country. The Rastafarian faith originated in Jamaica and the Baha'i faith in Iran, but now communities of both traditions are found in many parts of the world.

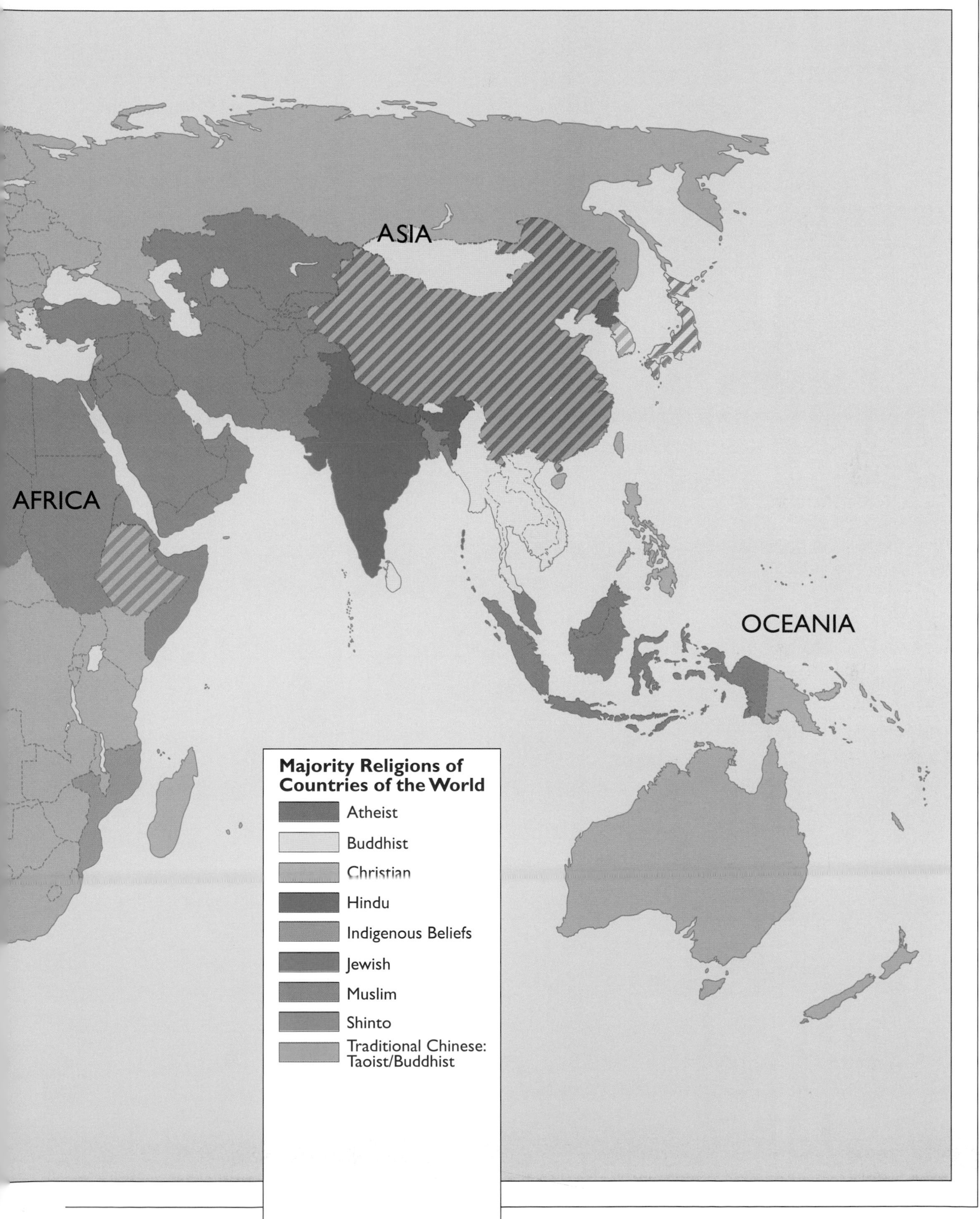
ASIA
AFRICA
OCEANIA
Majority Religions of Countries of the World
Atheist
Buddhist
Christian
Hindu
Indigenous Beliefs
Jewish
Muslim
Shinto
Traditional Chinese: Taoist/Buddhist

on Voyage
RED KOSHER
KIDDUSH
WINE
ANAVIM
ANAVIM

JEWISH FESTIVALS

At the heart of Jewish belief is the first commandment, the Shema:

Hear, O Israel: The Lord our God, the Lord is one; and you shall love the Lord your God with all your heart, and with all your soul, and with all your might. (Deuteronomy 6:4)

God is creator and Lord of all the universe. Images of God are forbidden, and many Jews will not write the name. Keeping the law is the Jewish people's part in the Covenant – the agreement made by God with Abraham, the father of the Jewish people. His faithfulness and obedience to God are related in the Bible, culminating in the Covenant, in which God promised that Abraham's descendants would form a great nation, saying, 'I will be your God and you will be my people.'

Famine and persecution

Abraham's descendants settled in Canaan. When the land was threatened by famine, Abraham's grandson Jacob (renamed 'Israel') left with his family for the land of Egypt. Several generations later, persecution in Egypt prompted the departure of the tribes of Israel under the leadership of Moses. God gave Moses laws for the people to live by, and renewed his promise to make them a great nation and give them a land to live in.

The most important of these laws are summarized as the Ten Commandments. They are also applied to varying circumstances in the teachings of Rabbis that were handed down over generations and collected in the Mishnah (second century AD) and Talmud (sixth century AD). Every aspect of Jewish daily life is guided by the Law.

The history of the Jewish people, and the development of the relationship between God and the descendants of Abraham, is at the heart of Jewish belief and practice. Almost the whole of Jewish history and teaching is embodied in its festivals, which pass the traditions on from one generation to another in stories, actions, symbolic food and songs.

The Seder Plate is the centrepiece of the Pesach meal. It holds symbolic reminders of the Israelites' escape from slavery in Egypt, as told in the second book of the Torah. Each year at the festival Jews retell the story.

After the Exodus

A head covering (often a skull cap) and a garment with tassels are worn by Jewish men as a constant reminder of their faith.

The Jewish people's departure from Egypt is known as the Exodus ('going out'). Eventually, they reached a land near the River Jordan. They conquered the people living there and settled in the land, which they believe was promised to them by God.

Around 1000 BC the Israelites formed a powerful kingdom under the great King David and his son, Solomon, who built the first Temple in Jerusalem. After Solomon, the Israelites split into two kingdoms, Judah and Israel. (The words 'Jew' and 'Judaism' derive from 'Judah', the name of Jacob's fourth son, whose descendants formed one of the largest tribes.)

The kingdoms fought against each other and against foreign invaders, until Jerusalem fell in 587 BC and the people were taken into captivity in Babylon. Although they were allowed to return forty years later, many of them decided to stay in Babylon. From that period on, the history of the Jewish people is characterized by a succession of powerful neighbours and conquerors. In AD 70 the Romans destroyed Jerusalem. The Jews were scattered all around the world and had no permanent homeland again until the modern state of Israel was created in 1948. For many Jews, this land, and the city of Jerusalem, is the centre of their faith.

The Middle Ages onward

In the Middle Ages, the long-established Jewish communities in Europe were affected by the cultures of the lands where they settled. Two groups of Jews developed with different religious customs. Those who lived in central and eastern Europe were called Ashkenazim (singular Ashkenazi), and those who had settled in Spain and Portugal were called Sephardim (singular Sephardi). The Sephardim were expelled from Spain in 1492. Some of them travelled to Europe, others to North Africa, but the majority migrated to Turkey and the Eastern Mediterranean. The two strands still exist. They both hold the same beliefs, but worship and celebrate with different traditional food, music and dance.

In 1800, the majority of the world's Jews lived in Europe. Between 1881 and

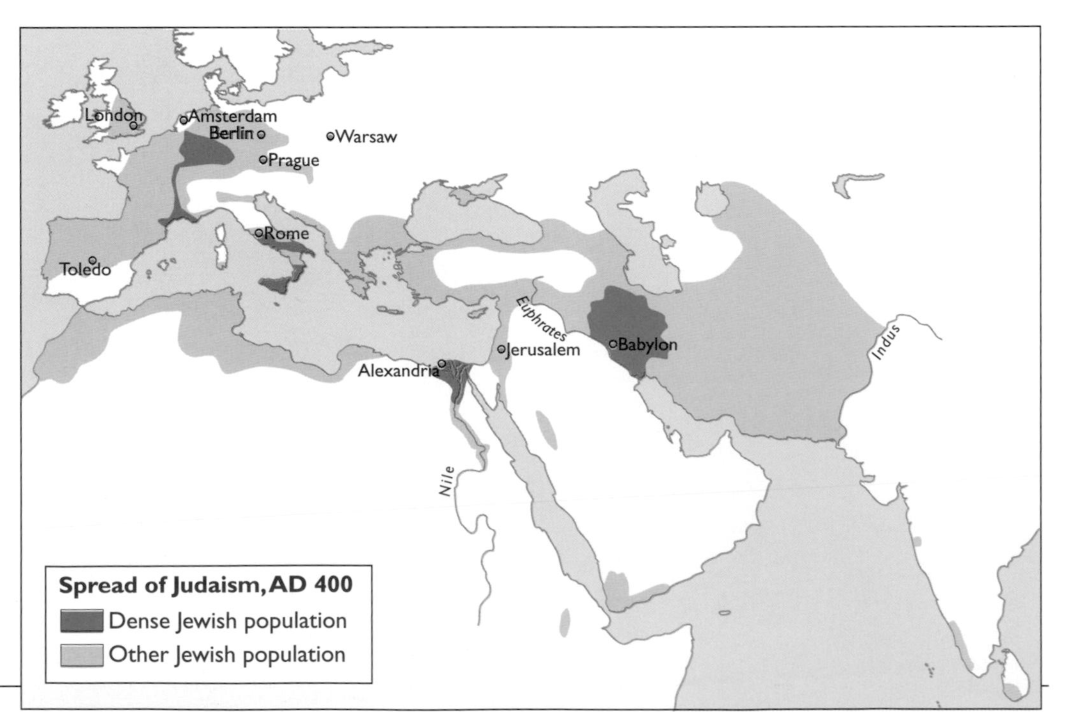

By AD 400, there were Jewish settlements through much of the Roman Empire. They were concentrated in eastern Europe and southern Italy, with other settlements around Alexandria, in Egypt, and, as a legacy of the Babylonian exile, near the Euphrates river in present-day Iraq.

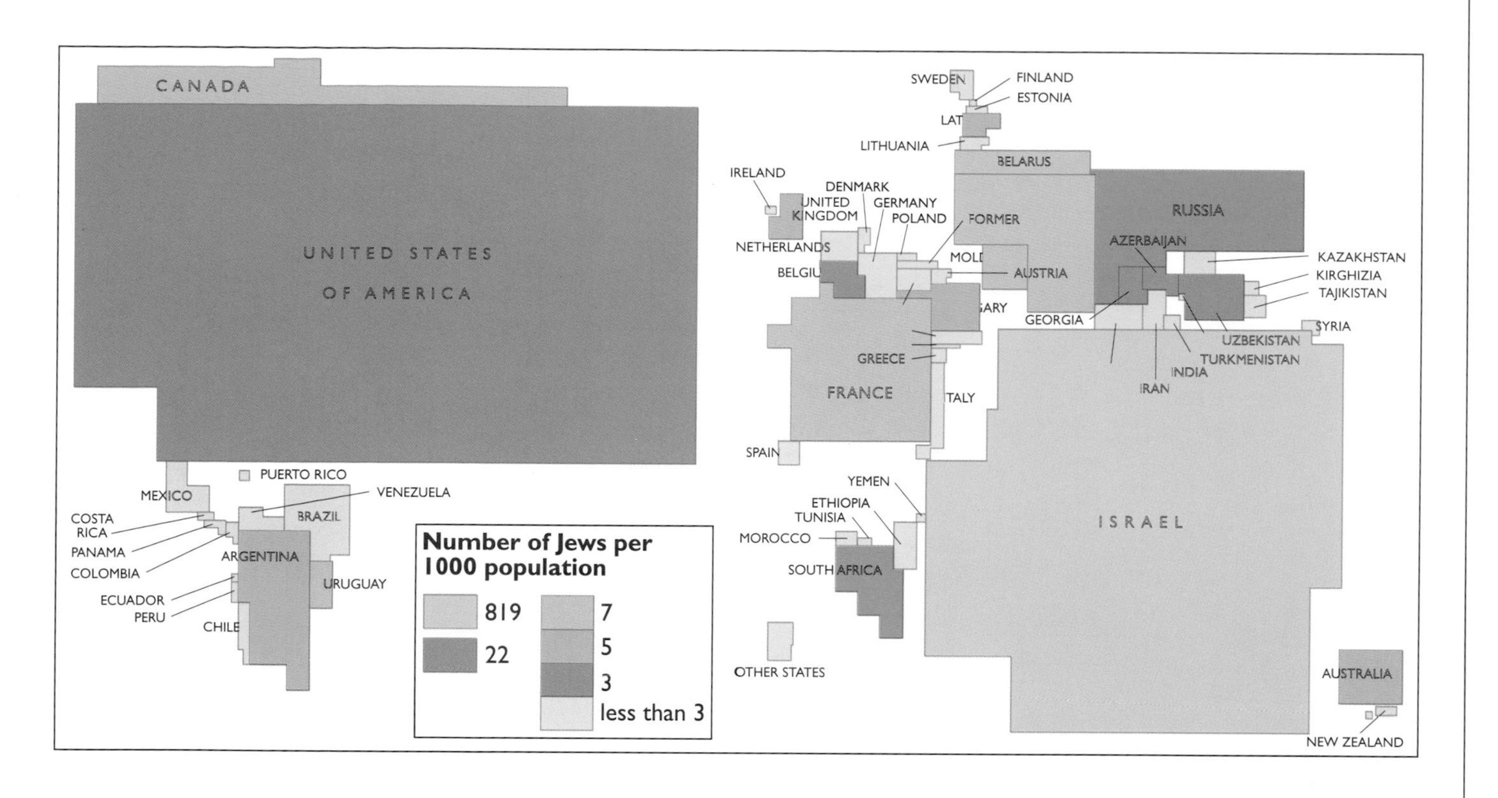

The size of countries on this diagram illustrates the number of Jews in the population. Israel is the only country in the world with a Jewish majority.

1914, more than 2.75 million Jews left eastern Europe, mainly for North America but also for South Africa, New Zealand and Australia. Increased anti-Semitism (prejudice against Jews) led to another wave of emigration between 1932 and 1939. In the years that followed, some six million Jews were killed in Europe by the Nazis in World War II. By the end of the war, hundreds of thousands more Jews had been displaced from their homes. Many sought a new life in the state of Israel, which was established in 1948. Today, nearly half of all Jews live in North America, and under a third in the Middle East.

The traditional teaching in the Haggadah, the form of service for the Pesach meal, distinguishes four types of person: the wise, the wicked, the simple and those who do not know how to ask. This illustration is from a modern American Haggadah.

Home and the Synagogue

THE HEBREW BIBLE
There are three types of book in the Hebrew Bible: the Torah, Prophets and Writings. The Torah, consisting of the first five books of the Bible, is believed to have been revealed directly to Moses by God. It includes stories of Creation, of Abraham and his descendants and of the Exodus from Egypt, as well as details of the Jewish law. The word 'Torah' is sometimes used to mean the whole Hebrew Bible. The Prophets recount both the actions and words of prophets such as Elijah, regarded by Jews as the greatest prophet, Elisha and Isaiah, and Jeremiah, who predicted and lamented the Babylonian exile. The Writings include poetry, such as the Psalms, and some of the later stories such as those of Ruth and Esther.

With the destruction of the Temple in Jerusalem in AD 70, and the scattering of the Jews to all parts of the Roman Empire, Jewish life, which earlier had centred on the Temple, began to focus on the home and the synagogue.

The home is where many Jewish festivals are chiefly held, and where the Sabbath, the seventh day of the week, is welcomed and celebrated with a special meal on Friday night. The details of the Law of Moses are lived out in the home every day in all sorts of ways. Jews will not eat certain foods, such as anything from pigs, rabbits or shellfish, and they prepare their food according to this Law. Food that Jews are permitted to eat is called 'kosher'.

Each synagogue has a set of scrolls on which the Torah is handwritten on parchment. These are kept in a special cupboard called the ark – here in the background centre – and covered in embroidered cloth and silver decorations.

A silver pointer is used when reading the Torah scroll to follow the words without touching the sacred text.

THREE TRADITIONS OF JUDAISM

Among those who see themselves as religious Jews, there are three main forms of contemporary Judaism: Orthodox, Conservative and Liberal or Reform.

Orthodox Judaism sees itself as the upholder of the true Jewish tradition. Hebrew is used in all the services and traditional Jewish law (halakhah) is observed in matters of food and behaviour.

Conservative Judaism is primarily American. It seeks to observe the traditional Jewish laws but to allow modifications so long as these are seen to be loyal to the law and developments of the laws over the centuries. For example, in 1960 the Conservative Jews agreed to the use of electricity on the Sabbath and to using the car to travel to the synagogue – something that Orthodox Jews would not permit.

Reform and Liberal Judaism arose in the early nineteenth century as an attempt to make Judaism a more modern faith, unencumbered by what its founders saw as outdated dietary laws and by the exclusive use of Hebrew in worship. It also embraced modern Biblical scholarship, and so, for example, does not teach that Moses wrote the five books of the Torah. Reform and Liberal Jews worship primarily in the language of their own country. They observe some dietary laws but only a fraction of those observed by Orthodox Jews. They are also often very engaged with social and political issues in their own countries.

Orthodox Judaism includes the Hassidic Jews, whose dress and lifestyle are those of 18th-century eastern Europe, where the Hassidic movement began.

Away from the home, the synagogue became the centre of Jewish community life. It fulfils three main functions: as a house of assembly, where the Jewish community can meet for any purpose; as a house of study where the Torah and Talmud are studied, and children learn Hebrew; and as a house of prayer, where services are held on the Sabbath and on festival days.

Times and Seasons

Festive Differences
Some festivals are celebrated for a day longer outside Israel than in Israel itself because, originally, the festivals were timed according to the sighting of the new moon in Israel. In days when communications were more difficult, other places could not be sure which was the right day.

The exceptions are Rosh Hashanah, which is thought too important to last for only one day, and Yom Kippur, which is one day everywhere because a strict fast for two days might cause health problems.

Many events in Jewish history are commemorated in the festivals, often by re-enacting or reliving the story. Five festivals are described as 'major' because they are laid down in the Torah. They are Rosh Hashanah and Yom Kippur, known as the Days of Awe, and three joyful festivals, Pesach (Passover), Shavuot and Sukkot (Feast of Tabernacles). Many of the 'minor' festivals have become popular even amongst non-religious Jews, and some, such as Hanukah, are celebrated more widely than some of the major festivals.

Shabbat, the Sabbath, is a weekly festival, welcomed as a queen. The best food is eaten, the best clothes are worn, and there is singing and celebration, mainly in the home. The Torah describes God's creation of the universe in six days, and his resting on the seventh, and Jews do the same, with no work and no travelling. On Friday night and Saturday morning, services are held at the synagogue.

The date for the beginning of each month is now found by calculation, but in earlier times it was fixed by observation of the new moon.

Most festivals are based on early Jewish history, especially the journey from Egypt to Canaan via Mount Sinai. Places on the map relate to episodes in different periods: Jerusalem did not exist at the time of the Exodus from Egypt.

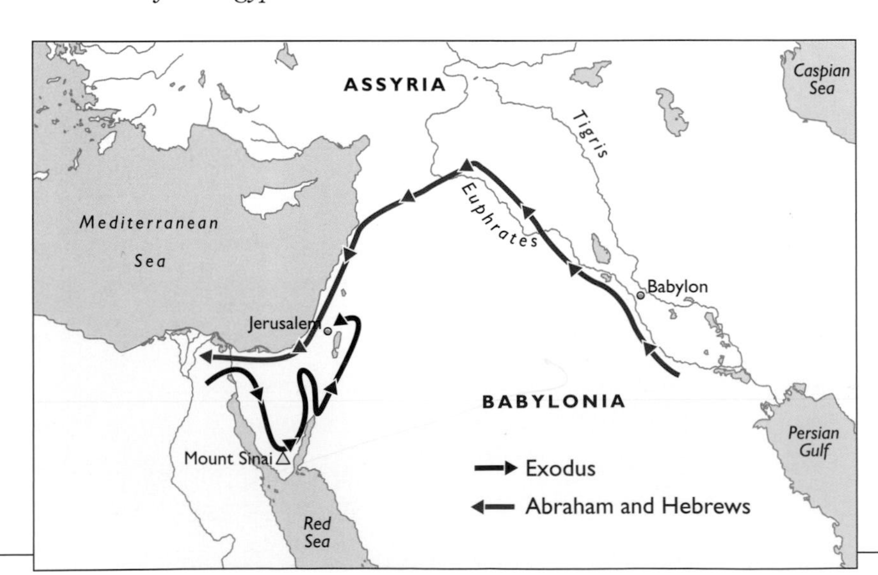

The Jewish Calendar

The Jewish calendar is lunar, but every few years a thirteenth month is added to keep in line with the solar year. The new day begins at nightfall, so festivals begin in the evening. The years are counted from the traditional Jewish dating of the creation of the world. Thus, the year AD 2000 was the year 5760 in the Jewish calendar.

1 Rosh Hashanah (1–2 Tishri)
The New Year is a time for recollection signalled by the blowing of the *shofar* (ram's horn).

2 Yom Kippur (10 Tishri)
The Day of Atonement. Jews fast for the whole day and ask God for forgiveness of their sins.

3 Sukkot (15–21 Tishri)
Also known as the Feast of Tabernacles, Sukkot is when Jews build small temporary shelters in memory of the Israelite wanderings in the desert.

4 Simhat Torah (23 Tishri)
Rejoicing in the Torah – the day when the yearly reading comes to an end and begins again. Congregations process round the synagogue, carrying the scrolls.

5 Hanukah (25 Kislev–3 Tevet)
Commemoration of a miracle, when the Jewish people re-dedicated the Temple in Jerusalem after their foreign rulers had desecrated it. Starting on 25 Kislev, one more candle is lit on each successive day of the eight-day festival.

6 Tu B'Shevat (15 Shevat)
The New Year for Trees. Familes and communities plant trees or support reafforestation projects in Israel.

7 Purim (14 Adar)
The Jewish queen Esther saved her people from annihilation. In the synagogue, the congregation sounds rattles and makes noises to drown out the name of the villain, as the story is read aloud.

8 Pesach (15–22 Nisan)
Pesach, or Passover, celebrates God's deliverance of the Israelites from captivity in Egypt. Unleavened bread is eaten to commemorate the hastily baked bread for the journey. The Seder – a meal consumed on the first night – includes many symbolic foods.

9 Holocaust Memorial Day (27 Nissan)
During World War II, 6 million Jews lost their lives in Nazi concentration camps, and others suffered forced labour.

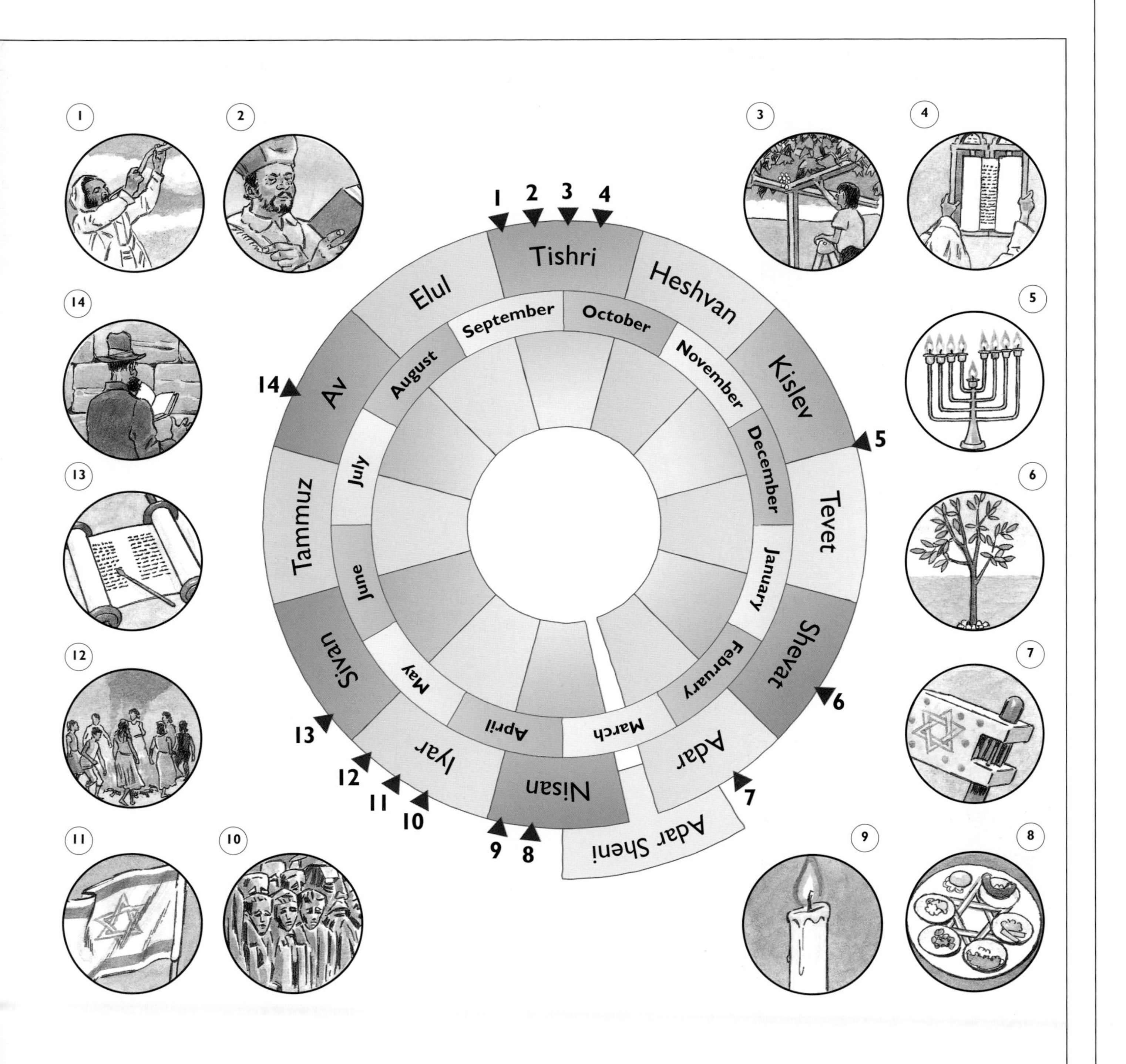

10 ISRAEL REMEMBRANCE DAY (4 IYAR)
The establishment of the state of Israel is regarded as a religious, as well as a national, achievement. On this day, those who died in the struggle to bring it about are remembered.

11 ISRAEL INDEPENDENCE DAY (5 IYAR)
Celebration of the founding of the modern state of Israel in 1948.

12 LAG B'OMER (18 IYAR)
This scholars' holiday commemorates teachers and students who risked death to study the Torah, especially Rabbi Akiva and Shimon bar Yohai. Children hold picnics and light bonfires.

13 SHAVUOT (6–7 SIVAN)
A celebration of the giving of the Torah – the Law – to Moses on Mount Sinai.

14 TISHAH B'AV (9 AV)
A day of mourning for several disasters that befell the Jewish people, in particular the destruction of the Temples in Jerusalem.

Rosh Hashanah and Yom Kippur

A GOOD, SWEET YEAR
A common seasonal greeting at Rosh Hashanah is 'May you be inscribed for a good year'. The food at that time is symbolic of wishes for a good year ahead – bread or sweet apple dipped in honey. Other symbolic actions include eating the head of a fish or a sheep to represent 'moving ahead'; wearing white to symbolize God's sustenance and mercy; and visiting a body of water to 'cast away' one's sins.

Nearly all Jewish festivals celebrate an event: an event in Jewish history or tradition, or a natural event such as a harvest, or, as is often the case, both. The exceptions are the High Holy Days (Yamim Nora'im), which begin with Rosh Hashanah on the first day of Tishri and end with Yom Kippur (the Day of Atonement) on day 10 of Tishri. They are a time of personal, rather than communal, recollection and repentance.

The Yom Kippur evening service is a time of solemn reflection. In this Reform synagogue, the congregation light candles as a sign of repentance.

Creation, remembrance and judgement

Rosh Hashanah ('Head of the Year') celebrates the birthday of the world, which God created, according to Jewish tradition, 3,760 years before the start of the general (AD) calendar. Yom Teruah ('Day of Blowing the Shofar') is the name given to Rosh Hashanah in the Bible (Numbers 29:1). The day is also known by other names that express the different themes within it:

Yom Hazikaron is the 'Day of Remembrance', when God, the creator of all things, remembers every living creature and their actions in the past year. Jews try to recall and reflect on their past deeds, in preparation for the judgement and repentance to come.

Yom Hadin is the 'Day of Judgement'. There is a tradition that, on this day, each person's fate is decided for the coming year and written in a book in Heaven. It is a day for rejoicing, to show confidence in God's mercy.

Fasting and atonement

Yom Kippur means 'Day of Atonement'. Many Jews who do not participate in other festivals diligently observe Yom Kippur.

Anything that would not be done on the Sabbath is not done on Yom Kippur either. The occasion is also a fast day, when Jews refrain from eating or drinking and do not bathe or wear perfume or leather shoes. However, no one for whom fasting would be dangerous is permitted to fast.

Even outside Israel, where most festivals are a day longer, the fasting lasts for just the one day. Some say that to fast on Yom Kippur is to become more like the angels, who have no need to eat, drink or wash. The day before Yom Kippur, people are expected to eat heartily, partly to prepare for the fast and partly to show that God's good gifts are not to be despised, even though one may refrain from them for a day.

On Yom Kippur, it is important to seek forgiveness for any wrongdoing before the book in Heaven is sealed. As Yom Kippur is the day to ask forgiveness from God, the day before is the last chance to ask forgiveness of others one has wronged, since God cannot forgive sins against others (the offended party has a duty to grant forgiveness when it is asked, subject to certain limits).

Revoking vows to God

In the evening, as Yom Kippur begins, Jews gather at the synagogue. The service begins with the Kol Nidrei, a prayer that is spoken or sung three times. The prayer repudiates and annuls any vows or promises that may be made in the year to come or, in some traditions, were made in the previous year. This has been subject to misunderstanding, but Jewish teachers emphasize that it refers to personal vows made to God, and is necessary because of human forgetfulness and weakness, and the immense seriousness with which vows are regarded. It does not affect promises made to others.

The service continues with communal prayers for forgiveness, which are repeated the following day in other services. As dusk falls, the shofar is sounded once more, and the fast is over.

Praying for Forgiveness

Many synagogues hold a Selichot service on the Saturday evening before Rosh Hashanah, to give people time to reflect on their deeds of the past year and ask for forgiveness. Selichot means 'prayers for forgiveness'. In the Sephardic tradition, the prayers are said for a month before Rosh Hashanah.

Blowing the Shofar

On each of the two days of Rosh Hashanah, and for a month beforehand, the shofar, a ram's horn, is blown to call the people to repent and to start afresh in the New Year. The sound is intended to induce self-awareness, prayer and repentance. Every Jew is commanded to hear the shofar on Rosh Hashanah, and to hear and say 'Amen' to the blessings recited.

The number of blasts sounded on the shofar is sometimes related to the story of Jael and Sisera in the book of Judges. Sisera, an enemy of the Israelites, was killed by Jael, as he lay sleeping. In one tradition, Sisera's mother is pictured weeping 101 tears for her son. The shofar is played 100 times to wipe out the tears shed in anger against the Jewish people, but the 101st tear is that of pure love of a mother for her son, and can never be wiped out.

In Sephardic tradition the number of blasts relates to the letter-values of the numbers: 101 blasts on the shofar signifies the name of Michael, the highest archangel. Other traditions have other patterns.

The shofar can produce a variety of sounds, from short, urgent, repeated notes to wailing and sighing, and is an intentionally awe-inspiring sound. It takes skill and practice to produce the right sounds.

At Rosh Hashanah, the Jewish New Year, the rabbi blows on the shofar in the synagogue.

Sukkot, Shemini Atzeret and Simhat Torah

The lulav for Sukkot consists of palm, myrtle and willow branches. The etrog carried with it is a kind of citrus fruit.

Although God had renewed his covenant with the Israelites when he gave Moses the Torah on Mount Sinai, the people had angered him by their grumbling and lack of trust. For forty years the people wandered through the desert, until the first generation that came out of Egypt had died out, and God led them to the land where they were to settle. Through all this time, they moved with their flocks from place to place, living in temporary shelters. God commanded them to remember this time, and how he had protected them and provided food and water.

A nine-day holiday

'Sukkot' means 'shelters' or 'booths'. The main feature of the Sukkot festival is the command to live in a shelter (*sukkah*) for seven days. It is also known as the 'Feast of Ingathering', at which thanks are given for God's provision of all the good things of the earth. Although Sukkot is a seven-day festival (15–21 Tishri), it is immediately followed by Shemini Atzeret and Simhat Torah, making a holiday period of nine days. Like other major festivals, it has a harvest festival element as well as being a commemoration.

In the synagogue, on each morning of Sukkot, the *lulav* (palm, myrtle and willow branches bound together) is carried in the right hand, and the *etrog* (a species of citrus fruit) in the left. The four species are shaken towards the four compass points, representing God's presence everywhere. At the end of the service, everyone carries their lulav and etrog in a procession, singing joyful songs.

Symbolic meanings

On the first day, you shall take the fruit of a goodly tree, palm branches, myrtle boughs, and willows and rejoice before The Lord. (Leviticus 23:40)

Traditionally, the four species have symbolic meanings: the mouth, the heart, the spine (uprightness) and the eyes, uniting in the service of God, or as the

Processing the Torah (Simhat Torah): a group of men in prayer shawls, each carrying Torah scrolls, approach the ark to put the scrolls away.

A recreation of an early Sukkot tent in the Negev desert in Israel.

The Sukkah

Blessed are You, O Lord our God, Ruler of the world, who has made us holy through your commandments and commanded us to dwell in the Sukkah.
Traditional blessing for Sukkot

Not only does the sukkah recall the rough shelters that the Israelites used in the desert, but its fragility symbolizes the need to rely on God for security. It must be constructed as a temporary shelter, and the roof covered with leafy branches that let in the light. It must have at least three walls capable of withstanding an average wind, and be big enough for at least one person. Reform congregations often have an ornate, semi-permanent sukkah at the synagogue, but in many traditions each family builds its own every year. They hang fruits, flowers and pictures on the walls as decoration, and use their best tableware at mealtimes.

The command to live in the sukkah is interpreted in different ways. Most Jews try to take at least some of their main meals in the sukkah, particularly on the first day of the festival. Weather permitting, they may sleep and perform most of their daily activities there, studying the Torah and welcoming guests as if at home, provided that this can be done without undue discomfort.

Jewish people in unity. Another interpretation is that the four species represent the four different types of person as defined by good deeds and learning, symbolized by taste and smell, respectively. Thus, the etrog, which tastes and smells good, is like the person who has both good deeds and learning; the myrtle, with smell but no taste, compares to a person of learning who is devoid of good deeds; the palm has taste but no smell, representing someone who does good but lacks learning; and the willow, which has neither taste nor smell, symbolizes someone in whom good deeds and learning are both lacking.

The Torah and the 'marriage' celebrations
The day after the seven days of Sukkot – 22 Tishri – is called Shemini Atzeret ('Eighth Day of Assembly'). It is a kind of prolonging of the festival, with a command to assemble and be joyful. Prayers for rain are said, since this is the time of planting in Israel.

The following day is Simhat Torah, which means 'rejoicing in the Torah'. Every week of the year, a part of the Torah is read out in the synagogue, so that over the year, the whole Torah is read. Simhat Torah marks the end of this annual cycle and the beginning of the next.

Some Jews see the festival as celebrating the 'marriage' of the Jewish people to the Torah, and the celebrations in the synagogue are very joyful. In Orthodox congregations, the man who reads the last portion of the Torah, at the end of Deuteronomy, is known as the 'bridegroom of the Torah', and the one who reads the beginning of Genesis to restart the cycle is known as the 'bridegroom of Genesis'. Before the readings, the scrolls of the Torah are taken from the ark and carried seven times round the synagogue, accompanied by singing, dancing and flag-waving from the whole congregation. As with a wedding, the dancing can go on all night.

Whereas Shavuot commemorates the giving of the Torah on Mount Sinai, Simhat Torah places more emphasis on the daily inspiration and guidance to be gained from reading the Torah.

Royal Guests
Jewish tradition places great stress on hospitality to the poor and friendless, so as well as welcoming friends and family into the sukkah, many families will also invite others to join them. It is said that Abraham, Isaac, Jacob, Moses, Aaron, Joseph and David – the seven 'faithful shepherds' of Israel – visit the festive meals: All seven spent some time as wandering outcasts with only God to protect them.

The Story of Hanukah

Judaism has many 'minor' festivals, defined as those that are not laid down in the Torah. Some of these have gained in importance and popularity over the centuries, so that they are now more widely known than many of the 'major' festivals, and are celebrated not only by non-religious Jews but also by non-Jews. Perhaps the best-known 'minor' festival is Hanukah. This is possibly because, in predominantly Christian cultures, Hanukah, whose name comes from a Hebrew word meaning 'dedication', offers a Jewish festival near the Christmas season.

The Meaning of Hanukah
For Jews, the meaning of Hanukah is poised between the two parts of the story, the emphasis changing in different contexts. On the one hand, it is a celebration of God's power to change impossible situations. On the other, it is a memorial to a successful armed struggle against a foreign power. It is also seen as a story about preserving one's religious distinctiveness and keeping faith alive.

Dissent and persecution

The story of Hanukah derives from two sources, each of which gives it a different emphasis. The first is from the books of Maccabees, which are not part of the Hebrew text of the Bible, but are included in the Greek version compiled later, perhaps in the second and first centuries BC.

In the second century BC, the Jews were ruled by a Greek dynasty known as the Seleucids. At first, these rulers recognized the Jewish religion and laws, but, around 175 BC, Antiochus Epiphanes, with support from some of the Jewish authorities, introduced practices from Greek religion. This caused considerable dissent, and eventually resistance, which gave rise to persecution. Antiochus pillaged the Temple in Jerusalem, instituted Greek sacrifices there and outlawed Jewish religious observance.

Resistance and triumph

Guerrilla warfare and resistance were conducted under the leadership of the Hasmonean family. Eventually, in 164 BC, the Hasmonean leader Judah Maccabee gained sufficient control of the country to allow the re-dedication of the Temple, a ceremony that lasted eight days, starting on 25 Kislev. It was proclaimed that these eight days should be celebrated every year 'with mirth and gladness' (1 Maccabees 4: 59).

In the troubled centuries that followed, the commemoration of this occasion seems to have been almost forgotten – there is no mention of it in the Mishnah (second century AD) – but by the time of the Talmud (up to the sixth century), there is a further part to the story.

At home and in the synagogue, a menorah – a special eight-branched candlestick – is lit for the festival: one candle on the first day, two on the second, and so on for eight days. The menorah should be placed where it can be seen from outside the house, to proclaim the miracle to passers-by.

When the army of Judah Maccabee set about purging and re-dedicating the Temple, they found that the consecrated oil used in the Temple worship had all been destroyed or defiled, except for one small flask that had been sealed by the High Priest. The oil was only enough to burn for one day, and it would take eight days to make more. But the lamp was lit, and by a miracle it burned for the whole eight days. The following year, a holiday was declared in joyful memory of this miracle.

Celebration

Since Hanukah is a minor festival, work during it is permitted, but there must be no fasting or signs of sadness. Many families hold parties and give gifts to the children. Pancakes and latkes (potato pancakes), often served with apple sauce, are a special feature of the festival, because the oil used to cook them recalls the miracle of the oil that did not run out.

Throughout the festival's eight days, services are held in the synagogue, with special additions to the normal prayers and readings. On the Sabbath, a verse from Zechariah that has become the motto of Hanukkah is read out:

Not by might, nor by power, but by my Spirit, says the Lord of hosts.
(Zechariah 4:6)

A Serious Game

It is said that during times of persecution, when it was dangerous to be seen studying the Torah, small groups of students continued to meet in secret. They brought small toys with them so that, if discovered, they would look as if they were just gambling or playing children's games. Playing a game with a spinning top known as a *dreidel* (from a Yiddish word meaning 'spin') is now a traditional celebration at Hanukkah.

Players start with an equal number of coins, counters or sweets. Each player then puts one or more of these 'tokens' into the pot in the centre. Players take turns spinning the dreidel, and act according to whichever Hebrew letter the dreidel falls on. Thus:

nun: player does nothing
gimel: player takes all the tokens in the pot
hey: player takes half of the tokens in the pot
shin: player must put one token into the pot

The winner is the player who takes all the tokens.

The letters on the dreidel stand for the Hebrew phrase 'Nes Gadol Haya Sham' – 'A great miracle happened there'. In Israel the last letter is *peh*, not *shin*, which stands for 'Poh' (not 'Sham'), meaning 'here', not 'there'.

Dreidels are found in many shapes and sizes, from ornate antique silver patterns to those made from card and a pencil stub.

Latkes (Potato Pancakes)

1 Mix the potatoes with the onion. Using a sieve or cloth, squeeze out as much liquid as possible.
2 Combine the potato mixture, flour, egg, and salt and pepper.
3 Heat a frying pan or griddle and cover with a thin layer of oil.
4 With the hands, press together about 2 tablespoons of the potato mixture, place in the pan and flatten with a wide metal spatula. Repeat to make one batch of latkes.
5 Cook for about 8 minutes, turning once, until browned on both sides. Transfer pancakes to a plate lined with paper towels to drain. Cover loosely with foil and keep warm. Repeat with the remaining potato mixture.
6 Serve with apple sauce or sour cream.

Latkes can also be made with other grated vegetables, or with cottage cheese.

Ingredients

1 kg potatoes, peeled and grated or shredded
3 tablespoons flour
1 medium onion, coarsely grated
2 eggs, beaten
salt and pepper, to taste
vegetable oil for frying

The Story of Purim

Purim in Jersualem
Because Shushan was a large, walled city, the Jews were permitted to fight for their lives on both 13 and 14 Adar. They did not celebrate until the day afterwards. So the tradition arose that the inhabitants of a great walled city should celebrate the festival on the 15th, while everyone else celebrates on the 14th. The only city recognized today as having comparable status to Shushan is Jerusalem, where the festival of Purim is still celebrated one day later than in the rest of the world.

Purim is a minor festival that has become more important in recent years. This is partly because of its theme – of the Jewish people, under threat of extermination, being saved by a woman – and partly because of the boisterous fun that accompanies its traditional celebration. The events that Purim commemorates date from the time of the Jewish Exile.

Plot to kill the Jews

King Ahasuerus, emperor of Persia, ruled in the city of Shushan (Susa). Among his officials was a Jew called Mordecai, who had adopted his beautiful niece Esther, after the death of her parents. When the king quarrelled with his wife and looked for a new queen, Esther won his favour. Mordecai also won favour with the king by uncovering a plot to kill him, but soon afterwards he offended the king's chancellor Haman, who decided to punish not only Mordecai, but his whole people. Haman went to the king and tricked him into agreeing to execute every Jew in the land, on a day that would be chosen by drawing lots (*purim* in Hebrew).

When Mordecai heard about this, he sent a message to Esther asking her to plead with the king to revoke the order. Although she knew that such interference might offend the king and cause her own death, Esther agreed.

She asked the Jews of Shushan to fast and pray for her, and she did the same, before approaching the king and inviting him and Haman to a banquet. The king was concerned at her pale appearance, but

Reading the scroll (Megillah) of Esther in the synagogue. As the story of Esther is read aloud, whenever the name 'Haman' is mentioned, everyone makes as much noise as they can, shouting, twirling rattles (known as 'graggers') or blowing horns, to drown the sound of his name.

she did not tell him her trouble, only inviting him and Haman to come again the next evening.

That night, the king reread the records of his reign and remembered how Mordecai had uncovered the plot to kill him. Finding that Mordecai had never been rewarded, he sent for Haman and asked, 'What should be done for a man whom the king wishes to honour?'

Thinking the king was referring to him, Haman replied, 'He should be given royal robes to wear, and a horse that the king has ridden. A crown should be put on his head, and one of the king's officers should lead him through the streets, proclaiming, 'This is how the king treats a man he wishes to honour!'

'Very good!' said the king. 'Go and do all that you have said to Mordecai the Jew.' With suppressed rage, Haman did as the king told him, and then set out to Esther's banquet.

Esther the saviour

Once again, they sat feasting, and once again the king asked her what was the matter, promising her she could have whatever she wished. As she pleaded for her life, and the lives of her people, the king realized he had been tricked. He ordered that Haman be executed on the very scaffold that Haman had prepared for Mordecai.

He gave Haman's house and all his riches to Esther, and Haman's job and the honour that went with it to Mordecai. He further gave permission for the Jews in all his empire to fight and defend themselves against those who had sought to kill them. On the thirteenth day of Adar, the Jews killed many of their enemies, and on the day after this victory, they feasted and rejoiced at their deliverance.

THE FOUR ESSENTIALS OF PURIM

A day of gladness, feasting and holiday-making, and the sending of gifts to one another (Esther 9: 18)

The day before the festival, people fast, commemorating the fast in the story. On festival day, there are four obligatory aspects of the celebration:

1 Reading the scroll (Megillah) of Esther
Everyone – young and old, men and women – should hear the story read aloud.

2 Festivity and rejoicing
At home and in the synagogue, the festival is full of boisterous fun. There is play-acting and dressing up, as well as good food and drink. A popular Purim dish is Hamantaschen ('Haman's ears') – tarts of pastry or dough filled with poppy seeds – and pinched into a three-cornered shape to resemble Haman's ears or his hat.

It is said that Jews have a duty to get so drunk on Purim that they can no longer distinguish between 'Cursed be Haman' and 'Blessed be Mordecai.' Costumes and masks recall the features of the story that revolve around mistaken or hidden identity: the king did not know that Esther was Jewish; Haman did not know that the king intended to honour Mordecai.

3 Giving gifts to the poor
Even those who are poor should give food, drink or clothing, or money to buy these things, to at least two people.

4 Giving gifts to each other
Friends and relatives exchange gifts of food and drink, preferably by messenger, since the Book of Esther uses the word 'send'. The gifts should be something that can be eaten or drunk without further preparation, such as cooked meat, cakes and wine.

One can send to any number of people, but the amount given should be more than a mere token: it must indicate regard for the recipient. However, it is better to be generous in one's gifts to the poor than to send large amounts to friends who already have plenty.

Jewish children dress up or put on fancy clothing for the festival of Purim and, in the synagogue, perform a play re-enacting the story of Esther and Haman.

Pesach – the Passover

The Awaited Guest
The Prophet Elijah is said to visit every Seder meal, and a cup of wine is set out for him. Towards the end of the meal, the door is left open in the hope that he will arrive and announce the coming of the Messiah, so that Pesach will be celebrated 'next year in Jerusalem'. The custom of leaving the door open may have originated in medieval Europe from the need to show Christian neighbours that no occult practices were going on.

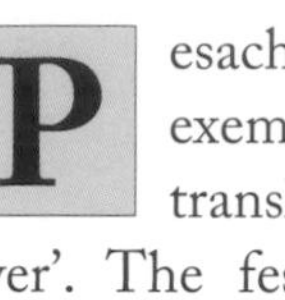

Pesach means 'to pass through', 'to exempt' or, as it is commonly translated into English, 'to pass over'. The festival is the beginning of the harvest season in Israel, but little attention is paid to this, as the emphasis is on the deliverance of the Israelites from slavery in Egypt.

'Let my people go'

The Patriarch Jacob and his twelve sons moved to Egypt, where they settled and prospered. Some generations later, the Pharaoh became concerned at the increasing number of Jews and began to persecute them. He subjected them to forced labour and ordered that Israelite boys should be killed at birth. However, one mother hid her baby son in a reed basket on the river, where he was found by the Pharaoh's daughter, who adopted him and named him Moses.

When Moses reached manhood, he fled, after killing an Egyptian slave-master. But God commanded him to return and to tell the Pharaoh, 'Let my people go'. Moses obeyed, and with his brother Aaron demanded permission for the Israelites to leave the country.

Pharaoh refused, and increased his oppression of the Jews. In punishment, God sent one disaster after another on the Egyptians: the waters of the Nile turned to blood; the land was invaded by frogs, then mosquitoes, then horseflies; the live-stock died; the people were afflicted with boils; hail destroyed the crops; locusts stripped the land and the trees bare; darkness covered the land for three days.

The youngest member of the family reads from the Haggadah. Pesach is very much a family celebration.

The angel of death

Throughout, the Israelites remained immune from the trouble. After each disaster, Moses renewed his demand for them to leave, but the Pharaoh either refused point-blank or gave permission and then withdrew it. Finally, the tenth plague brought death in one night to the first-born son of each Egyptian family and to their livestock. God told the Israelites to slaughter a lamb for each household and smear the blood on the doorposts so that the angel of death would recognize and pass over the Israelite houses.

Overwhelmed by the catastrophe, the Pharaoh finally let the Israelites go. They departed in such haste that there was no time to bake bread for the journey. Instead, they made flat cakes of flour and water. In memory of the hasty departure from Egypt, Jews eat only unleavened bread – matzah – for the nine days of the festival (eight days in Israel), which is also known as the 'Festival of Unleavened Bread'.

The Seder Plate

The high point of Pesach is the Seder, which is both a meal and a religious service, held on the first night. On the festive table stands a plate with three pieces of matzah, and the Seder plate.

As well as the symbolic food on the Seder plate, there is wine and a festive meal, which should be the best that the household can provide. A few drops of wine are spilled to recall the suffering of the Egyptians as the plagues came upon them.

The text of the Pesach Seder is written in a book called the Haggadah. It combines symbolic food, symbolic actions, talking, singing and blessings. At one point, the youngest child present asks four questions, beginning, 'Why is this night different from other nights?' – a cue for telling the story.

Clearing Out the Yeast

Flour ground from grain rapidly develops a natural yeast when water is added, so matzah is only considered lawful for Pesach if it has been completely cooked within 18 minutes of coming into contact with water. Any other form of grain or flour, known as chametz, must be cleared out.

A thorough cleaning starts weeks beforehand, to rid each house of any trace of chametz. Just before the start of the festival, a special search is made, traditionally using a candle to show up any remaining traces of breadcrumbs, and a feather and bag to whisk them away to be burned. It is customary to hide a few pieces of chametz in the house so that the search will not be in vain.

Unleavened Bread
Matzah, the unleavened bread for Pesach, is made from nothing but flour and water, mixed, flattened and baked very quickly. Its full-sized form is about 25 centimetres square, but it is also used finely ground to make cakes and biscuits, coarsely ground like breadcrumbs, and in small pieces like pasta.

Roasted lamb bone
A reminder of the lamb that was killed by each household.

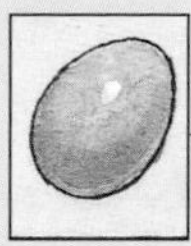

Roasted egg
A symbol of mourning, recalling the destruction of the Temple in Jerusalem.

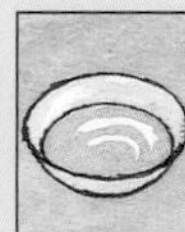

Salt water
Symbolizing the bitter tears of slaves, the green vegetable is dipped in it.

Bitter herbs
Usually horseradish, symbolizing the bitterness of slavery.

Green vegetable
Usually lettuce, parsley or celery. Some people say this represents the humble origins of the Jewish people.

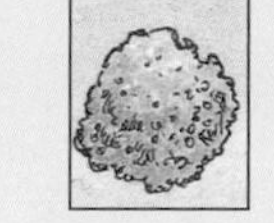

Charoset
A sweet mixture resembling the mortar used by the Israelites during their forced labour, made sweet in the end by God's kindness.

Shavuot – the Feast of Weeks

RUTH THE FOREIGNER
The Book of Ruth tells of a love story that took place at harvest time. Ruth the Moabitess, widow of an Israelite, left her homeland out of love for her mother-in-law Naomi, and settled in Israel. A second marriage brought love and comfort to her and Naomi. She was the great-grandmother of King David. Her story is celebrated at Shavuot because, although a foreigner, she was willing to take on the commandments of the Torah.

Shavuot comes seven weeks, or a 'week of weeks', after Pesach. It is also known as the 'Feast of Weeks' and as 'Pentecost', from the Greek for 'fifty', since it falls on the fiftieth day. In Hebrew it can be called Zeman Matan Toratenu, ('The Season of the Giving of Our Law'), as its main focus is the giving of the Law to Moses and the people of Israel. In Israel, Shavuot is also a time of celebration for the wheat harvest.

Moses on Mount Sinai

After the Israelites had escaped from slavery in Egypt, they travelled through the desert. God protected them and provided for them, giving them manna to eat and fresh water when they needed it. After three months, they came to the foot of Mount Sinai. There, God spoke to Moses, and promised that if the people were prepared to obey him, he would make them a special nation.

The people agreed, and Moses told them to wash and prepare themselves to hear God's voice, and then, on the appointed day, to wait for the sound of the ram's horn before they approached the mountain. Two days later, at dawn, there was thunder and lightning, the sound of the ram's horn echoed through the camp and the people saw smoke rising from the mountain. Moses alone was allowed to go up the mountain, where God spoke to him and gave him the laws for his people, written on tablets of stone.

The Feast of Weeks

The Torah gives instructions for the Feast of Weeks fifty days after Pesach, but does not describe the occasion as a celebration of the giving of the Torah. This aspect came later, for reasons that are not clear. The main focus of the festival now is the study of the Torah, with many Jews spending the night in study.

Shavuot is also one of the traditional days for children to begin their Torah studies. When the Temple still stood in Jerusalem, Shavuot was one of the great pilgrimage festivals, when all who could do so made their way to Jerusalem, bringing the first fruits from their land. In

Flowers, singing and dancing are important ways of celebrating Shavuot. These children in a kindergarten in Jerusalem have made wreaths and decorated their classroom.

recent years there has been a movement to revive the pilgrimage, with hundreds of people making their way on foot to the Western Wall at sunrise for a service.

Homes and synagogues are beautifully decorated with flowers, greenery and stalks of wheat, recalling the tradition that Mount Sinai was green and covered with flowers, as the earth rejoiced at the giving of the Torah.

Many Jews spend the night of Shavuot studying the Torah, as a celebration of its special place in Jewish life..

A tradition of Shavuot is the eating of dairy foods, for which various possible reasons have been given: perhaps because it recalls the biblical promise of a land 'flowing with milk and honey'; or else that, when the Israelites were first given the Torah, it took them a little time to learn to follow the new laws about how to prepare meat, and so they ate dairy foods instead.

Counting the Days
The Torah gives instructions for offering a sheaf (*omer* in Hebrew) of barley in the Temple on the second day of Pesach, and counting forty-nine days from that day (Leviticus 23:15). The interval between Pesach and Shavuot is known as 'the period of counting the Omer'. Traditionally, it is a time of semi-mourning, when no weddings or celebrations are held.

The Ten Commandments

God gave Moses many detailed laws for the Jewish people, beginning with the ten most important ones – the Ten Commandments.

1. You shall have no other gods before me.
2. You shall not make for yourself a graven image, or any likeness of anything that is in heaven above, or that is on the earth beneath, or that is in the water under the earth; you shall not bow down to them or serve them
3. You shall not take the name of the Lord your God in vain
4. Observe the Sabbath day, to keep it holy, as the Lord your God commanded you. Six days you shall labour, and do all your work; but the seventh day is a Sabbath to the Lord your God; in it you shall not do any work.
5. Honour your father and your mother.
6. You shall not kill.
7. Neither shall you commit adultery.
8. Neither shall you steal.
9. Neither shall you bear false witness against your neighbour.
10. Neither shall you covet your neighbour's wife, or anything that is your neighbour's.
(Extracts from Deuteronomy 5: 6–22). Another version is given in Exodus 20:2–17.

'This book of Torah shall not depart from your mouth, and you shall meditate upon it day and night.' (Joshua 1:8). The Ten Commandments are often carved in stone or wood above the ark where the Torah is kept.

Some Minor Festivals

ISRAEL REMEMBRANCE DAY
Yom Hazikaron– Israel Remembrance Day – takes place on 4 Iyar, a week after Holocaust Day. It commemorates those who died fighting to establish and defend the state of Israel. Two 2-minute silences, one at 8 pm and another at 11 am, are observed across the nation, and a ceremony of remembrance is broadcast.

A number of festivals commemorate events in Jewish history, or aspects of the Land of Israel, which has religious as well as national importance for Jews. Some of these festivals are joyful, others filled with sadness.

A solemn occasion

Tishah B'Av, on 9 Av, is a solemn festival. According to tradition, a number of disasters for the Jewish people occurred on that day. First, God decreed that, because the people would not trust him, those who had left Israel should not enter the Promised Land, and all would spend forty years in the desert. Then, in 586 BC and AD 70 respectively, the First and the Second Temple in Jerusalem were destroyed. Later, in AD 135, the last Jewish fortress fell, during a rebellion against Roman rule, and, in 1492, King Ferdinand of Spain decreed that all Jews must leave Spain by that day.

Many of the observances of Tishah B'Av are similar to the customs followed by those in mourning for a death in the family. Only plain and simple food is eaten, many Jews refraining from meat for three weeks before the day. In the synagogue and at home, people may sit on the floor or on a low stool rather than on chairs, and at services, special prayers of mourning are said. The readings are from the Book of Lamentations, and the sanctuary is darkened.

Many Jews do not even study the Torah on Tishah B'Av, as that would be a source of joy. Instead, they may study the Book of Job, which is a reflection on the problems of undeserved suffering.

Suspended mourning

The period between Pesach and Shavuot, known as 'counting the Omer', is a time of semi-mourning: Jews do not cut their hair and they refrain from any merrymaking. However, the mourning is suspended for one day – Lag B'Omer – which means 'the thirty-third day of counting the Omer'. The festival of Lag B'Omer is celebrated on 18 Iyar, and commemorates a time when bad things began to get better. In the first century AD, the students or followers of Rabbi Akiva suffered a great plague, which killed 24,000 of them.

Many Israeli schoolchildren and others plant trees for Tu B'Shevat. People in other countries give money to finance reafforestation in Israel.

What this plague was is unknown, and some speculate that it may refer to the 'plague' of Roman rule, against which they were waging guerrilla warfare. However, on the thirty-third day of counting the Omer, the plague ceased, and Rabbi Akiva's remaining followers rejoiced.

The day is also celebrated as the anniversary of the death of another great teacher, Shimon bar Yohai. In Israel, it is an occasion for many people to visit his grave, hold wedding celebrations or have a haircut. For some Orthodox Jews, it is the traditional time for a three-year-old child to have its hair cut for the first time.

Being associated with the students of Rabbi Akiva, the day is also celebrated in Israel as a schoolchildren's holiday. One of the traditional games played was bows and arrows, underlining the theme of armed resistance. Another custom is going on picnics, which may recall times when students had to study the Torah in secret and meet in remote rural areas.

New year for Trees

Tu B'Shevat (15 Shevat) is celebrated as the New Year for Trees. It is mentioned in both the Mishnah and the Talmud, but fell out of use during the early Middle Ages. However, the festival is gaining in importance as an environmental festival – a time to celebrate God's goodness in the natural order, and humanity's duty to care for nature.

A Tu B'Shevat Seder, similar to the Pesach Seder, is a reviving tradition. It includes recitations and songs, drinking four cups of wine and eating the fruits for which the Torah praises the land of Israel, such as wheat, barley, grapes, figs, pomegranates, olives and dates.

Israel Independence Day

Jews worldwide celebrate 5 Iyar as Israel Independence Day. On this day, in 1948, the modern state of Israel was established, fulfilling the hopes of many Jews for a return to the land promised by God. The occasion is marked by huge public celebrations, with fireworks, and addresses to the nation by the President of Israel and the Chief Rabbi.

Holocaust Memorial Day

Soon after coming to power in 1933, Hitler's extreme right-wing, anti-Semitic National Socialist (Nazi) Party brought in severe restrictions on the Jewish communities of Germany.

Between 1940 and 1945, six million Jews were killed by the Nazis and their collaborators. This amounted to more than a third of the number of Jews in the world at the time. Millions of Jews and non-Jews were murdered in concentration camps, or died from disease or starvation. This period is known as the Holocaust, a word from the Greek version of the Hebrew Bible, referring to a sacrifice consumed by fire, or in Hebrew as the *shoah*, 'catastrophe'. Many countries have now adopted a national day of remembrance and mourning for the victims. In Israel, Holocaust Day occurs on the 27 Nissan. The main ceremony is broadcast from Yad Vashem, the Holocaust memorial in Jerusalem, in the morning. At 10 am, the sirens are sounded, marking two minutes of national silence and stillness, during which all transportation comes to a halt. Since 1961, all places of entertainment have been required to close on Holocaust Day and the previous evening. Some religious Jews do not participate in Holocaust Day, regarding it a secular festival. Outside Israel, some countries hold a simpler day of remembrance on 19 April.

Two minutes' silence is kept at Yad Vashem, in front of the flame and the lowered flag which commemorate the six million Jews murdered in the Holocaust.

CHRISTIAN FESTIVALS

Christianity is the biggest of the world religions in terms of the number of its followers. A majority in Europe and the United States describe themselves as Christians, and the numbers of Christians in South America, Africa and the Far East are growing rapidly. Christian festivals have become an established part of western culture, even if today some of them have become detached from their original religious meanings.

The life of Christ

Christians believe that the man Jesus, born to a Jewish couple in Palestine in the first century AD, was the Christ, a Greek word meaning the 'anointed', or 'chosen one of God'. He is thus sometimes described as the 'Son of God', or 'God in human form'.

When aged about 30, Jesus spent three years as an itinerant preacher and healer near his home town of Nazareth, and in Jerusalem. He died, according to Christian belief, by crucifixion (a Roman method of executing criminals) and was raised to life again by the power of God. His life, death and resurrection, Christians say, can reconcile humanity with God. Most Christian festivals celebrate the life of Jesus, from birth to death and resurrection.

Christian denominations

Of the many different Christian groups, the three largest are Roman Catholics, Orthodox Christians and Protestants. The Catholic and Orthodox traditions place greater emphasis on festivals, using much colour and ceremony. In the Catholic Church, the Virgin Mary, the Mother of Jesus, is an especially important figure, and Catholic festivals often focus on her life or on the lives of Christian saints.

The Protestants, who split from the Catholic Church in the sixteenth century, have, for historical reasons, generally made less use of ceremony and festivals, seeing them as part of the tradition against which they had rebelled. Under extreme forms of Protestantism, such as the Puritan government of Oliver Cromwell in seventeenth-century England, many festivals were banned, including even Christmas.

Christian belief and festivals centre on Jesus, known as the Christ, God's anointed one. This stained glass window depicts his baptism in the river Jordan.

History and Belief

Jesus' death and resurrection are central to Christian belief, and the cross is the universal Christian symbol. When the figure of Jesus is shown, as in this example from the church of San Damiano in Assisi, it is known as a crucifix.

Almost all the available information on Jesus concerns the short period (probably three years) from when he was about thirty years' old to his death. During that time, he preached a message about the 'kingdom of heaven', gathered many followers around him and appointed twelve of these disciples – the Twelve Apostles – to be with him and hear more of his teaching. At the end, he was arrested, was crucified and died on the cross. According to the Gospels, he was punished largely because of the religious opposition he had aroused among the Jewish leadership.

Two days after his death and burial, and over the next forty days, Jesus' disciples had several encounters with him. This convinced them that he had been brought back to life by the power of God: the event that is celebrated at Easter. At the end of this time he is described as ascending into Heaven, and was seen no more in the flesh.

The early Christian Church

After Jesus' ascension, his disciples continued to meet with each other. Before long, they underwent a powerful experience of God the Holy Spirit, filling them with enthusiasm and with the power to preach, perform miracles and make converts. This episode is commemorated at the festival of Whitsun, or Pentecost, and is often regarded as the true beginning of the Christian faith.

From then on, an increasing number of people came to believe in Jesus as the Messiah, the anointed one of God. The original disciples travelled widely, teaching and converting others to their faith. The converts in turn established local Christian groups, so that very soon there were groups of Christians – churches – all around the Mediterranean, in Egypt, Greece, Italy and Asia Minor.

Evangelists, saints and martyrs

Almost immediately, the new faith came under attack from the authorities of the Roman Empire, as Christians refused to worship the Roman gods or to recognize Roman emperors as gods. In the early years, tens of thousands of Christians were killed for their beliefs, but still their numbers continued to grow.

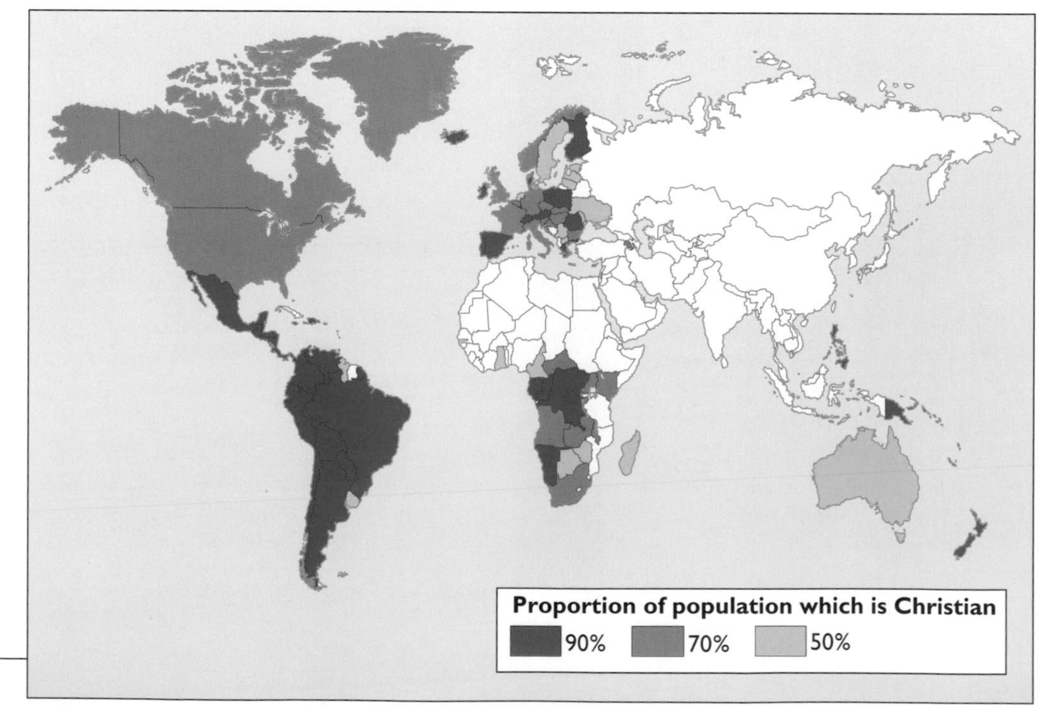

The map shows the strength of Christianity in South America and southern Africa. Figures in North America and Europe are hard to judge since different organizations collect data in different ways, and regular church attendance is much lower than the number of people who describe themselves as Christian.

The faith continued to spread in the third and early fourth centuries, despite the persecution of Christians across the Roman Empire. Beyond its borders, the Kingdom of Armenia became the first Christian state. There were also sizeable communities of Christians in southern India, southern Arabia, the Nile valley and Sudan, the Horn of Africa and the Caucasus and in the Persian Empire.

Soon, a system of local organizations headed by bishops developed. From time to time the bishops would meet, in an attempt to preserve the unity of Christian teaching against the various local variations that arose. Many of these were condemned as heresies by the bishops' conferences, but some groups continued to teach and make converts, such as the Nestorians and Monophysites, who took Christianity to Asia and as far as China.

Acceptance and Influence

In AD 313 the accession of Constantine as Roman Emperor changed everything. He first tolerated and then adopted the new faith. As the Romans expanded their empire into northern Europe, Christianity spread with them. Many countries of Europe commemorate those who are credited with spreading Christianity in that country, such as St Patrick in Ireland, St Boniface in Germany, or St James (Sant Iago) in Spain.

Christian teaching represents God as Three in One. This symbolic picture shows God the Father, holding the Son (Jesus) who is part of him, and the Holy Spirit represented as a dove.

Christian Scriptures

In the Christian Bible, the Old Testament contains almost all of the same writings as the Hebrew (Jewish) Bible; the New Testament is a collection of writings dating from very soon after the life of Jesus. It includes the Gospels, the Acts of the Apostles, which tell the story of the few years after Jesus' death, several letters explaining the faith to new groups of Christians, and the book of Revelation, which describes a vision of the end of time.

The Gospels

The main events of Jesus' life, death and resurrection, and his teachings, are recorded in the Gospels. These were written within a hundred years of Jesus' death, and are probably based on earlier accounts given soon after the events that they describe. Four Gospels appear in The Bible – Matthew, Mark, Luke and John – though others of more doubtful accuracy or authenticity also exist. There are also many traditional legends about Jesus, particularly about his birth and childhood, which are often retold and celebrated at festivals.

Differences and Divisions

Worship and Celebration
Styles of worship vary greatly between denominations, from noisy to quiet, from dancing to sitting motionless. Most gatherings involve some singing and reading from the Bible and include a service that is called the Mass, Eucharist or Holy Communion. In it, worshippers share bread and wine, recalling Jesus' words the night before he died: 'This is my body', as he shared bread, and 'This is my blood', as he shared wine.

From its very earliest days, Christianity has had groups within it with widely differing ideas. Over centuries, the differences became divisions and various traditions of Christianity came into being.

When the Roman Empire divided into East and West, Christianity centred on the two respective capital cities, Rome and Constantinople (modern Istanbul). In time, differences of teaching and authority arose between them, which finally caused a split in the Church in 1054.

In the western Church, Rome had a unique place because it alone in western Europe had a tradition going back to Peter, the chief of the Apostles. Consequently, the bishop of Rome, who by now was known as the Pope, became the head of the western, Roman Catholic Church. The eastern Orthodox Church, meanwhile, was expanding northwards, reaching Russia in the year 988. When Constantinople fell to the Turks in 1453, the Church in Russia became the cultural and spiritual centre of eastern Christianity.

The Reformation

In 1517, Martin Luther, a Catholic monk, disagreed publicly with the teachings of the Catholic Church, and was eventually expelled. The creation of national churches allied to dissatisfaction with the power of the Pope and the Catholic Church caused these churches to break away. These ruptures led to numerous wars of religion in Europe and to further splitting of different groups or denominations, which continues to this day.

As European countries expanded their territories abroad, western forms of Christianity were brought to their new outposts of empire. The religious divisions and disputes within Europe were

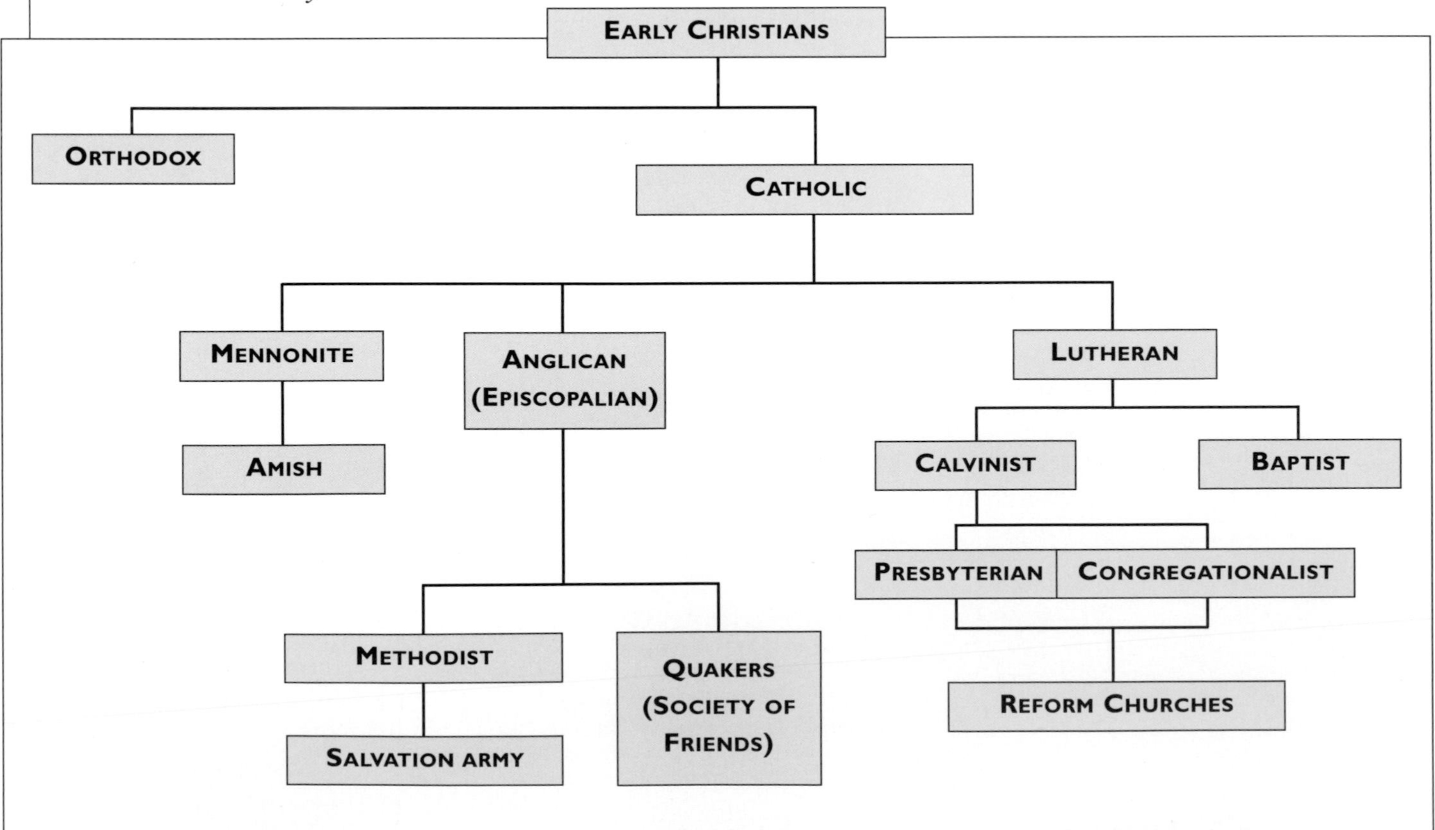

The development of Christian denominations. This chart indicares the links and 'family resemblances' between some of the churches we know today.

carried on across the world. Today, the type of Christianity found in former European colonies very often depends on which European country was the occupying power.

CHRISTIAN TRADITION AND OTHER CULTURES

In the past, converted Christians in Africa and Asia often adopted the culture, including the language, of the missionaries who taught them their faith.

However, in recent years local churches have developed their own ways of expressing their faith based on their own language and culture, using their own music and art forms, rather than European models. As a result, this has meant the development of a new group or denomination.

At the same time, among the older traditions, the Catholic Church has been particularly successful in presenting its beliefs, worship and celebration in ways appropriate to local cultures.

In Europe and North America, churches of all denominations are trying to develop new ways of adapting to the culture and interests of the secular world.

This has led not only to the growth of Christian TV channels and 'televangelists' in the USA, but also to the use of presentation skills taken from the world of entertainment in western churches. The use of rock music, visual effects, video and internet websites have a part to play in many churches in the twenty-first century.

Villagers in Guatemala celebrate Good Friday with designs in coloured sawdust. This one shows the angel Gabriel blowing his horn.

A re-creation of a historical Harvest Festival procession in Santa Fe, New Mexico, USA.

Times and Seasons

Christian festivals celebrate the main happenings in the life of Jesus, the Christian year telescoping the events of his thirty-three years into one year. Because the exact dates of many of these episodes are not known, dates were sometimes fixed to make an appropriate succession of events rather than with any historical accuracy. Particular days were allotted to festivals in a variety of ways that were mostly to do with local conditions in Europe as the Christian faith developed.

Creating the calendar

According to the Gospels, Jesus died at the time of the Jewish festival of Passover and was raised to life on a Sunday – the day after the Sabbath. From earliest times, Christians have celebrated his resurrection on a date based on the Jewish lunar calendar. Since Easter is always a Sunday, and Passover has no fixed day of the week, several different methods were developed to calculate the date, but still there is no worldwide agreement. The series of festivals from Ash Wednesday through Pentecost and beyond are fixed in relation to Easter, so the dates of these festivals vary from year to year in ways that are quite complicated to calculate.

THE ORTHODOX CALENDAR
Orthodox Churches use a calendar different from that used by other major Christian groups. This is partly because of a different method for calculating Easter, but also because some Orthodox Churches, though not all, still use the Julian calendar, rather than the modern Gregorian one. In the Julian calendar, dates are thirteen days later than in the Gregorian calendar

In Britain, the harvest festival in September is a time for giving thanks for the harvest, for God's provision of food for the coming winter.

THE CHURCH YEAR

The traditions and festivals of the Christian Church developed over time as the faith spread. The church year always starts with Advent.

1 BEGINNING OF ADVENT
Preparation for the coming of Jesus, and the start of the Christian year, which begins four Sundays before Christmas.

2 CHRISTMAS DAY (25 DECEMBER)
Celebration of the birth of Jesus in Bethlehem.

3 EPIPHANY (6 JANUARY)
Literally, 'Showing forth' – the visit of the wise men to the infant Jesus. In the Orthodox Church especially, Epiphany also celebrates his baptism as an adult and the start of his preaching career.

4 ANNUNCIATION (25 MARCH)
The Angel Gabriel tells Mary that she is to bear God's son.

5 SHROVE TUESDAY
The day before the start of Lent.
Lent is a period of six-and-a-half weeks of penitence and fasting in preparation for Good Friday (40 days not counting Sundays).

6 ASH WEDNESDAY
The first day of Lent. Many Christians receive a mark of ashes on their forehead as a sign of penitence.

7 MOTHERING SUNDAY
Two weeks before Easter, Christians honour either their natural mother or their 'mother' church or monastery.

8 PALM SUNDAY
One week before Easter, Jesus rode into Jerusalem on a donkey, to the acclamation of the crowd.

9 MAUNDY THURSDAY
Jesus shared the Last Supper with his disciples, and instituted the Eucharist, or Holy Communion.

10 GOOD FRIDAY
Jesus' trial, crucifixion and death. Many Christians attend a service between 12 noon and 3 pm, the time that Jesus was suffering on the cross.

11 EASTER SUNDAY
Celebration of God's raising of Jesus from the dead. Churches are decorated and filled with candles and light.

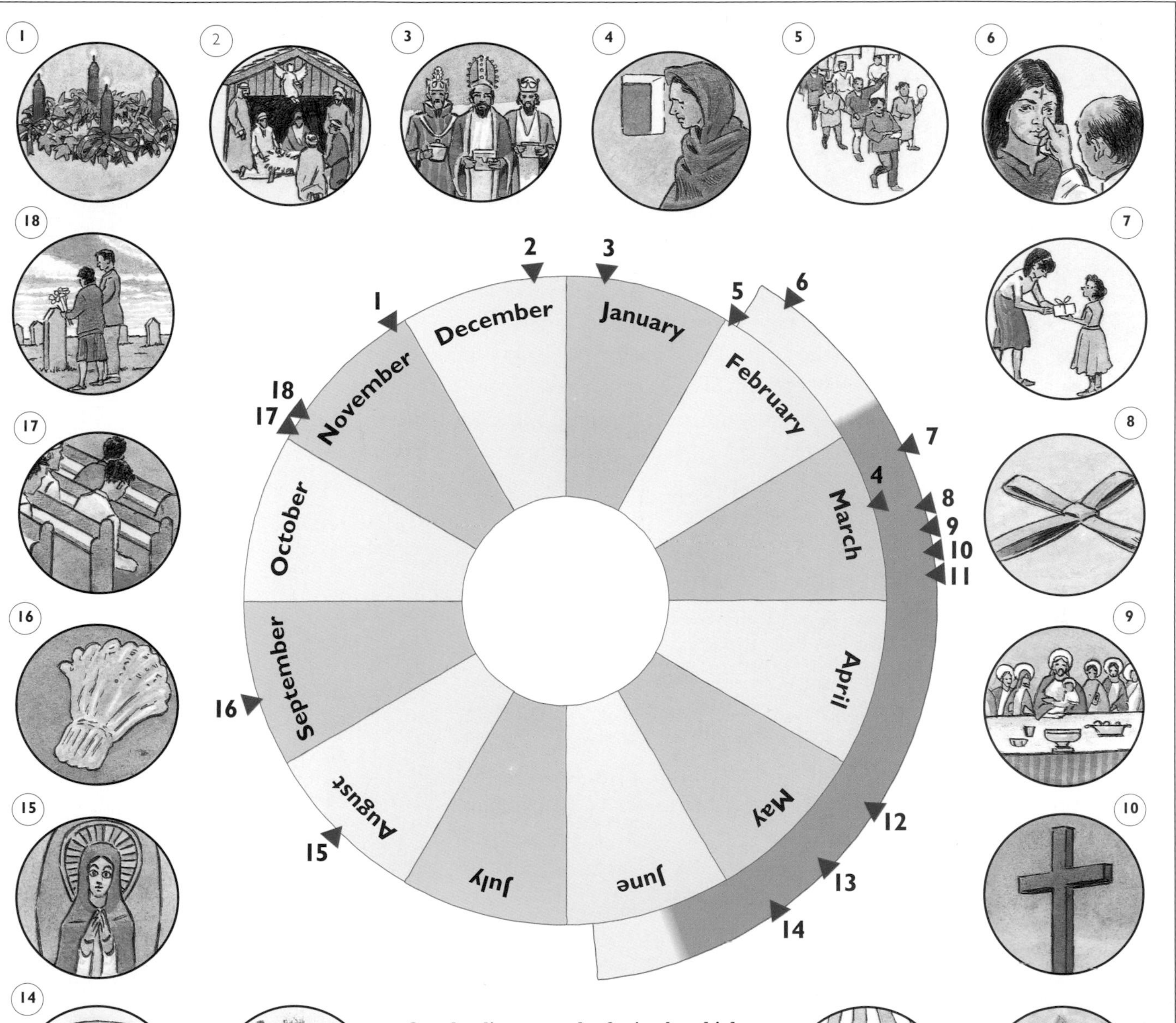

On the diagram, the festivals which move with Easter are marked on the outer segment. The lighter shaded area shows the earliest and latest dates for these festivals.

12 ASCENSION
Always a Thursday, 40 days after Easter. The last time Jesus was seen in the flesh. The disciples saw him taken up into heaven.

13 WHITSUN/PENTECOST
Always a Sunday, seven weeks after Easter. The disciples felt a great wind and saw flames, and were filled with the power of God. They began to preach that Jesus was the Messiah.

14 CORPUS CHRISTI
In Catholic and Orthodox Churches, a celebration of the Eucharist as the body and blood of Christ. This takes place either 10 days after Pentecost or the following Sunday.

15 FEAST OF THE ASSUMPTION (OR DORMITION) OF MARY (15 AUGUST)
In Catholic and Orthodox Churches, Mary the mother of Jesus is believed to have passed straight to Heaven at the end of her life on earth.

16 HARVEST FESTIVAL
Not an official church festival, but often held in the northern hemisphere in September to give thanks for food and the harvest.

17 ALL SAINTS' DAY (1 NOVEMBER)
Commemoration of all Christian saints.

18 ALL SOULS' DAY (2 NOVEMBER)
Commemoration of all Christians (or for some churches, all good people) who have died.

The Period of Advent

The Christian year officially starts four Sundays before Christmas Day. This is the beginning of Advent, the period of preparation for Christmas. If 25 December falls on a Sunday, Advent will be four weeks' long; if on a Monday, then Advent will last just over three weeks. Many secular customs simply take Advent as starting on the 1st of December.

Advent means 'coming' or 'arrival'. The emphasis is on preparedness for the arrival of Jesus, whom Christians believe to be God in human form. Mary's pregnancy is remembered, and the preparations she had to make for the birth of her son. Christians also think about preparing to celebrate Christmas at their own home with their family, and – above all – about the need to prepare one's inner self to receive Jesus in spirit. As well as looking backwards to the birth 2,000 years ago, Advent is also a time for looking ahead to prepare for the promised second coming of Jesus in glory at the end of time, when, Christians believe, all human beings will be judged.

The Christmas story

The story of the birth of Jesus starts with the visit of the Angel Gabriel to Mary, a young girl of Nazareth, who was betrothed to a man called Joseph. The angel told her that she would bear a son by the power of God, although she was a virgin, and that the child's name should be Jesus. Joseph was suspicious of her pregnancy at first, but took her as his wife after a dream in which God reassured him.

Not long before her baby was due, a decree from the Roman ruler of the region commanded that every man should return with his family to his ancestral home for a census to be taken. Joseph was descended from King David, whose home town was Bethlehem, near Jerusalem, so he and Mary travelled there together. Luke's Gospel relates that 'there was no room for them in the inn', and tradition has added details of their journey from house to house seeking lodging, with Mary heavily pregnant and both of them weary from the journey.

The 4th century Saint Lucia is celebrated in Advent, on 13 December. In Sweden, on St Lucia's day, girls fasten candle crowns to their heads, and visit the family first thing in the morning with coffee and special spicy buns.

Christingle

The Christingle began in the Moravian Church. It consists of an orange, symbolizing the world, a candle, the symbol for Christ, a red ribbon and sticks, to represent his wounds at the crucifixion, and raisins or sweets on the sticks, standing for the fruits of the earth given by God. Many churches now hold a service during Advent in which every person, or every child, receives a Christingle.

Posada

In Mexico and other Latin American countries, the last twelve days of Advent re-enact Joseph and Mary's journey to Bethlehem and their search for lodgings (*posada* in Spanish). A couple with a donkey travel from house to house, accompanied by a choir of children. They knock on each door, and are refused entry. When the procession reaches the church, a Mass is celebrated, followed by a party at one of the houses.

Advent Wreath

Many families and churches prepare an Advent wreath, or crown. Greenery is bound to a wheel shape, and four candles are fastened round the edge, with a taller one, usually white, in the middle. One of the candles round the edge is lit on the first Sunday in Advent, two on the second, and so on, until on Christmas Day all four are lit as well as the central candle.

Dating Christmas

No one knows the date, the time of year or even the year of Jesus' birth for certain. Early Christians in Europe began to celebrate the birth around the time of the winter solstice. This was possibly to fit in with pre-Christian traditions of feasting at this time, but also because of the symbolism of Jesus coming as a light into a dark world, as stressed in John's Gospel.

The spread of Christianity worldwide means that many people now celebrate Christmas in mid-summer, but the symbolism of light coming into the darkness is still powerful among Christians, even in the tropics where there is little difference in the length of days,

The system of numbering years AD (Anno Domini –the year of the Lord) did not begin until the sixth century. It was based on an estimate of the year in which Jesus was born, which is now thought to be inaccurate. Modern scholarship puts his birth at about 4 BC.

SANTA CLAUS

Within the period of Advent there are several Saints' Days that have been assimilated into Advent and Christmas customs. The saint who has become most closely associated with Christmas is Nicholas, fourth-century Bishop of Myra (in modern-day Turkey), who is more familiar as Saint Nicholas or Santa Claus.

Very little is known about him as a historical figure, but a host of legends celebrate his generosity and kindness, especially to needy children. He was renowned for bestowing his gifts secretly, at night. His feast day is 6 December, and in many Christian traditions it is this day, not Christmas Day, that is the time for giving presents. Children put their shoes outside the door when they go to bed on 5 December, so that St Nicholas can come and fill those belonging to good children with sweets and cakes. In Holland, 'Bishop Nicolas' tours the streets giving presents to children.

The picture of a jolly old man in a red coat, riding in a sleigh pulled by reindeer, developed in the nineteenth century from a poem by Clement C. Moore, an American, and a series of illustrations by Thomas Nash in *Harper's Weekly* magazine. This figure also became associated with Father Christmas, an older character in European folklore who probably originates in pre-Christian mid-winter customs.

Preparations for Christmas often follow local traditions such as this Russian Nativity house depicting various scenes from the Christmas story.

The Twelve Days of Christmas

St Francis and the Crib
In 1223, St Francis of Assisi wanted to help poor people understand the poverty and hardship of Jesus' birth. Francis brought an ox and and ass into a cave in a wood, and spread hay over a stone. When Francis preached his sermon in the cave many of his audience, it is said, saw a living, moving child lying on the hay. St Francis was not the first to make a Christmas crib, but his devotion meant that the custom spread rapidly across Europe.

Mary and Joseph eventually found some sort of lodging in Bethlehem, where Mary's baby was born. Traditionally, they are believed to have stayed in a stable or cowshed, because Luke's Gospel says that Mary laid the baby in a manger 'because there was no room for them in the inn'.

Not far away, some shepherds out at night looking after their sheep saw an angel who told them the joyful news. A whole chorus of angels then sang praises to God, and the shepherds decided to go and see the baby. They told people what they had heard from the angel and returned to their sheep, rejoicing and praising God.

The Three Wise Men

Some time after Jesus was born, 'wise men from the East' came to Jerusalem asking for the child who had been born 'king of the Jews'. They had seen his star and wished to pay him homage. When Herod, King of Judaea, heard about this, he was disturbed. He told the wise men to come back and tell him when they found the child so he could worship there too. The star led the wise men to Bethlehem where they found Jesus, knelt down and presented their gifts.

The wise men had a dream warning them not to return to Herod, as he only wanted to kill the child. Joseph was also warned in a dream to flee with Mary and the baby to Egypt. Herod was furious when he discovered that the wise men had tricked him. He ordered that every boy in and around Bethlehem under two years old be killed, as it was two years since the wise men had first seen the star.

From earliest times, there have been traditions about the wise men to complete the brief account in Matthew's Gospel. There were thought to be three of them because they brought three gifts. The tradition that they were kings may have arisen from the value of the gifts and the expense of the journey. They might also have been Magi, Zoroastrian priests from the area of modern Iran who made a study of astrology. Their names – Caspar, Melchior and Balthazar – appear in very early tradition, and from the fifteenth century Balthazar is often portrayed as African. Their gifts are symbolic: gold for a king, frankincense (a resin that burns with a beautiful smell) to worship Jesus as God, and myrrh (a plant oil used to prepare bodies for burial) to show that he would one day die and be buried.

Crib-making has now become a worldwide tradition, drawing on local popular art-forms.

From Christmas Day to Epiphany
Many churches hold a service beginning before midnight on 24 December, because midnight marks the beginning of Christmas Day, when the first act of the worshippers is to receive Holy Communion. Around the world, the services held on Christmas Day vary enormously in length and style, as do public and private celebrations. This is the first of the twelve days of Christmas.

The end of the twelve-day Christmas season is marked by the feast of Epiphany (Greek 'showing forth'). Depending on the tradition, this is held on 6 January or on the first Sunday after Christmas. Epiphany celebrates the arrival of the wise men, the first people from outside the Jewish world to see and believe in the infant Christ. Many churches also celebrate the 'showing forth' of Jesus as an adult, when he was identified at his baptism as God's son.

Christmas food
The food eaten at Christmas varies from country to country, often depending on what is locally available for a feast. In the United Kingdom, turkey has replaced the goose or boar of earlier centuries. In France, a carp, a large fish, is a traditional Christmas dinner. Mince pies, which are pastry cases filled with dried fruit, were originally oval in shape to represent the infant Jesus lying in the manger. Italians eat a special cake called panettone. Norwegians bake bread known as Julecake, filled with raisins, spice and candied peel.

Children sing Christmas songs around a large open-air Christmas tree in San Antonio, Texas.

Traditional Christmas fare –goose with stuffing, mulled wine and cookies for dessert.

CHRISTMAS TREES AND OTHER PLANTS

The custom of Christmas trees started in Germany, around the sixteenth century, when families would either bring in a tree or make a small pyramid of wood, and decorate it with ornaments.

A story tells that it began with Martin Luther, the founder of Protestantism. Apparently, walking home one Christmas Eve he saw stars shining. He thought them so lovely that he tried to recapture that beauty by tying candles to the branches of a fir tree.

Germans and Ukrainians often decorate their trees with mock spider webs; Swedes often make decorations from straw.

Christmas plants include mistletoe, holly and ivy. The use of winter plants predates Christianity. The Romans used holly at their Saturnalia festival, and the Norse associated mistletoe with the death and resurrection of the sun god, Baldur. Kissing under mistletoe is an eighteenth-century custom.

The Easter Story

Nearly three months of the Christian year are devoted to celebrating the events that surrounded the end of Jesus' life on earth: his death by crucifixion and his rising to life again and ascending to heaven. The period begins on Shrove Tuesday and continues through Holy Week and Easter to Ascension Day. The dates of these festivals are fixed in relation to each other, but Easter varies from year to year between late March and late April.

The name 'Easter' probably comes from a Germanic pre-Christian goddess called Eostre, who had a festival around this time. In many languages the festival is called by some variation of 'Pesach', the Jewish Passover festival when these events first took place.

THE HARROWING OF HELL
Medieval plays and paintings describe the 'Harrowing of Hell', the occasion when, Christians believe, Jesus descended into Hell and released all the good people imprisoned there since the beginning of the world. In Orthodox churches it is celebrated in a long service whose high point is when the congregation bang their seats as loudly as they can, to represent Jesus bursting down the gates of Hell.

According to the Gospels
The story of Jesus' death and resurrection is told in all four Gospels, with varying details.

In three years of public preaching, teaching and healing, Jesus aroused considerable opposition from both the Jewish religious authorities and the Roman administration. At the same time, he won enormous popular acclaim. When he entered Jerusalem a week before the Passover festival, riding on a donkey, a crowd of people greeted him, shouting their praises and waving palm branches.

The following week, he angered his opponents further by his words and controversial actions. The religious auth-

THE STATIONS OF THE CROSS

Many Christians, especially Catholics, in some way trace Jesus' last walk, from Pilate's judgement hall to where he met his death. Some follow what is believed to be the actual route, the Via Dolorosa ('sorrowful road') in Jerusalem, while others re-enact the walk on a street in their homeland or trace it in their imagination with the help of pictures. Tradition refers to fourteen events, not all of which are recounted in the Gospels.

1 Jesus is condemned to die.

2 Jesus carries his cross.

3 Jesus falls the first time.

4 Jesus meets his mother.

5 Simon helps Jesus carry his cross.

6 Veronica wipes Jesus' face.

7 Jesus falls the second time.

8 Jesus meets the women of Jerusalem.

9 Jesus falls the third time.

10 Jesus is stripped.

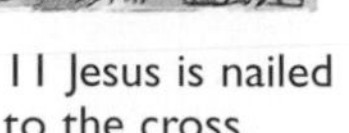
11 Jesus is nailed to the cross.

12 Jesus dies on the cross.

13 Jesus is taken down from the cross.

14 Jesus is laid in the tomb.

orities wanted to arrest him and silence him, but they were afraid of how the people might react if he were seized in public. Then Judas Iscariot, one of the twelve men closest to Jesus, offered to help facilitate his arrest when he would be alone, in exchange for thirty silver coins.

Betrayal, death and resurrection

On the night of Passover, Jesus and the twelve disciples gathered for a meal, now known as the Last Supper. First Jesus took on the role of the most menial servant, and washed the feet of his disciples. As they ate, he shared bread and wine with them, telling them that the meal was his body and blood. He told them that one of them would betray him, and that they would all desert him. Peter, one of Jesus' closest disciples, protested that he would never do that. Jesus told him that before the cock crowed next morning, Peter would deny him three times.

Then they left the house and went to a garden called Gethsemane, where Jesus prayed in great agony about his forthcoming ordeal. Soon, Judas returned with soldiers to arrest him, identifying Jesus to the soldiers by kissing him. All the disciples, including Peter, ran away, although some followed secretly. The next day, Jesus was tried, first before the religious authorities, then before Pontius Pilate, the Roman governor. He was condemned to be crucified, a standard Roman punishment for insurrection. He was crucified alongside two criminals, and died after three hours.

The following day was the Sabbath, when Jews could do no work, so Jesus' disciples obtained permission to take down the body and bury it in a tomb, donated by Joseph of Arimathea. A huge stone was rolled across the entrance to prevent any tampering with the body.

As soon as possible after the Sabbath, a group of women went to the tomb to anoint and prepare the body properly, which they could not do on the eve of the Sabbath. They found that the stone had been rolled away and the tomb was empty. Angels appeared before them, telling them that Jesus had risen from the dead by the power of God. For the next forty days, people close to Jesus had experiences that convinced them that Jesus was indeed alive, in the same body that had been broken on the cross.

Candles and eggs are symbols of resurrection and new life at Easter.

Symbolic Bread

Bread and yeast cookery is a powerful symbol of Easter, since the dough rises again after being 'knocked back'. People in many countries bake a traditional Easter bread or yeast bun. This is usually rich in eggs, milk and sugar – all of which would have been given up in Lent (see page 54). Hot-cross buns are the British equivalent. In eastern Europe, loaves are brought to church to be blessed early on Easter morning, and then taken back home for a festive breakfast.

Russian Easter Bread

Ingredients

- 1 cake of yeast or two packets of dry yeast
- 1 cup milk
- 1 cup cream
- 10 eggs
- 2 cups sugar
- 1 cup butter (2 sticks)
- 1 tablespoon lemon extract
- Lemon rind
- Sifted flour
- pinch of salt

Soften yeast in a cup of warm water. Mix and scald milk and cream. Beat the eggs well and add to cooled milk and cream. Combine the sugar, salt and butter and add to egg and milk mixture when lukewarm. Add softened yeast, lemon extract and lemon rind. Beat the flour to make a soft dough and then add more flour to make a stiff dough. Knead until satiny. Let rise till it doubles in volume. Punch down and knead slightly. Divide into three parts. Roll into smooth ball and place each one into a greased can such as a large coffee can. Fill can approximately one half full and let rise till doubled. Bake at 140C for about 1 hour. Cover domed top with foil after first 15 minutes to keep from getting too brown.

Russian cooks often ice and decorate the top quite elaborately.

Holy Week and Easter

Central to the Christian religion is the belief that God in human form voluntarily suffered and died in degrading circumstances, but that death could not hold him, and his true godly nature was revealed in the resurrection. These events, as described in the Gospels, are celebrated in a series of solemnities and festivals leading up to and beyond Easter.

Easter Garden
Some congregations or families build an Easter Garden – a small model of Jesus' tomb, made of earth and stones – which is placed either in the church or garden. Sometimes it includes three crosses on a hill, representing Jesus and the two the criminals who were executed with him.On Easter Sunday, the stone barring the tomb is rolled away, showing the empty grave.

Giving up for Lent

Lent is a time of preparation, both mental and physical, for the events of Good Friday and Easter Day. It also recalls the forty days that Jesus spent in the desert, without food or water, as a preparation for his public teaching and healing activities. For many Christians it is a time of self-discipline and solemn reflection: some refrain from eating meat and other animal products, such as cheese and eggs; others do not get married at this time or make love; while yet others give up some favourite item such as sweets or cakes.

On Ash Wednesday, the first day of Lent, church services are held in which Christians receive a mark of ashes smeared on their forehead in the shape of a cross, as a sign of repentance.

From Palm Sunday to Maundy Thursday

The week before Easter Sunday is known as Holy Week. It begins with Palm Sunday, which recalls Jesus' triumphant entry into Jerusalem, riding upon a donkey, while the people waved palms and shouted 'Hosanna! Hosanna!'

On Palm Sunday, churches are decorated with palm leaves, if available, or evergreen tree leaves and facsimiles of palm leaves. Often there is a procession around the church or through the streets, with singing and waving leaves or branches.

The Thursday of Holy Week is called Maundy Thursday. 'Maundy' is derived from the Latin *mandatum novum*, meaning 'new commandment'. This refers to Jesus' words at the Last Supper, as reported in John's Gospel:

'I give you a new commandment, that you love one another.'

Christians remember how Jesus, the master, washed his followers' feet. The story is often re-enacted on Maundy Thursday,

Easter Eggs
Since the fourth century, the egg, with its potent connotations of new life and rebirth, has been associated with Easter. In the West, the custom is generally to give chocolate eggs, which are a twentieth-century invention. In Orthodox countries, such as Russia, Greece and parts of eastern Europe, the custom is to hollow out eggshells and paint them in bright colours. Children often crack their eggs against each other's, like chestnuts, seeing whose will break first.

Christians from all over the world visit Jerusalem for Holy Week. In the Good Friday procession, a simple wooden cross is lifted high for all to see, as the pilgrims make their sad way towards the place of the crucifixion.

with someone of conventionally high status, such as a priest or monarch, washing the feet of those with lower status. In medieval Europe, kings washed the feet of specially invited poor people, and afterwards gave them food, clothes or money. The custom has survived in the tradition of the British monarch giving 'Maundy money' to a selected number of senior citizens. The money nowadays consists of specially minted coins that do not resemble normal currency.

Some Christians celebrate an *agape* – a communion in the form of a meal – in memory of the Last Supper. Church services are usually quiet and meditative, and end with the stripping of all decorations and candles from the church as the congregation remembers the arrest and impending death of Jesus.

From Good Friday to Easter Sunday

It may seem strange that the day that Jesus died is called Good Friday. However, Christians believe that as a result of his death and resurrection, good triumphed. Jesus accepted suffering and death to bring all humanity back to God. Many churches hold a meditative service from noon until 3 p.m., to mark the length of time that Jesus was on the cross before he died.

Late on Easter Saturday evening, many churches begin a vigil which lasts until the early morning of Easter Day. After midnight, the church is decked with light and colour again, as people exchange the traditional Easter greeting: 'Christ is risen!' – 'He is risen indeed – Alleluia!' Easter morning services are joyful and full of music.

Ascension Day and Pentecost

In Lancashire and Yorkshire, 'Whit walks' during the week following Whitsun were common in the nineteenth century and the first half of the twentieth, and still take place in some areas today. The procession was often led by a Rose Queen, perhaps to represent the Virgin Mary, followed by girls in new white dresses who carried flowers. The walkers, accompanied by a brass band, wound their way round every part of the parish, as if celebrating the preaching of the gospel by the first Apostles.

For forty days after Jesus' crucifixion and resurrection, a large number of his friends saw him alive in the flesh. He spoke to them of going away, but also of sending in his place 'another comforter', or 'one who strengthens'. At the end of the forty days, he led his friends out of the city of Jerusalem to a village called Bethany. He told them to wait in Jerusalem until they received power from heaven, then he disappeared from sight. In some accounts, he was seen being lifted up into heaven, and two men in white robes appeared saying that he would return in the same way.

Pentecost

The disciples duly waited in Jerusalem until the Jewish festival of Shavuot (also known by its Greek name 'Pentecost'), which takes place seven weeks after the Passover festival. That day, when they were all together in one room, they suddenly became aware of a strong rushing wind and saw tongues of fire, which separated and rested on the head of each one of them. They were filled with the power of God and rushed out of the house to tell people that the man executed as a dangerous criminal was in fact the Chosen One of God, and had been raised to life by God's power.

As they spoke, those who heard them experienced different things. Some thought they were drunk, but others – visitors to Jerusalem from many different countries – were astonished to hear themselves addressed each in their own language. From that time on, the group of Jesus' friends and disciples, who had run away when Jesus was arrested, now risked arrest themselves, and faced beatings and

Pentecost, or Whitsun, was the day on which new members to the church were traditionally admitted by being baptized. They often wore white –hence the name Whitsun, meaning 'white Sunday'.

Forty days after he rose from the dead, Jesus left his disciples once more. He is traditionally portrayed as 'going up' into Heaven, as in this Bible illustration.

other punishments because they would not stop telling others that Jesus was risen from the dead. On that first morning alone, 3,000 people believed their words and became followers of Jesus. The power from on high, the Holy Spirit, had come.

A new religion

The events of that morning, known to Christians as Pentecost or Whitsun, are regarded as the beginning of the Christian faith, the time when followers of Jesus took on the responsibility and the power to act without the physical presence of Jesus, because the Holy Spirit was working in them.

Whitsun falls seven weeks after Easter Sunday. The importance that is given to it by the Church varies considerably according to the particular Christian tradition. Some churches – known as 'Pentecostalist' – regard the ecstatic speaking in unknown languages as an important part of Christian worship, and give this festival special prominence.

Ascension Day

Sometimes referred to as Holy Thursday, Ascension Day is always celebrated forty days after Easter Day, and therefore falls on a Thursday. Church services are held to mark the occasion, but it is no longer a major church festival in most traditions.

Various traditional practices have survived. For example, in Germany groups of men go off together for hunting and drinking parties, which is perhaps why the day has also become known as 'Father's Day'. In Britain Ascension Day, or the previous Sunday, was the day for 'beating the bounds' – a procession around the parish boundaries to establish that fences and boundary markers were still in good order and had not been moved.

Food on Ascension Day traditionally included a bird of some sort, because birds can 'fly up to heaven'. There was also the belief that it would rain on Ascension Day because of the hole that Christ made in the sky!

THE QUEEN OF THE MARSHES

In southern Spain, the Pentecost weekend is the time of pilgrimage to the shrine of the *Virgen del Rocio* in the marshes near Almonte. No motor vehicles are allowed, and nearly a million people make their way on foot, on horseback or by ox-cart from the surrounding countryside, and from the cities of Seville, Madrid and Barcelona. They dress in traditional Andalusian costume, the women in flamenco-style dresses and the men in short jackets and wearing wide-brimmed hats. From the village of Almonte, the pilgrims travel across the marshes to the shrine, singing and playing flutes, tambourines and guitars. Then the image of the Virgin Mary is carried around the fields as the crowd shouts *'Viva la Reina de la Marisma!'* (Hail to the Queen of the Marshes!).

WHITSUNTIDE ACROSS EUROPE

A vast number of Whitsuntide customs are found in different parts of Britain and Northern Europe. In most cases, the religious significance of the day has merged with customs that are probably pre-Christian, but these traditions also reflect the fact that this is a holiday in early summer.

Different European countries associate different plants and flowers with Whitsun, which is probably due to differences in climate.

In Hungary, Germany and Lithuania birch twigs are the traditional Whitsun decoration, woven into wreaths or tied in bunches round the house.

In Italy, rose petals are scattered in churches to recall the flames seen on the disciples' heads, and in Russia girls carry flowering branches. In western Hungary, there is a custom of leaving all the doors of the houses open so that the Holy Spirit can blow in freely, while in France they used to make blowing noises with their mouths to recall the rushing wind in the story.

In many parts of Northern Europe, Whitsun is the traditional time for the cattle to be driven to their summer pastures, often with their horns decorated with green branches, ribbons and bells. The first animal to reach the pasture is regarded as especially blessed.

Corpus Christi and Festivals of Mary

MAJOR FEASTS OF MARY
1 January Feast of the Incarnation by the Virgin Mary

2 February Purification

25 March Annunciation by Gabriel ('Lady Day')

31 May Visitation by Mary to Saint Elizabeth

15 August Assumption into Heaven

8 September Mary's Birthday

8 December Mary's Immaculate Conception

Not all Christian festivals are celebrated by all Christians. Certain festivals important to some Churches may be downplayed or ignored by other denominations. Moreover, the same occasion is often celebrated in different ways in different parts of the world, according to the local tradition. One such festival is that of Corpus Christi.

Corpus Christi (Body of Christ) commemorates the institution of the Eucharist (Holy Communion). It is celebrated ten days after Pentecost, a Thursday, or in the United States and some other countries, on the Sunday two weeks after Pentecost.

Jesus' actions and words at the Last Supper are remembered on Maundy Thursday. However, because on that day there is so much emphasis on the imminent death of Jesus, a new festival of thanksgiving and celebration was instituted in the Catholic and Orthodox Churches.

The origin of the feast

In 1208, Juliana, a nun in Liège, Belgium, had a vision of a dazzling bright disc like the moon, but on one side there was a dark spot spoiling its beauty. She believed that God was telling her that this was because the church calendar had no solemn feast to honour the Blessed Sacrament (the body and blood of Jesus present in the Eucharist).

Officially sanctioned by Pope Urban IV in 1264, by the fourteenth century the observance had become universal in the western Church. There was often a procession of local dignitaries and church leaders and this soon became the main feature of the feast. In rural areas it turned into an agricultural festival as the procession made its way through the fields.

Music and dancing

In some parts of the world, especially South and Central America, the festival merged with local traditional festivals, incorporating plays, music, dancing and feasting. Statues newly dressed in fine robes are paraded through the streets, and churches are decorated.

In Cuzco, Peru, a statue of the patron saint of each church is carried through the streets in a colourful procession to

During the traditional celebration of Corpus Christi in Poland, girls scatter flowers in front of the procession carrying the Blessed Sacrament.

Throughout Catholic countries, statues of the Madonna and child (Jesus and Mary, his mother) are widespread, in homes, wayside shrines and churches.

the cathedral, where the saints remain for a week before being returned to their home churches. Every village community is involved: as musicians and dancers; carrying the statues; or providing a great feast for all the participants. Before the festival begins, new clothes are made for the saint and the statue is refurbished and painted. Each community tries to put on the best show with their saint. The ceremony probably derives from an ancient Inca festival in which a procession carried the mummified bodies of Inca emperors.

In Seville, Spain, the Sacrament (the consecrated bread and wine) is carried through the streets amid cheering, singing crowds. The church bells ring out. Part of the festivities commemorates the reign of Ferdinand and Isabella in the fifteenth century, and the expulsion of Muslims from Spain. The festival also features young boys in sixteenth-century costume performing the traditional Seise dances.

DORMITION AND ASSUMPTION

Nothing is known for certain about the date or the details of the Virgin Mary's death. From the fifth century, it was traditionally believed that, after she had died and been buried, her grave was reopened and found to be empty, as if she had been taken body and soul into heaven.

In different traditions, the date varies between three and fifteen years after Jesus' death and resurrection. The place is believed to have been either Jerusalem or Ephesus. The Orthodox Church celebrates the Dormition (falling asleep) of the Virgin Mary on 15 August, but is less specific about the Assumption.

The Feast of the Assumption has been celebrated on 15 August probably since the seventh or eighth century, but other dates are also recorded. It seems that, from that time onwards, a great procession was a feature of the festival. In many parts of Europe the festival falls in harvest time, and has become associated with other Christian and non-Christian harvest festivals, such as the Celtic festival of Lughnasa. The celebrations include singing, feasting, dancing and thanksgiving. In Germany there was a custom of collecting plants with healing properties and bringing them into church for a blessing on Assumption Day.

As part of the celebrations for the Assumption of the Virgin Mary, girls inthe Seychelles process a statue of the Virgin Mary on a palaquin adorned with flowers.

Saints and Martyrs

ST SWITHUN'S DAY

When Swithun, the ninth century Bishop of Winchester, died, he gave instructions that he was to be buried outside his church, but his remains were later moved into the new Cathedral. The story is told that it rained for forty days after this, and now if it rains on July 15, his feast day, it is said it will rain for forty days afterwards; if not, it will be fine for forty days.

The word 'saint' means 'holy or sacred one', but for centuries there have been differences among Christians over who is to be regarded as a saint. In the New Testament, the Greek equivalent of the word referred to anyone who believed in Jesus as the Christ, whereas in the Orthodox and Catholic Churches the title is reserved for persons of outstanding holiness. The Catholic Church, in particular, has a very rigorous process to go through before anyone can be declared a saint. Generally, Protestant Churches have reverted to the earlier meaning of the word, but they also recognize as saints particular people who are deemed worthy of memorial as examples to all Christians.

Many Christian traditions venerate saints, but they are particularly important in the Catholic and Orthodox Churches, for whom almost every day is dedicated to three or four saints. However, the Catholic and Orthodox Churches revere different saints.

Most saints' days are not marked by any special celebration, unless a church or an institution is dedicated to a particular saint, when an appropriate service may be held. In countries of eastern Europe, the day dedicated to the saint after whom someone is named – known as their 'name day' – is often an occasion for the same kind of celebrations and giving of gifts as birthdays in Western countries.

The Feast of All Saints

By the end of the third century there were so many martyrs that it became impossible to celebrate them all, and many of their names were unknown. This is probably the origin of the Feast of All Saints, when thanks are given for the lives of all those who can be regarded as saints. The occasion is also traditionally known as 'All Hallows' Day', from an old word for 'saint', and its eve – the night before – gave rise to Hallowe'en.

The celebration of All Saints' Day varies greatly according to the Church tradition. Catholics and Orthodox Christians pray to the saints or ask the saints to pray for them. Protestant traditions place the emphasis of the day on giving thanks for the lives of Christians down the ages, remembering one's own family and loved ones and holding a

This Russian Orthodox icon portrays the Virgin Mary surrounded by saints.

service for someone dear who has died. In Catholic and Orthodox churches this last aspect is celebrated the following day.

All Souls' Day

All Souls' Day, on 2 November, commemorates the souls of the faithful departed. The Catholic Church makes a distinction between saints and other Christians, many of whom are believed to be in purgatory, still awaiting full redemption. This is why Catholics are encouraged to pray for the dead, as do Orthodox Christians. In many countries, people visit the family graves and pray for their dead relatives on All Souls' Day. Some also pray for those good people who lived before the time of Jesus and therefore had no chance of becoming Christians.

HOLY INNOCENTS
The name refers to the children killed by order of King Herod when Jesus was born. Herod feared for his throne because of the story of a 'new-born king' and did not want to take any chances. On Holy Innocents' Day any children who have suffered or died are remembered.

SAINTS' DAYS

This calendar combines several different traditions, showing some saints of major importance and some of particular local or regional interest. Since the traditions vary, you may well find dates other than these given in other sources.

January
1 Basil the Great (or 2 Jan)
3 Genevieve
7 John the Baptist (Orthodox)
8 Thorfinn
10 Gregory of Nyssa (Orthodox)
12 Aelred
13 Hilary of Poitier
14 Kentigern (Mungo),
16 Priscilla
17 Antony of Egypt
18 Athanasios and Cyril (Orthodox)
20 Sebastian
21 Agnes
24 Francis de Sales
25 Paul
26 Timothy and Titus
28 Thomas Aquinas

February
1 Brigid (Bride) of Kildare
3 Blaise
5 Agatha of Sicily
10 Scholastica
11 Caedmon
14 Valentine
15 Onesimos (Orthodox)
18 Colman of Lindisfarne
19 Conrad
23 Polycarp
24 John the Baptist (Orthodox)
25 Tarasios (Orthodox)

March
1 David
2 Chad
4 Gerasimos of the Jordan (Orthodox)
7 Perpetua, Felicity
9 Frances of Rome
17 Patrick
19 Joseph of Nazareth (or20 March)
20 Cuthbert (or 4 September)
24 Gabriel the Archangel
25 The Repentant Thief

April
1 Mary of Egypt (Orthodox)
5 Theodora of Thessalonica (Orthodox)
11 Stanislaus
16 Bernadette of Lourdes
19 Alphege
21 Anselm
23 George
25 Mark
29 Catherine of Siena

May
1 Philip and James, (or 3 May)
2 Athanasius
5 Irene
8 Apostle John (Orthodox)
10 Simon the Zealot (Orthodox)
12 Pancras
13 Julian of Norwich
14 Matthias the Apostle
15 Dympna
16 Brendan the navigator
17 Simeon Stylites (orthodox) (or January 5)
19 Dunstan
20 Alcuin
*21 Helena
22 Rita
24 David I of Scotland
25 The Venerable Bede
26 Augustine of Canterbury
27 Melangell
30 Joan of Arc

June
1 Justin
2 Erasmus (Elmo)
3 Kevin
4 Petroc
5 Boniface (Wynfrith)
6 Norbert
9 Columba
11 Barnabas the Apostle
13 Anthony of Padua
15 Vitus
22 Alban
23 Etheldreda (Audrey)
24 John the Baptist
27 Cyril of Alexandria
28 Irenæus
29 Peter and Paul

July
3 Thomas the Apostle
4 Elizabeth of Portugal
9 Thomas More
11 Benedict of Nursia
12 Veronica
13 Silas
15 Swithun
16 Helier
19 Gregory of Nyssa
20 Margaret
22 Mary Magdalene
23 Bridget of Sweden
25 James the Apostle; Christopher
26 Anne and Joachim, Parents of the Blessed Virgin Mary
29 Mary, Martha and Lazarus
31 Ignatius of Loyola

August
1 Alphonsus
5 Oswald
8 Dominic
10 Laurence
11 Clare of Assisi
14 Maximilian Kolbe
16 St. Stephen of Hungary
18 Helena (or 21 May)
20 Bernard
23 Rose of Lima
24 Bartholomew the Apostle
27 Monica
28 Augustine of Hippo
31 Aidan of Lindisfarne

September
3 Gregory the Great
9 Ciaran
10 Finnian
13 John Chrysostom
15 Cyprian
16 Ninian
17 Hildegard
20 Eustace
21 Matthew
24 Gerard
25 Finbar
27 Vincent de Paul
28 Wenceslas
29 Michael and All Angels
30 Jerome

October
1 Therese of Lisieux
4 Francis of Assisi
6 Bruno
9 Denys
12 Wilfrid
13 Edward the Confessor
15 Teresa of Avila
16 Hedwig
18 Luke
21 Ursula
24 Raphael the Archangel
25 Crispin and Crispinian
28 Simon and Jude
29 Colman

November
1 All Saints' Day
2 All Souls' Day
3 Hubert
5 Zachariah and Elizabeth
6 Leonard
10 Leo the Great
11 Martin
16 Margaret of Scotland
17 Elizabeth of Hungary
19 Hilda
20 Edmund
22 Cecilia
23 Clement
25 Catherine of Alexandria
30 Andrew

December
3 Francis Xavier
4 Barbara
6 Nicholas
7 Ambrose
12 Finnian
13 Lucy
21 Thomas
26 Stephen
27 John the Apostle
28 Holy Innocents
29 Thomas Becket

Carnivals and Family Feasts

ST VALENTINE
We know almost nothing of St Valentine, nor why he has become the Patron Saint of lovers. By the fourteenth century, courting couples were known as each other's 'Valentine', and there was a tradition that birds choose their mate on this day.

Virtually everywhere that Christianity has taken root, earlier local customs have been adapted and given a Christian message. At the same time, some festivals that were primarily Christian have taken on a life of their own, are celebrated in colourful and exciting ways and now have very little religious content. Notably, the feasts of Christmas, Corpus Christi and St Valentine's Day have incorporated local beliefs and earlier traditions. Sometimes it is hard to say whether a festival derives from Christianity, or whether the Christianity is little more than a veneer covering an ancient ritual, and a good excuse for a party.

Mardi Gras traditions in Nice, France, date back to the 13th century. Part of the celebration is the parade of enormous pasteboard caricatures known as 'big heads'.

Mardi Gras

Shrove Tuesday, the last day before Lent, is called 'Mardi Gras' in French. Literally, this means 'fat Tuesday' since it was a time of overindulgence to compensate for the forty days of fasting and self-deprivation that lay ahead till Easter. In the British Isles and North America, the dish of choice is normally pancakes, which use up eggs, sugar and milk. In England, the tradition of pancake races still survives.

The carnivals that take place all over Europe at this time may have their roots in the Roman carnival of Saturnalia, which was an occasion for great celebration and feasting. The origin of the word 'carnival' is a matter of some dispute: whether it derives from *carne-vale* – Latin for 'farewell to flesh (or meat)' – or from the Latin *carrus navalis* – the 'ship of fools', in reference to pre-Christian festivities.

Mardi Gras is no longer directly linked to religious practice. In many cities of the United States it is marked by highly colourful parades that originated in New Orleans, in the state of Louisiana. Started by students in 1827, the celebration is in effect a huge, vigorous street party that lasts several days – though the preparations to design the carnival floats and costumes may take many months. As the timing of the festival is linked to Easter, the dates change but it is always held in February or March, just before Ash Wednesday, the official beginning of Lent.

Carnivals across the world

The day – or, in some cases, the week – before Ash Wednesday is celebrated in similar ways in many parts of the world. In the Caribbean, carnival processions include traditional characters derived from folklore traditions that have contributed to the local culture. In Trinidad, for example, one of the characters, Dame Lorraine, is thought to be a caricature of the eighteenth-century French planters on the island, while Jab Molassie is one of several devils, who tries to smear onlookers with his tin of black oil. In many parts of Greece, similar festivities, featuring outrageous costumes accompanied by feasting and drinking, are thought to date back to ancient Greek spring festivals.

In German-speaking countries, the same period is known as Fastnacht ('eve of the fast'), or Fasching. Especially in south Germany, it is a time for wild parties and dressing up in exotic masks and costumes. The start of the Fasching carnival has gradually moved further and further back from Ash Wednesday, and now begins at any time from early February. On Shrove Tuesday, 'Fools' Guilds' hold parades and sometimes exercise traditional rights to hold 'Fools' trials' in which they dispense their mock justice.

April Fools' Day

It is not clear how, or when, 1 April became known as the day for hoaxing and playing practical jokes. Some attribute it to the weather in the northern hemisphere – the joy that winter is over, and a reflection of the capriciousness of spring weather.

Some have drawn a parallel with the Hindu festival of Holi, which happens at about the same time and also involves practical jokes and boisterous games. Others have associated it with the Roman festival of Hilaria, which took place on 25 March to celebrate the resurrection of the god Attis, or with the Norse god Loki, the trickster.

Yet another account links it to the change to the dates in the seventeenth century, when the Gregorian calendar was introduced, and those who still kept the old New Year festival at the end of March were treated as 'fools'. There is no clear evidence for this, but in parts of Europe the New Year was celebrated at the Spring Equinox, with several days of festivities, which might have lasted until 1 April.

In Anglo-Saxon countries, the victim of the hoax is an 'April Fool'. In France, the unfortunate is a 'poisson d'avril' ('April fish'), though no one seems to know why.

In many Spanish-speaking countries, similar customs are found on 28 December – Holy Innocents' Day – which commemorates the babies killed by King Herod. However, why this festival has become associated with pranks and hoaxes is not clear.

On Mother's Day, many churches hold a special service at which children receive flowers to give to their mothers.

Mother's Day

As Christianity spread through Europe, new communities were founded as 'daughter-houses' of older monasteries or churches. On the fourth Sunday in Lent, it became customary to visit one's 'mother-church'. In the later medieval period, this Sunday became the day when house-servants and apprentices had permission to visit their mother. In England, the family baked a Simnel cake, covered with almond marzipan, to celebrate. 'Mothering Sunday' gradually became the secular 'Mother's Day'.

Father's Day

A day to celebrate fathers arose in different ways in different countries. In Germany, Father's Day is on Ascension Day. Some Catholics celebrate fatherhood on 19 March, St Joseph's Day, since Joseph acted as father to the young Jesus. In many English-speaking countries the festival is on the third Sunday in June.
In the United States a special day for fathers was first suggested by Mrs John B Dodd in 1909. She wanted to honour her father, a Civil War veteran who had brought up six children after his wife died. In 1924 President Calvin Coolidge supported the idea of a national Father's Day, but it did not become official until 1966.

Thanksgiving and Hallowe'en

WALPURGIS NIGHT
Why 30 April, the eve of the festival of the eighth-century abbess St Walburga, should be associated with certain night-time festivities in Germany and Scandinavia is unclear. Some suggest that the abbess has been confused with the ancient fertility goddess Waldborg. In Germany, the Walpurgisnacht festival is similar to Hallowe'en. Traditionally it is associated with hobgoblins and evil spirits, and with mischief and mayhem in the streets. Witches were believed to gather, especially in the Harz mountains; bonfires were lit for protection against evil spirits. In Sweden, the bonfires have no sinister associations, and large crowds gather to sing around the fire.

Thanksgiving is not a religious holiday, but Americans – whatever their beliefs – see it as a time for family and friends to give thanks for the good things in their lives. Thanksgiving commemorates a meal shared between Pilgrims and Native Americans in the seventeenth century.

Does the Hallowe'en party game Bobbing for Apples have its origins in ancient beliefs about the journey of the soul 'across the water' into the underworld?

The first Thanksgiving

'Pilgrims' was the name given to those settlers who founded the first colony in New Plymouth, Massachusetts to escape religious discrimination in England. They had set sail from Plymouth, England, on 5 August 1620, aboard the *Mayflower* and *Speedwell*, but were forced to abandon the *Speedwell* and continue their journey to America on the *Mayflower* alone.

In September 1620 the Pilgrims landed at Cape Cod. During their first, harsh winter, more than half their community died of hunger and disease. The small group that survived did so with the help of the Native Americans, who showed them how to grow crops, including maize and sweet potatoes. The Pilgrims celebrated their survival with the first 'Thanksgiving' in 1621. These first settlers have become known as the Pilgrim Fathers.

Many of them were seeking peace and religious freedom, but later colonists often did not share these ideals. Some religious groups in America now see Thanksgiving as an occasion for mourning the subsequent exploitation and killing of Native Americans by European colonizers.

Hallowe'en

One festival that has encouraged a lot of myths about its origins is Hallowe'en. This very old celebration takes place on 31 October, the eve (night before) All Saints', or All Hallows' Day. Some churches hold celebratory services, but to most people Hallowe'en is no longer a religious festival.

It has long been believed that the spirits of the dead come out on Hallowe'en. Customs from different parts of the world – from mummers' plays to building fires

The Thanksgiving meal of turkey, cranberry sauce, sweet potatoes and pumpkin pie recalls the celebratory meal shared by the Pilgrim settlers and the Native Americans in Massachusetts.

and carving crosses above the door – are designed to ward off any malign influence that they might have. Nowadays, Hallowe'en is more of an occasion for slightly macabre fun. People attend Hallowe'en parties dressed as ghouls and goblins. They carve pumpkins into lanterns (a practice that dates back to around 1900) and tell spooky ghost stories. The tradition of 'trick-or-treat', whereby children in fancy dress wearing masks go from door to door asking for small presents, harks back to earlier alms-giving traditions practised on that night, especially in Scotland.

Some aspects of Hallowe'en celebrations may have derived from the Celtic festival of Samhain, which marked both the 'end of summer' and was a commemoration of the dead. The spirits of the departed were believed to visit their kinsfolk in search of warmth and good cheer as winter approached. It was a time when both good and evil spirits returned to the living. The association of witches with Hallowe'en dates from the nineteenth century, when German immigrants to the United States brought with them the traditions of Walpurgisnacht.

Weird food

Many different traditions at Hallowe'en feature food in unusual ways. For example, there are old Scottish recipes – most of them pretty unappetizing – telling young women what to eat in order to dream of their future husband. They include over-salted bread eaten with no water; a cake with soot in it; a kipper (smoked herring) eaten whole, bones, head and all. Such traditions may have given rise to some modern party recipes in which food is disguised as something disgusting. Alternatively, these latter dishes may have their origin in the witches' concoctions for their spells in Shakespeare's *Macbeth*, such as 'eye of newt and toe of frog, wool of bat and tongue of dog' among other nasties.

A Hallowe'en Warmer

Colcannon is an Irish dish traditionally cooked for Hallowe'en. It is warm and filling, and the ingredients are readily available at this time of year.

Boil the potatoes in salted water until soft. Cook the cabbage and onion together with about 25g (1oz) of the butter and a small amount of water so that it steams, until tender. Mash the potatoes with the remaining butter and a little of the milk.

Stir in the cabbage and onion mixture.

Warm the remaining milk and stir in to make a soft consistency.

Add salt and pepper to taste.

Ingredients

- 2 lb. (900g) potatoes, peeled and cut into pieces
- 1 Large cabbage, cut up and stalks removed
- 1 Large onion, quartered and sliced, or a bunch of green 'spring' onions cut small
- 4 oz (115g) butter (or margarine)
- pepper and salt
- Half a pint (285ml) of milk approximately

The tradition of carving turnips into frightening faces may have originated in Scotland as a way of warding off the spirits that were believed to be about on Hallowe'en. Today it is more common to use pumpkins.

Chapter Three

Muslim Festivals

The formal religion of Islam (Arabic for 'submission') began in Arabia in the seventh century AD, guided and led by the Prophet Muhammad. Muslims believe it is the original religion of humanity, however, preached and practised by all God's prophets from Adam onwards, including many found in Jewish and Christian scriptures, such as Abraham, Moses and Jesus.

Muslims believe that God gave a true message to these prophets, but that it became distorted or incomplete because it was not carefully recorded. Muhammad is seen as God's final prophet because God's complete message – the Qur'an – was revealed to him and written down, word for word. Since Muhammad was the messenger of God, Muslims honour him. They seek to follow the example of his life, but do not worship him.

The central belief of Islam is summarized in the shahada, or 'testimony': *I bear witness that there is no god but God, and Muhammad is the messenger of God.* A Muslim is one who can say this with sincerity and understanding. The Arabic word *muslim* means 'one who submits' (to the will of God). God ('Allah' in Arabic) is the creator and sustainer of all that is, and is the only being who should be worshipped.

There are over a billion Muslims worldwide: in the Middle East and North Africa, where in many countries more than 90 per cent of the population is Muslim, and in southern and eastern Europe and Malaysia. There are two main branches of Islam: Sunni, which accounts for 80 per cent of all Muslims; and Shi'a, whose members are found mainly in Iran, Iraq, Yemen and Bahrain.

The practice of Islam places emphasis on observance of God's commands in daily life including a number of annual obsevances. Consequently, the celebration of festivals is less important than in many other faiths.

On a Muslim's house, drawings showing the mosque and Ka'ba at Makkah (Mecca), in Saudi Arabia, announce that the owner is on the annual pilgrimage (the Hajj) to the holy city of Makkah.

The Beginnings of Islam

In the days before printing, the Qur'an was copied by hand and often decorated with geometric patterns inspired by natural objects. The Qur'an is divided into sections called surahs.

Muslims worship one God (Allah) who is the creator and ruler of the universe, is all-powerful and has no equal. Islam is a total way of life, not just concerned with the 'spiritual' aspects. The Prophet Muhammad is respected and honoured as the final and most faithful messenger of Islam, which is deemed to have existed from the beginning of the world. When Muslims say or write Muhammad's name, they add 'Peace be upon him' as a sign of this respect. They distinguish between love and respect for the Prophet and worship, which is due to God alone.

Life of Muhammad

Muhammad was a trader in Arabia in the seventh century AD. He was well known as an honest, upright and reflective man. In 610, at the age of forty, he was meditating in a cave at Hira, outside the city of Makkah (Mecca), when he had a vision of the angel Jibra'il (Gabriel). The angel told him, 'Recite!' Muhammad refused three times, until at last the angel said, 'Recite in the name of your Lord who created!' The angel gave him words that now form part of the Qur'an, proclaiming the oneness of God.

Muhammad began to preach this message in the city of Makkah, but met with opposition from those who believed in many gods. He and his followers eventually moved to the city of Medina, where the first Islamic community was founded. Muslim dates are all calculated from this journey (the Hijrah) in AD 622, which is year 1 AH (After Hijrah). Throughout his life, Muhammad continued to receive further revelations, which were written down by his followers as he recited them.

A period of missionary, political and military activity followed, so that, by the time of the Prophet's death in 632, Islam was established on most of the Arabian peninsula, including Makkah itself.

The Holy Qur'an

Muslims believe that the Qur'an was written by God and that it was revealed to Muhammad at intervals, from the time of his first vision, when he was forty, until he

The last of God's messengers

Muslims believe that, from time to time, God has sent prophets, such as Adam, Ibrahim (Abraham), Musa (Moses) and Isa (Jesus) to teach successive generations, but their wisdom has frequently been forgotten or misinterpreted. Of the twenty-five prophets named in the Qur'an, all but Muhammad also feature in the Jewish or Christian scriptures. There can be no prophets after Muhammad, Muslims say, because he transmitted God's message perfect and complete.

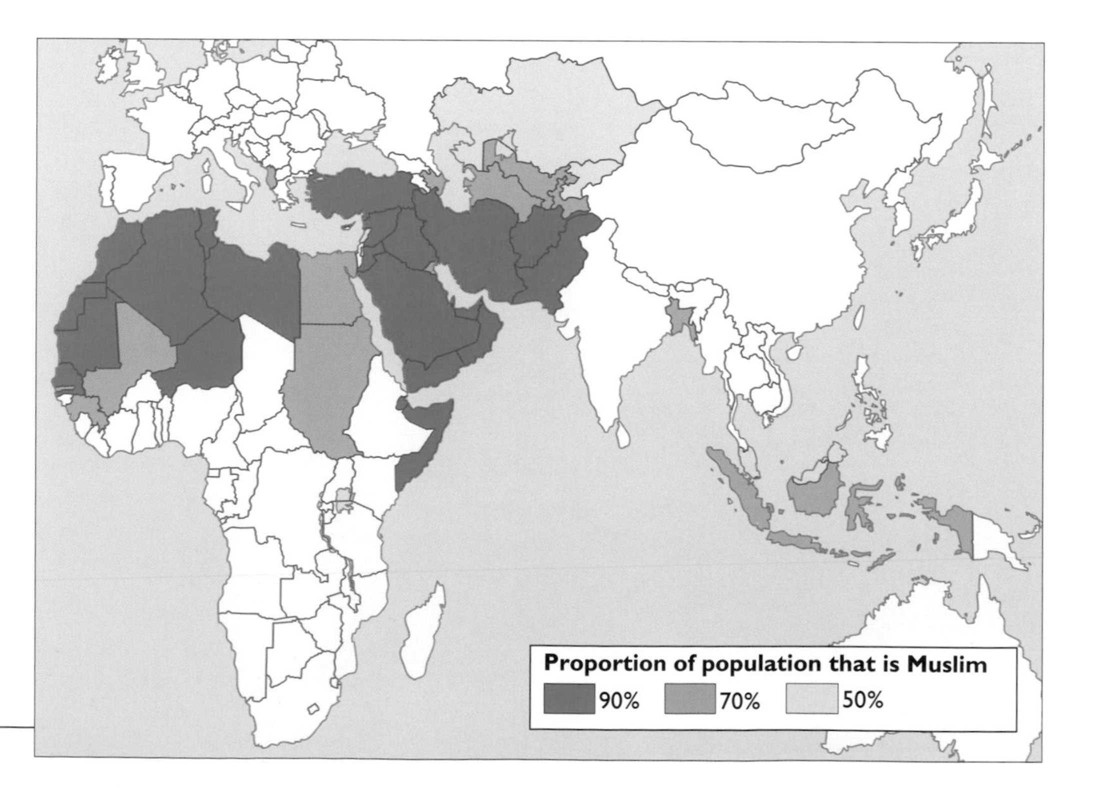

Islam is concentrated in the Middle East and North Africa. However, there are significant numbers of Muslims around the world, arising from immigration and conversion.

died, aged sixty-two. He memorized it and taught it, word for word, to his followers. The revelations were written down and collected into one volume soon after the Prophet's death. Since the words are regarded as the direct transmission from God himself, the Qur'an is read and studied in the original Arabic, and translations are never used in worship. The beauty of the Arabic of the Qur'an is often cited as one proof of its divine nature, and it is considered to be the foundation of all other knowledge.

Hadith

And whatsoever the Messenger gives you, take it and whatsoever he forbids you, abstain from it. (Qur'an, Surah 59:7)

Muhammad is believed to have interpreted the word of God by his actions (sunna). Stories of his life and his sayings were handed down and collected for more than 200 years. They were examined for authenticity by scholars who checked the reliability of the line of transmission. These records are known as Hadith, and are a source of guidance for Muslims where there is no specific guidance in the Qur'an. The combination of the Qur'an and Hadith forms the basis of Islamic law.

THE FIVE PILLARS OF ISLAM

Muslims express and uphold their faith in their daily lives by practising the Five Pillars of Islam, described as the actions that arise out of belief.

1 The declaration of faith
A Muslim is one who can say with understanding and sincerity: 'There is no god but God and Muhammad is the messenger of God.'

2 Prayer (*salah*)
Five daily prayer times are laid down: before sunrise, after midday, late afternoon, after sunset and before midnight.

On Fridays, Muslims meet together in the mosque for the after-midday prayer. Friday is not a 'holy day': business may go on before and after the midday prayers, and in all other respects it is like any other day.

3 Fasting (*sawm*)
The month of Ramadan is laid down as a month of fasting during daylight hours.

4 Welfare tax (*zakat*)
Zakat is the right that a community of Muslims has to all the surplus wealth of an individual.

It is frequently calculated at an annual rate of 2.5 per cent and is usually distributed among the poor and needy. The zakat is the minimum amount an individual is expected to give. Many Muslims offer far more in private donations or charity.

5 Pilgrimage (*Hajj*)
All Muslims are expected to go on a pilgrimage to Makkah at least once in a lifetime if they can afford to do so.

In many countries, those who have made the pilgrimage are known by the title 'Hajji'.

Muslims praying at Lahore Mosque, Pakistan. As well as congregational prayers on Fridays, Muslims often say one or more of their daily prayers at the mosque.

COMMUNITY SPACE
Islam teaches that the whole world is a mosque, because one can pray to God anywhere. Building a mosque provides a convenient place for the Muslim community to meet, and there is no distinction between the sacred and the everyday. In many parts of the world one can see travellers resting or sleeping in the mosque, since it is for the general use of the community.

The Growth of Islam

Makkah
Muslims believe that the Ka'ba at Makkah was first built by Adam as a house of worship, and later rebuilt by Ibrahim (Abraham) and his son Isma'il (Ishmael). Makkah was also the place where Muhammad grew up, and where he first received the revelations of the Qur'an. When Muslims pray, wherever they are in the world, they face in the direction of the Ka'ba. No non-Muslim is allowed to enter the city of Makkah.

After Muhammad's death, the leadership of the Muslim community passed to a succession of caliphs, ('deputies') under whom Islam continued to spread. From the Arabian peninsula, Arab forces moved northward and westward, conquering Palestine, Jerusalem and Syria, Egypt and North Africa and penetrating into Spain. In the east, Islamic forces conquered the Persian Empire, and by the early eighth century were fighting the Chinese. Damascus, Baghdad and Cairo soon rose as major social, political and religious centres of Islamic power.

In 711, Muslim forces in the south crossed the Indus River into India, and in the north entered Spain. Their farthest northward expansion was in 732, when a Muslim army was defeated near Tours in France.

Christian forces of northern Europe fought back and, over many centuries, regained control of Spain, finally expelling the Muslims in 1492. In the fourteenth century, Ottoman Turks crossed into eastern Europe from Anatolia and took over most of the Balkans.

Meanwhile, under the Abbasid caliphate in Baghdad (750–1258), control spread eastward through northern India to the Bay of Bengal. From 1526, the Mughal Empire in India controlled most of the subcontinent of India, but gradually lost control of outlying areas, before finally being deposed by the British in 1858.

For each country where Islam is the majority faith, the map shows which branch of Islam is predominant. However, in several Sunni countries there are significant minority groups of Shi'a Muslims, and in Iraq there is a considerable number of Sunni.

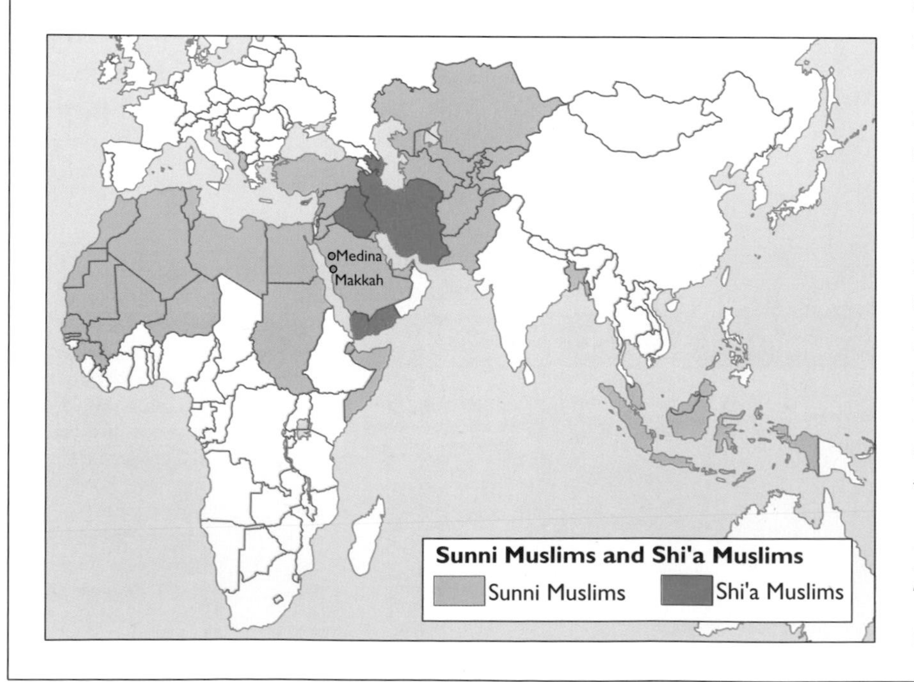

Sunnis, Shi'as and Sufis

During the caliphate of Ali in the mid-seventh century, Islam split over the source of religious authority within the faith. This marked the beginning of the two major divisions: the Sunni (meaning 'majority') and the Shi'a (meaning 'partisans')

Sunni Muslims hold that the first three caliphs were all Muhammad's true successors. The Shi'a believe that Ali was Muhammad's first true successor. 'Shi'a' originally referred to the partisans of Ali, and his sons Hassan and Hussein, who were killed in AD 561. Today, there are a number of Shi'a groups, the largest being the Ithn'Ashariyah, found mainly in Iraq and Iran, and the Isma'iliyah, whose members are spread around the world.

From about the eighth century AD, a more mystical tradition arose in Islam, emphasizing the inner spiritual state of love and devotion to God. This tradition became known as Sufism, and many different Sufi orders arose, some of which still survive. In contrast to other forms of Islam, Sufi Muslims developed the use of music, drumming and dance in worship. In recent years Sufism has experienced a considerable growth in both eastern and western hemispheres.

Islam across the world

There are more than a billion Muslims in the world today. They are concentrated in the Middle East and North Africa, but they are also found in numbers in West Africa, southern and eastern Europe and Malaysia. In addition, there are significant Muslim communities in western Europe and in North America. Most of these consist of migrants from Islamic countries, but converts are growing in number, too, especially in the United States, where the Nation of Islam movement has converted many Afro-Americans to Islam.

Islamic rules of modestly require men to cover the body from the neck to the knees; some women cover the whole body, while others cover their hair but not their face.

The entrance to Lotfallah mosque, Esfahan, Iran. Islam discourages pictures of living creatures. Instead, Islamic art makes use of shapes inspired by natural objects, and intricate geometric patterns.

Times and Seasons

Eid Festivals
The great festivals of Islam – and the only ones observed by all Muslims – are the two Eids and the three holy nights. Both Eids can last for two or three days. However, the prescribed rituals and prayers must be performed on the first day of each festival.

The Islamic calendar is entirely lunar, but unlike most other lunar calendars, no adjustments are made to keep in step with the solar year. Each month begins with the observance of the new moon. Since the lunar year is ten or eleven days shorter than the solar year, Muslim dates change constantly in relation to the Western, solar calendar. Years, in AH (After Hirjah) are counted from the Prophet Muhammad's move to Medina in AD 622. The year 1424 AH starts in March 2003.

Observances and Festivals

The Arabic word *eid* ('time' or 'season') is reserved for the observances instituted by the Prophet Muhammad. Although not normally regarded as a festival, the congregational prayer in the mosque on Fridays is an 'Eid' in the Islamic sense, since it is a recurring, joyful time. There are few major, universally celebrated festivals in Islam, but many local celebrations each with its own traditions. Certain groups also have their own festival days.

Bedouin men singing at the festival of Eid ul-Fitr.

A Calendar Ordained by God

Truly, twelve months is the number of the months with God, according to God's Book, ever since He created heaven and Earth.
(Qur'an, Surah IX, 36)

A new month does not begin until two reliable witnesses have seen the new moon. Since this can vary with different longitudes and weather conditions, a Muslim festival can fall on different days in different countries.

1 Al-Hijra (1 Muharram)
New Year's Day. The date of the Prophet's move from Makkah to Medina, from which all Muslim dates are counted.

2 Ashura/Muharram (9–10 Muharram)
Originally a day of fasting instituted by the Prophet; today, among Shi'a communities, it commemorates the death in battle of Hussein, the Prophet's grandson.

3 Maulid al-Nabi (12 Rabi 1)
The birth and death of the Prophet Muhammad.

4 Anniversary of 'Abd al-Qadir al-Jilani (11 Rabi' 2)
'Abd al-Qadir al-Jilani founded one of the most widespread Sufi orders. The anniversary of his death is celebrated in India and Pakistan with sermons, stories and a commemorative meal.

5 Lailat ul Mir'aj (26–7 Rajab)
The 'Night of Ascension' commemorates a journey that Muhammad made from the mosque at Makkah to the Al-Aqsa mosque in Jerusalem, and thence up into Heaven.

6 Lailat-ul-Baraa (14–15 Sha'ban)
The 'Night of Repentance' or 'Night of Record', when forgiveness is granted to those who repent. Some Muslims believe it is a night when God is setting the coming year's course for each person. It is therefore a time to ask for God's blessings or make any specific request. It is said that there is a tree in Heaven that sheds a number of leaves on this night, each one containing the name of someone destined to die in the coming year.

On 15 Sha'ban, Shi'a Muslims celebrate the birthday of Imam Mahdi, the hidden Imam who is expected to return one day.

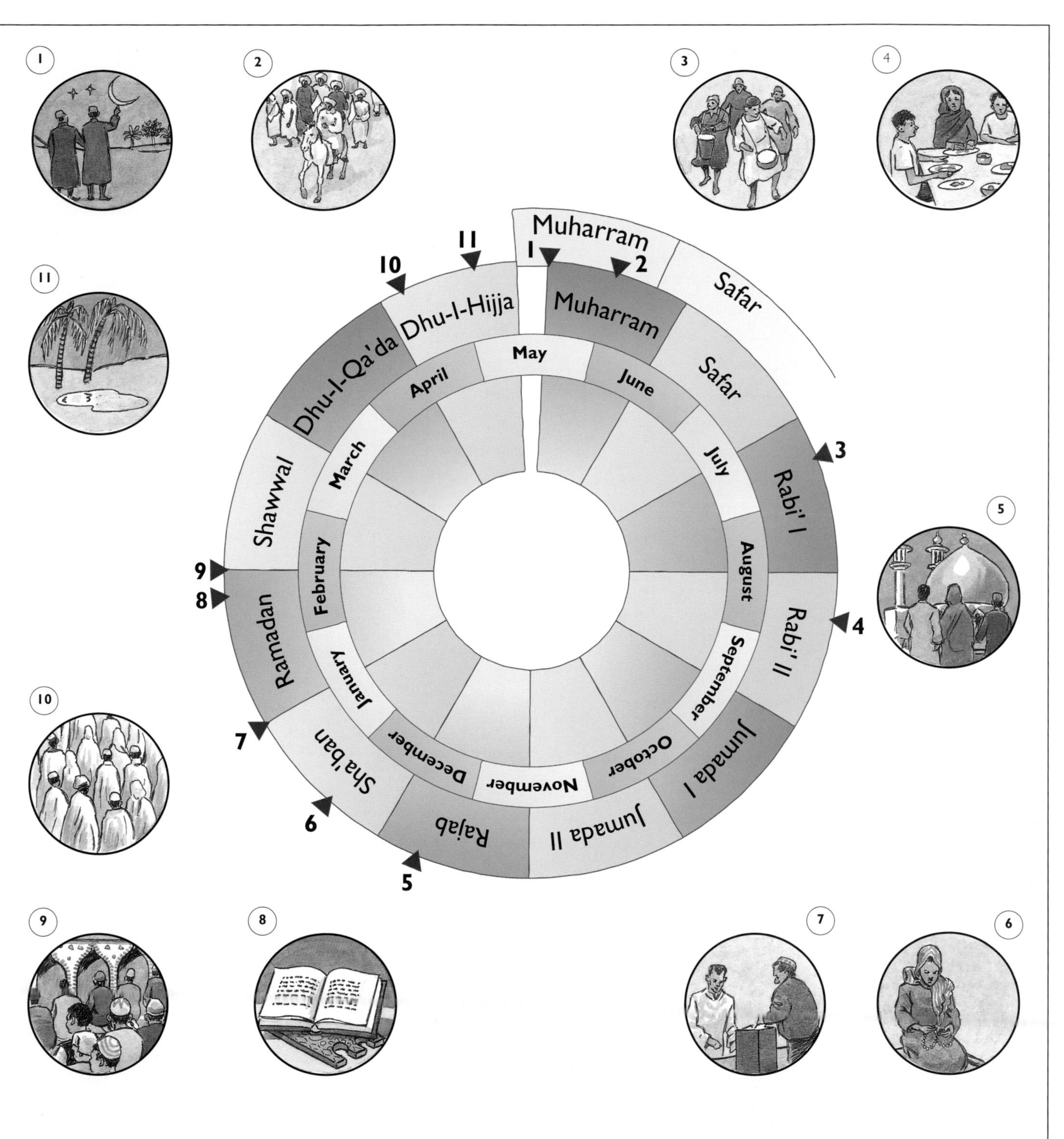

7 RAMADAN
The month of fasting from dawn until dusk, when the zakat contribution is collected.

8 LAILAT UL QADR (27 RAMADAN)
The 'Night of Power', when the Qur'an first began to be revealed to Muhammad.

9 EID UL-FITR (1 SHAWWAL)
A festival to celebrate the end of the month of fasting. Also known as the 'Lesser Eid'.

10 EID UL-ADHA (10 DHU-L-HIJJA)
The 'Festival of Sacrifice', and culmination of the Hajj, the annual pilgrimage.

11 EID AL-GHADIR (18 DHU AL-HIJJAH)
The 'Feast of the Pond'. The Shi'a community celebrates the day on which it is said that Muhammad invested 'Ali as his successor near the pond Khumm.

Ramadan and Eid ul-Fitr

Why fast?
O you who believe, fasting is prescribed to you as it was prescribed to those before you, so that you may learn self-restraint. (Qur'an, Surah 2:183)
Besides this clear instruction in the Qur'an, Muslims point to other benefits of fasting:
- Self-control builds confidence in one's faith.
- Knowing that millions of Muslims worldwide are also fasting promotes a sense of community.
- Fasting builds solidarity with the poor and hungry.

Pancakes or samosas filled with curd cheese and nuts and dipped in syrup are a popular sweet during Ramadan. People often buy them on their way home for the iftar meal.

Ramadan, the ninth month of the Islamic calendar, is the month in which the Prophet is believed to have received the Qur'an from the angel Jibra'il (Gabriel). It is a time of fasting, when everyone except children, pregnant women, travellers and those suffering from severe illnesses fasts from sunrise to sunset. Because the Islamic calendar is a lunar one, the time of year for Ramadan changes. In latitudes far from the equator observing Ramadan can be much more difficult in summer than in winter, because of the long days. The beginning and the end of Ramadan are marked by the first appearance of the new moon.

Fasting and prayer

Children are gradually encouraged to fast from quite an early age. They first try for part of a day, then one day a week, then on consecutive days, so that when the time comes to fast for the whole month, they have a sense of achievement. Those who miss days because of illness or for other reasons will make up the days missed as soon as they can do so, after the festival of Eid. Those who cannot fast at all make donations of money or food to the poor. Anyone who is not fasting should eat and drink in private, and in Muslim countries public eating or drinking in Ramadan is forbidden during daylight hours. In the evening, family and guests gather to await the call to prayer, which signals the end of the day's fast. Each night, about one-third of the Qur'an is recited at the mosque and special prayers are said.

During the evenings, people visit their relatives and friends, and also try to heal any broken relationships. Some stay up most of the night, sleeping just after dawn and before sunset. During the day, people still go to work, but in Middle Eastern countries the working day is often shortened by an hour or two.

The Night of Power

Muhammad received the first words of the Qur'an from the angel Jibra'il on an odd-numbered day in the last ten days of Ramadan (usually celebrated on 27th). It is called Lailat ul Qadr – the Night of Power. The Qur'an describes this night as

Crowds gather together at the end of the special month of Ramadan: when the new moon rises, it is a sign that the month is over, and celebrations take place.

'better than a thousand months', adding 'On this night the prayers of the sincere Muslim are certain to be answered.'

Eid ul-Fitr

Towards the end of Ramadan, Muslims clean their house, prepare new clothes and gifts and plan a great feast for when the sighting of the new moon marks the end of the fast. Street parties and family parties are held, and greetings and cards are exchanged with the words 'Eid mubarak' ('A blessed Eid') or the Turkish 'Elveda, ey Ramadan!' ('Goodbye, Ramadan!')

The early morning Eid prayers often take place out of doors to accommodate the large crowds who come in their best clothes to celebrate and give thanks to God. Later, families often visit the graves of relatives, then spend their time celebrating, exchanging gifts and feasting.

Sugared almonds are a speciality of the festival, as well as chocolates and nuts. For the main feast, a dish such as a whole, stuffed lamb is served, accompanied by plenty of side dishes.

RAMADAN FOOD

Each culture has its own specialities for Ramadan meals. There are no rules. Most of the following examples are from Muslim countries of the Middle East.

SUHOOR - BEFORE SUNRISE

The Prophet (peace be upon him) said: 'How excellent are dates as the believer's Suhoor.'
(From the Hadith: traditions of the Prophet Muhammad's words and deeds)

Suhoor foods should be filling but not salty, with plenty to drink:
- Bread with olive oil
- Date bread or raisin bread
- Rice or wheat porridge, or other cereals
- Boiled eggs
- Curd cheese or yoghurt cheese – unsalted, and maybe sweetened with sugar or honey, and flavoured with rosewater
- Dates or other fruit
- *qamer ed-din*, a drink made from apricots, popular in Jordan
- Sweet tea

IFTAR - AFTER SUNSET

To break (or 'open') the fast:
- A few dates, traditionally an odd number
- Small savoury pastries with cheese
- Pistachio nuts
- Fruit drink – apricot or sweetened tamarind juice are popular
- An infusion of hibiscus flowers or liquorice root

All these help to balance fluid in the body and prepare the stomach gently for the bigger meal to come.

Charity

One way of celebrating the end of Ramadan is to give *zakat* (charity), in recognition of God's good gifts, the worldwide family of Islam and the needs of the hungry. This is called Zakat ul Fitr, and is in addition to the obligatory zakat that is one of The Five Pillars of Islam. It should be done before the start of the Eid prayer, though many Muslims give before the end of Ramadan, so that those in need can prepare to celebrate the festival like everyone else.

After maghrib (evening prayer):
- A nourishing soup of lentils, or chick-peas, or a chicken and noodle broth
- A hearty meat or vegetable stew, with rice flavoured with spices and dried fruit
- Salad with lemon and mint
- Pickles and other relishes such as chick-pea or aubergine dips
- An array of sweets, often pastries or pancakes filled with soft cheese and nuts, and soaked in syrup or honey

At any time during the night
- Snacks, such as dried fruit and nuts
- Drinks, especially herbal tea and fruit juice

Hajj and Eid ul-Adha

THE HOLIEST PLACE
The Ka'ba in Makkah, a simple, cube-shaped stone building, has been a religious site since very early times. Some Muslims believe it was built by Adam as a house of worship, but later rebuilt by Ibrahim and Isma'il. At the time of Muhammad, it had become a centre of polytheistic worship, with statues of gods. When the Muslims took control of Makkah, they removed these statues and re-dedicated the Ka'ba to the worship of the one God.

THE BLACK STONE
In one corner of the Ka'ba there is an oval stone mounted in a silver frame. According to some traditions, this is the only surviving part of the house of worship built by Ibrahim and Isma'il. When pilgrims circle the Ka'ba, they try to kiss or touch the stone, as the Prophet Muhammad is reported to have done.

The annual pilgrimage to Makkah – the Hajj – and the Festival of Sacrifice (Eid ul-Adha) have their roots in the story of the founding, long ago, of the holy city of Makkah by Ibrahim and his son Isma'il.

A place in the desert

The Prophet Ibrahim (Abraham) was a friend of God and a staunch upholder of the oneness of God, in the face of the people around him, who worshipped many gods. For years, Ibrahim had no children, but then God promised him a son by his second wife Hejira (Hagar). When this son, Isma'il (Ishmael), was still a small baby, God commanded Ibrahim to leave the mother and child in the desert, with a supply of water, at the place where the city of Makkah now stands. This spot would be the foundation of a community where the one God would be worshipped.

When the water ran out, the baby cried for thirst. Desperately searching for water, Hejira ran seven times to and fro between two small hills, now known as Safa and Marwa, but there was no water. Then the angel Jibra'il came to her aid, struck the ground, and a spring of water erupted. That spring, now contained in a well, is known as Zamzam. The mother and child drank, and settled by the well. Ibrahim visited them from time to time, and when the child Isma'il was older, father and son rebuilt the Ka'ba – the first mosque – for the worship of God. They called on peoples from all around to make an annual pilgrimage to that place.

But then came an even harder test for Ibrahim: God commanded him to sacrifice his son Ishmael. Ibrahim waited until Ishmael was in his teens, then sadly told him of God's command. To his surprise, the lad told him that he was willing to undergo whatever God had asked. So they set off for Mina, the intended place of sacrifice. On the way, Satan tried three times to tempt Ibrahim from his obedience, but Ibrahim threw stones at him, and he disappeared into the ground.

When God saw that Ibrahim and his son were willing to carry out his command, he stopped them just in time, and ordered Ibrahim to offer a goat instead.

Festival of Sacrifice

Eid ul-Adha (Festival of Sacrifice) commemorates the willingness of Ibrahim and Isma'il to sacrifice everything for God. The three-day festival, known as the Greater Eid, starts on the tenth day of the last month of the Islamic year. This is the month – called Dhu-l-Hijja – of the Hajj, the pilgrimage to Makkah, which is one of the Five Pillars of Islam.

The festival starts with dawn prayers, and family members all wearing new clothes. Then, either a lamb or a sheep is sacrificed, its head pointing towards Makkah. The meat is shared out among

Every year, at the time of the Hajj, more than 2 million people come to Makkah and walk seven times around the Ka'ba in the courtyard of the mosque.

THE RITES OF HAJJ

On arrival in Makkah
Men put on ihram, with a prayer that begins:
Here I am, O God, at Your service! Here I am at Your service!

8 Dhu-l-Hijja
Travel to Mina, a small, uninhabited village east of the city.

9 Dhu-l-Hijja
To the plain of 'Arafat where pilgrims stand (*wuquf*), in meditation until sunset. Muslims around the world gather at the local mosque for prayer in spiritual solidarity with those at 'Arafat.
Return to Muzdalifah to collect a number of small pebbles.

10t Dhu-l-Hijja
Throw seven stones at each of three white rock pillars of Mina, as a reminder of Ibrahim's resistance to temptation.
Make the sacrifice.
Take off ihram and put on everyday clothes. Cut hair – whole head for men, a symbolic lock for women.

Visit Makkah for:
tawaf, walking seven times round the Ka'ba, reciting a prayer during each circuit. Then pray and drink the water of Zamzam.
sa'y (running) Run between Al-Safa and Al-Marwa, two small mounds about 500 metres apart in Makkah, in memory of Hagar's search for water.

11–13 Dhu-l-Hijja.
Return to Mina to throw remaining pebbles at the rock pillars.
Before leaving Makkah pilgrims usually circle the Ka'ba again to bid farewell to the Holy City.

Standing in meditation

Tents for the pilgrims

Mina - throwing stones at the pillar

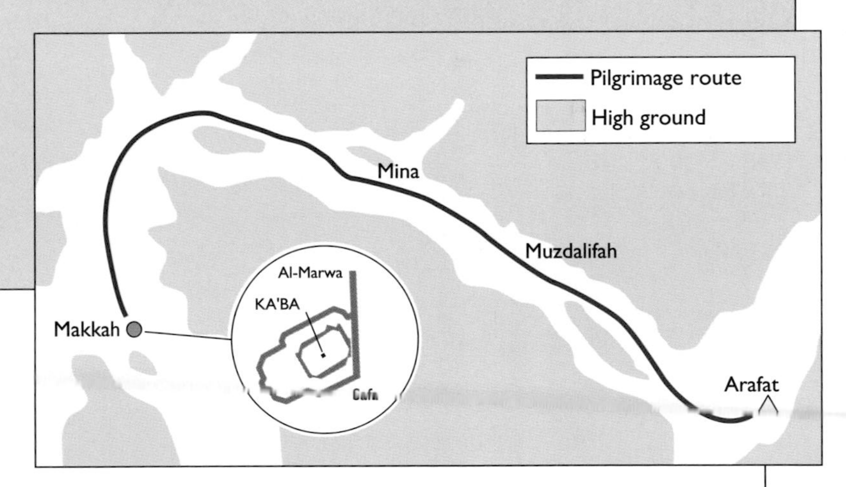

the family, neighbours and the poor, and cards and gifts are exchanged. Many different ways of preparing the lamb have been devised for this festival, including roasting it whole with a sweet in its mouth.

Children look forward to the feasting with great glee because they are given special care, lots of attention and presents.

Pilgrimage to Makkah
For the 2.5 million or so Muslims each year who make the journey to Makkah, the Hajj is the peak of their religious life. Before setting out, pilgrims should pay all debts and make sure that they can afford the journey and provide for their family without hardship.

During the Hajj, Muslims try to act towards each as brothers and sisters. To conceal any distinctions of wealth or class, male pilgrims wear only two white sheets of cotton (ihram), and women wear a simple dress covering them from head to foot.

The map shows where the rites of Hajj take place. The distance from Makkah to 'Arafat is about 24 kilometres. Safa to Al-Marwa (inset) is about 400 metres.

Ashura, Maulid al-Nabi, Lailat ul Mir'aj

Some Muslim festivals, such as Maulid al-Nabi and Lailat ul Mir'aj, did not originate with the Prophet, or were not acknowledged by him, and there is much discussion and disagreement among religious authorities as to whether they should be observed at all. Another festival – Ashura – was recognized by Muhammad, but its significance has changed since the early days.

Ashura is celebrated on the ninth and tenth days of Muharram. It may have originally derived from the Jewish festival of Pesach. Apparently, Muhammad, following the custom of the Jews of Medina, instituted a two-day fast, but reportedly said that it was not obligatory.

The 'Respected' Month
'Muharram' – the name of the first month of the Muslim year – means 'respected'. The Islamic calendar counts months from the Hijra, the time of the Prophet Muhammad's emigration from Makkah to Medina. The first day of Muharram is known as Al-Hijra. On that day, Muslims visit the mosque to hear and tell stories of the Prophet and his companions.

The Dome of the Rock in Jerusalem marks the place from which Muhammad experienced his journey to heaven.

The festival now commemorates the events that are traditionally said to have happened on those days. They include the safe grounding of the ark of Nuh (Noah) after the flood, and the birth of the prophet Ibrahim, who later built the Ka'ba. However, Ashura is of greatest importance to Shi'ite Muslims, who remember and mourn the death of Muhammad's grandson, Hussein, killed at the Battle of Karbala.

Honouring the Prophet

According to tradition, the Prophet Muhammad was born in Makkah on 12 Rabi ul-Awal in AD 570, and died in 632 at about the same time of year. The festival of Maulid al-Nabi both celebrates his birth and mourns his death. It lasts for the first twelve days of the month, in memory of the twelve days of the Prophet's last illness. There are considerable variations in the way the occasion is observed, depending on local folk customs. The Sufis taught that it was a time for an expression of love and respect towards the Prophet.

Night Journey to Heaven

Glory be to God Who took His Servant For a journey by night From the Sacred Mosque To the Farthest Mosque Whose precincts We blessed So that We might show him some of our signs. For He is the One Who hears all and sees all.
(Qur'an, Surah 17:1)

Lailat ul Mir'aj (Night of Ascension) recalls the journey that Muhammad undertook from the mosque in Makkah to the Al-Aqsa mosque in Jerusalem, and from there up to Heaven. Muslims debate whether this was a purely spiritual experience or an actual physical journey that miraculously took place all in one night. The festival is traditionally celebrated on

THE MARTYRS OF KARBALA

In the time of confusion and dispute about the leadership of the Muslim community, Hussein, the grandson of the Prophet Muhammad, became the ruler in what is today Iran.

According to Shi'a tradition, the inhabitants of Kufa, a town in present-day Iraq, asked Hussein to become their ruler in place of Yazid, whose rule was unjust. In 51 AH (AD 561), Hussein set off with his family and seventy followers to Kufa, believing he had popular support there. But Yazid instructed his soldiers to surround them in the desert and keep them from reaching Kufa. At Karbala, Hussein's party of men, women and children were starved of food and water, before being attacked and slaughtered by a large army. Shi'ites relate how Hussein's baby son was killed in his arms, and when Hussein himself eventually fell, his head was carried to Yazid in triumph.

For Shi'ite Muslims, Karbala has become a place of pilgrimage second only to Makkah. The whole of the first ten days of Muharram are set aside as a time of mourning. The main event of this Shi'ite festival is a huge procession through city streets in remembrance of the martyrs.

The procession includes *taziahs* (ornate bamboo and paper replicas of Hussein's tomb), the green flags of Hussein's army and a white horse. Wrestlers, dancers and actors re-enact the battle of Karbala, and prayers of mourning are said while young men beat their breasts and cry, 'Oh Hussein, we were not there.'

Muslims in New Delhi, India, prepare a taziah, a replica of Hussein's tomb, for the Muharram procession.

the night before the 27 Rajab. In the mosque, accounts of the journey and sermons on the meaning of the many signs that the Prophet saw on the way are read.

The Prophet's detailed account of the experience, recounted by more than one of his hearers, tells that in the middle of the night, he prayed in the mosque in Makkah and then fell asleep. The angel Jibra'il woke him, and gave him a miraculous beast, Buraq, on which he rode to Jerusalem, stopping at intervals to pray along the way. At the Al-Aqsa mosque in Jerusalem, Muhammad led a host of earlier prophets in prayer.

Then Jibra'il took him upwards from the rock, step by step, to the seventh heaven, and finally, to the presence of God. God instructed him about the way of life for Muslims, including fifty daily prayers. On the advice of Musa (Moses), Muhammad asked several times for this number to be reduced; people would never manage so many. When the prayers were reduced to just five, Muhammad asked for no further reduction.

HINDU FESTIVALS

Hinduism is the indigenous religion of India. It grew over thousands of years into a body of teaching and culture and is named after the Western word for India, formerly called 'Hind', the land on the other side of the Indus river. India's own name for its religion is Sanatan Dharma, which means 'the eternal occupation of the soul' or 'eternal truth'. Religion in India has always been a natural part of daily life: for the body the natural thing is to breathe and to eat; for the soul it is religion.

Reality and illusion

The original source of teaching for this practice of religion is the Vedic hymns: poems passed down from ancient times by word of mouth, and written in the Sanskrit language in their earliest form around 1500 BC. The central theme of these poems is the soul's search for liberation from suffering and ultimately for release from the cycle of birth and death.

The temporary, changing world of birth and death, through which everyone travels, is taught to be an illusion, for reality is unchanging and eternal. This eternal reality exists everywhere as spirit or Brahman – the energy that sustains the universe. God is manifest in all the different deities and in the countless living beings on earth.

Social duties

Over thousands of years, Hindu society developed an elaborate social order within which everyone had a part to play. Central to this order is the concept of Dharma, or duty, which requires some to be manual workers, others merchants, others leaders and others teachers.There are also duties associated with the family and with each stage of life, and community members carry a responsibility to participate in important rites of passage such as birth, marriage and death. All duties, however, are intended to lead to the ultimate duty: the obligation to understand one's true self as summed up in the Sanskrit saying, '*Tat Tvam Asi*' ('You Are Spirit').

Hindus listening to scriptures being read by a Brahmin as they bathe in the sacred River Ganges.

The Roots of Hinduism

Shiva Nataraja, or Lord of the Dance, symbolises the eternal rhythm of destruction and creation.

The teachings of Hinduism – the Vedas – began as an oral tradition passed from one generation to another through stories and songs, and preserved by spiritual teachers. Called *Brahmins*, these teachers traced their wisdom back to the first created being, Brahma, who had himself been taught by Vishnu, the 'Supreme Lord' who exists outside time and space. It was Brahma who, after receiving inspiration from Vishnu, created the universe. Today the oldest school of Hinduism is still known as the Brahma Sampradaya, meaning 'the teaching that descended from Brahma'.

Fusion of three cultures

According to modern scholarship, the Vedas show the influence of the early Indo-Iranians, the most easterly group of the Indo-European peoples who lived in what is now Iran. There is evidence that these people, who called themselves

Devotees gathered at a Krishna temple in Jaipur to hear a guru expound on the teachings of the Bhagavad Gita.

Karma and the Journey of the Soul

The law of action and reaction, called karma, governs the movements of all beings. It is sometimes understood as being simply a process of punishment and reward. On a deeper level, however, it is to do with fulfilling the desires of the soul and the working out, on the material plane, of the journey of the soul.

Krishna teaches, in the Bhagavad Gita, that the soul is reincarnated into a new body after death and that this body is designed to fulfil its wishes exactly, such as offering the ability to fly like a bird, or be peaceful and affectionate like a cow. For those who desire wisdom, a human birth is offered, which opens the path to self-understanding and ultimately to liberation from the cycle of birth and death. It is therefore said that the greatest prize is to be born as a human being.

'Aryans', migrated into India between 3000 and 1500 BC.

In Northern India the Aryans met a culture already well established, such as at the city of Mohenjo Daro (today in Pakistan), where they found paved streets and meticulous sanitation. Southern India had the Deccan Neolithic culture, which flourished for 1,500 years until about 1000 BC. Early Hinduism was the result of the fusion of these three cultures.

Sacred literature

About 3,000 years ago in Hindu reckoning, Kali Yuga, or the 'Age of Iron', began and human intelligence and memory started to decrease. Therefore the Vedas had to be written down to preserve them for future generations. The original hymns were divided into the four books called the *Rig Veda*, *Sama Veda*, *Atharva Veda* and *Yajur Veda*. These later expanded into a vast body of spiritual learning known as the Vedic literatures, which include the Upanishads, containing philosophical treatises, and the Puranas, or epic histories.

Two great epics, or Puranas, have come to form the central books of Hindu faith and devotion. They are the *Ramayana* and *Mahabharata*, which tell the stories of Rama and Krishna and include the essential teachings of the Hindu tradition. They are today the most popular of the Hindu scriptures. Besides these there is the *Bhagavata Purana*, a detailed account of the life of Krishna, which incorporates much older wisdom from the Vedic scriptures.

The 'Song of God'

The *Mahabharata* includes the Bhagavad Gita, or 'Song of God', which for many Hindus is the essential book of Hindu wisdom. This is a dialogue between Krishna and his friend Arjuna in which Krishna teaches the path of bhakti, devotion to a personal God, as the easiest path for all to follow.

THE IMMORTAL ATMAN

Vedic wisdom teaches that the true self, called the *Atman*, is an immortal soul which is reincarnated from one body to another. Thus each living being in this world, whether human or animal, is an eternal soul inhabiting a temporary body.

The individual Atman cannot be burned by fire, moistened by water, or withered by the wind. It is without beginning or end. By its presence as the self, the Atman gives energy to the body.

Each soul has its own desires to enjoy the world, and to fulfil these desires it enters the cycle of rebirth, called *samsara*.

When the soul leaves one body, that body dies, and the soul is then reincarnated into another body, like an actor changing clothes. Whilst it is moving from body to body in search of happiness, the soul passes through all forms of life, from insect to god:

"As the self passes in this body from childhood to youth to old age, so when this body dies the self passes into another body. The wise are not deluded by this change." (Bhagavad Gita 2.13)

Because the soul is eternal, it finds satisfaction not in the temporary pleasures of this world, but in the eternal realm of the spirit. *Moksha* – release from samsara – is possible with the realization that the inner Atman and the universal spirit of Braham are identical. When this happens, the Atman is freed from rebirth and reunited with Brahman.

Krishna teaches that all living beings are the eternal children of God who find happiness if they surrender their every action in devotion to God. This will release the self from the cycle of birth and death and allow it to return to the eternal spiritual realm, to be reunited with God. Krishna's advice is to be active in the world but without attachment to results: it is the motive that is important – by working unselfishly for the sake of pleasing God, one will find freedom and peace:

Whatever you do, whatever you eat, whatever you offer and give away, and whatever austerities you perform – do these as an offering unto Me. In this way you will be freed from bondage to work and its auspicious and inauspicious results. With your mind fixed on Me in this principle of renunciation, you will be liberated and come to Me.
(Bhagavad Gita 9.26–28)

A Brahmin performing puja beside a shrine to Hanuman at Khajuraho, north India.

Hindu Deities

HOME WORSHIP
The path of *bhakti*, or devotion, which is taught in the Bhagavad Gita, has become very popular in Hinduism. Most Hindu homes have their own shrines where daily worship, called *puja*, takes place. The family honours their deities by chanting prayers, offering the sacred *arti* flame and sanctifying food. In this way, the home is transformed into a small temple, where the daily life is pursued in harmony with the Divine.

There are more than 750 million Hindus worldwide and the majority live in South-East Asia. In addition to the UK, USA, Canada and South Africa, there are communities numbering more than 300,000 in Mauritius, Fiji, Guyana, and Trinidad and Tobago.

Hindus believe in one ultimate Being who has unlimited forms. The two great deities of Hinduism are Vishnu and Shiva, both of whom are aspects of this Being. They each have their own ardent devotees who honour them as the Supreme Deity, and their own separate traditions of learning and worship. Together with Brahma, they form the great trinity of Brahma, Vishnu and Shiva, who became known as the gods of Creation, Maintenance and Destruction, respectively.

Vishnu and Shiva are balanced by the Goddess Devi. She is revered as the Mother Goddess, accompanying Vishnu in the form of Lakshmi, and Shiva as Parvati. Other gods and goddesses are all intermediaries of the three great deities, Vishnu, Shiva and Devi, and ultimately of the one Supreme Spirit.

The Preserver
Vishnu is the background to existence. He gives birth to Brahma, the creator, and then enters the universe as Narayana, 'the One Who Lies on the Waters of Life'. He sleeps at the base of the universe, attended by the goddess Lakshmi. Whenever there is disturbance in the balance of the universe, he takes human form to restore religious teachings and protect righteousness. His role as a just and dutiful ruler is exemplified in his incarnation as Rama, whose story is recounted in the *Ramayana*. He takes the role of teacher in his incarnation as Krishna, who taught the Bhagavad Gita.

The Dissolver
Shiva is associated with the powers of death and dissolution. He is easily pleased and is merciful to his devotees. When the universe meets its end, it is by the power of Shiva, who carries a small drum which he beats to accompany his dance of destruction.

Riding on the bull Nandi, he wears on his head a crescent moon and a symbol of the descending waters of the Ganges, which he caught in his hair to save the mountains from being crushed by the river's weight. His mountain home is Mount Kailash in the Himalayas, and he has many followers in this region. He is also said to live in cremation grounds, where he smears his body with ashes and sits in a trance of meditation.

The Ten Incarnations of Vishnu
Vishnu comes into this world ten times as an avatar - 'One Who Descends '- to restore the balance of good and bad. The ten avatars of Vishnu take progressively more developed forms, from aquatic through mammal to human form. The stories of these incarnations have had a profound influence on Hindu culture:

1. Matsya the Fish, who saved the Vedic hymns and all creatures from the universal flood.

2. Kurma the Tortoise, who helped the gods gain immortality.

3. Varaha the Boar, who rescued the

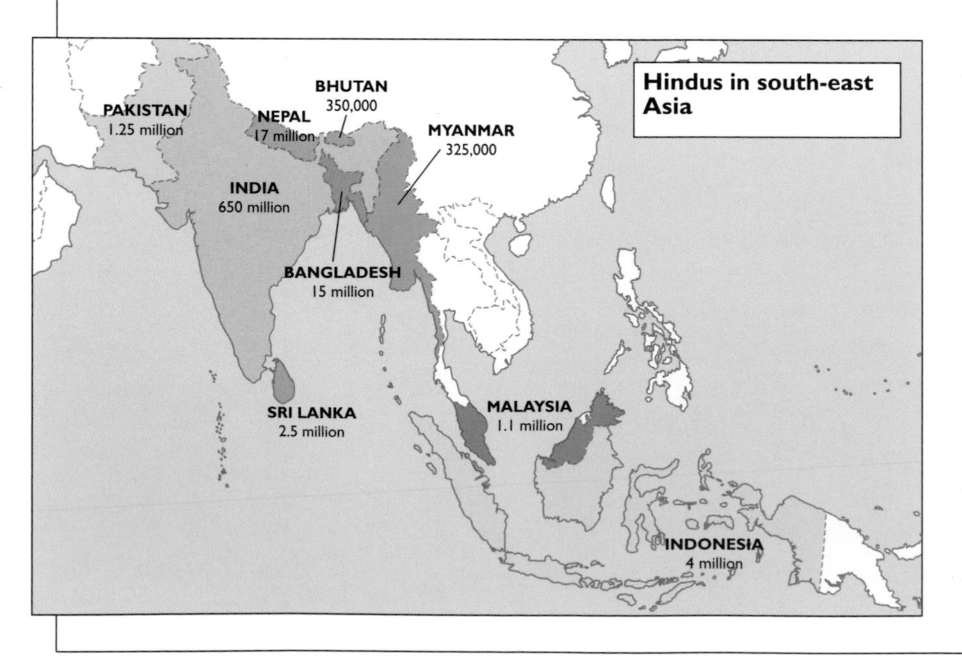

earth from the bottom of the universe.

4. Narasimha the Man-Lion, who killed the demon Hiranyakasipu and rescued his son Prahlad.

5. Vamana the dwarf, who defeated the powerful king, Bali.

6. Parasurama, who defeated the war-like kings and established peace.

7. Rama the hero of *Ramayana.*

8. Krishna, the cowherd boy, and teacher of the Bhagavad Gita.

9. Buddha, who taught non-violence and compassion.

10. Kalki, who will come at the end of time to vanquish the demons and inaugurate a new cycle of the universe.

Boys performing puja to Vishnu at the temple of Budhanilakanath in the Kathmandu Valley, Nepal. Carved from black stone and half submerged in the waters of a small lake, Vishnu reclines on the body of the cosmic serpent Anantasesh.

A group of women, who have made the pilgrimage to Varanasi from their village in north India, perform puja on the banks of the sacred river Ganges.

Times and Seasons

Sadhus representing all Hindu religious groups throughout India gather every twelve years at the Maha Kumbha Mela. The millions of people attracted to the fair bathe at the confluence of the Ganges and Yamuna rivers, and at the point where the historical river Sarasvati is said to emerge from underground

The Hindu calendar is written in Sanskrit, the ancient language of India. It follows a cycle of twelve lunar months each made up of thirty lunar days, or *tithis*. The month is divided into two halves, or *paksha*, of fifteen days each.

The appearance of the new moon marks the fortnight called *suklapaksa* (bright half of the month) while the full moon begins the fortnight known as *krsnapaksa* (dark half of the month). When Indian dates are given, the bright half is often abbreviated to '*sudi*', and the dark half to '*badi*'. Thus, the festival of Janmashtami, which falls on the eighth day of the dark fortnight of the month of Sravana, appears as Sravana badi 8.

The lunar year

Since a lunar month has $29\frac{1}{2}$ days, the lunar year lasts only about 354 solar days, so, every two or three years, the lunar and solar calendars are reconciled by inserting an extra lunar month. This 'intercalary' month was traditionally added after the months of Asadha or Sravana.

Due to the seasonal patterns in different parts of India, the start of the new agricultural year varied, thereby affecting what was traditionally regarded as the New Year. In some parts it begins with Chaitra, which falls between March and April, while in others it begins at Kartik. The phase of the moon that marks the start of a new lunar month also varies, beginning in some regions at the new moon, and at the full moon in others.

ASTROLOGICAL DATES

The astrological months, based on the twelve signs of the zodiac, are used to date certain religious festivals or determine auspicious days. The Sankranti, or day when the sun passes from one sign of the zodiac to the next, is considered an auspicious day. The Maha Kumbha Mela, the great religious fair and mass ritual bathing that takes place every twelve years at Allahabad, begins on the Sankranti between Makara (Capricorn) and Kumbha (Aquarius).

THE HINDU CALENDAR

Across India a wide variety of local and regional festivals take place, to honour deities associated with a particular area or community, celebrate a stage in the agricultural calendar or commemorate historical figures and events. Some festivals are celebrated by those belonging to the Vaishnavite tradition; others are significant for the Shivite tradition. Even festivals such as Divali, celebrated in most areas of India, have regional variations in religious ritual, food and associated stories or legends.

1 SARASVATI PUJA (5TH DAY OF THE BRIGHT HALF OF MAGH)
Sarasvati, the goddess of learning and the arts, is honoured at this festival celebrating the start of spring.

2 MAKARA SANKRANTI (A SOLAR FESTIVAL, WHEN THE SUN PASSES FROM THE TROPIC OF CANCER TO THE TROPIC OF CAPRICORN)
This harvest festival marks the end of winter; in north India it is an auspicious day for ritual bathing. In Tamil Nadu and Andhra Pradesh it is called Pongal, and in the Punjab, Lohri.

3 MAHASHIVARATRI (13TH OR 14TH DAY OF THE DARK HALF OF MAGH)
The god Shiva, who destroys for creation to begin again, is honoured on 'The Great Night of Shiva'.

4 HOLI (FULL-MOON DAY OF PHALGUN)
The grain harvest in India is celebrated with bonfires and the boisterous throwing of coloured water and powder in the streets.

5 RAMA NAUMI (9TH DAY OF THE BRIGHT HALF OF CHAITRA)
The birthday of Rama, the seventh incarnation of the god Vishnu, hero of the epic Ramayana.

6 HANUMAN JAYANTI (FULL-MOON DAY OF CHAITRA)
The birthday of the monkey god, Hanuman, honoured for his strength, energy and devotion to Rama.

7 RATHA YATRA (2ND DAY OF THE BRIGHT HALF OF ASADHA)
A famous example of this chariot festival is that of Lord Jagganath, in the town of Puri.

8 NAGA PANCHAMI (5TH DAY OF THE BRIGHT HALF OF SRAVANA)
Snakes (*nagas*), which are considered semi-divine, are honoured and placated.

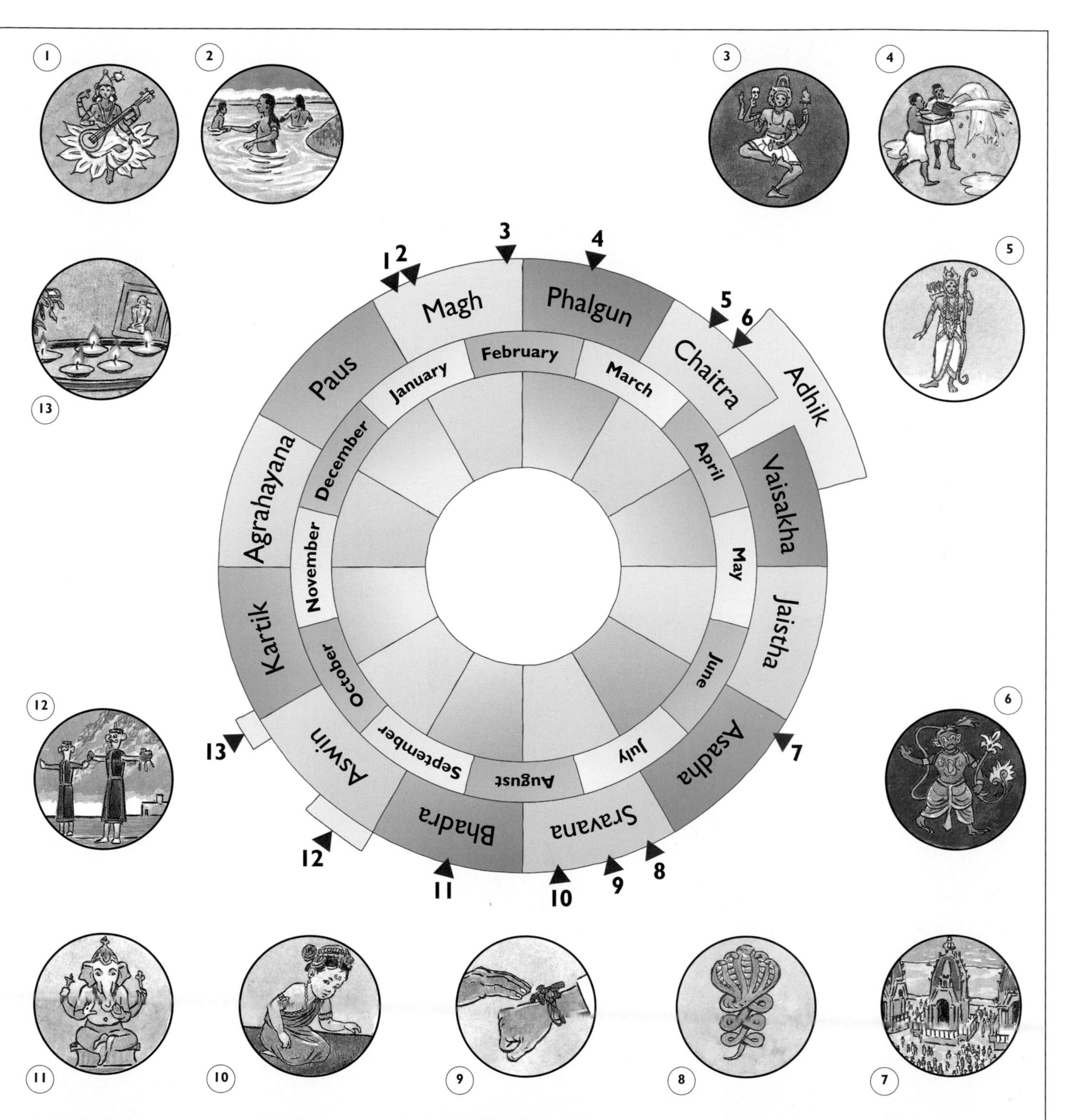

9 Raksha Bandhan (full-moon day of Sravana)
Sisters tie *rakhis* around the wrists of their brothers to signify the bonds of affection and protection between them.

10 Janmashtami (8th day of the dark half of Sravana)
Birthday of Krishna, the eighth incarnation of the god Vishnu and teacher of the Bhagavad-Gita, the 'Song of God'.

11 Ganesh Chaturthi (4th –14th days of the bright half of Bhadra)
A festival honouring Ganesh, the elephant-headed god, son of Shiva and Parvati, who is regarded as the remover of obstacles.

12 Durga Puja or Navaratri (1st day of the bright half of Aswin and lasts for nine nights). Dussehra (10th day of Aswin)
Devi, the female form of the divine power is worshipped in various forms.

Dussehra celebrates Durga's victory over the demon Mahishasura and Rama's victory over the demon Ravana.

13 Divali (13th day of the dark half of Aswin)
This festival of lights, lasting five nights, honours Lakshmi, the goddess of prosperity, and celebrates the triumphant return of Rama and Sita to their kingdom after fourteen years of exile. For many Hindus it marks the start of a new year

Sarasvati Puja and Mahashivaratri

THE RITE OF SPRING
Vasant Panchami – the ancient festival that marks the flowering of spring – is known as Sira Panchami in the states of Bihar and Orissa. Using rice paste and vermilion powder, auspicious marks are made on ploughs, which are then laid on land that has been purified and decorated with flour or rice grains in *rangoli* patterns. The land is then ceremonially ploughed, making the first furrows after the winter season, to bestow fertility.

The festival of Vasant Panchami, honouring Sarasvati, goddess of wisdom, learning and the arts, falls on the fifth day of the bright half of Magh. In northern India it heralds the arrival of spring. To mark a fresh start to the agricultural year, the colour yellow – symbol of royalty and of spring – is worn and displayed in garlands. Many people mark yellow *tilaks* on their foreheads, using turmeric, and prepare kesar halva, a dish made of nuts, sugar, flour and ghee (clarified butter).

Sarasvati is particularly popular in Bengal where huge images of the goddess are paraded through the streets, accompanied by the joyful sounds of musicians. After puja has been offered to Sarasvati, the statue is immersed in a river, recalling her role as a water deity and goddess of the Sarasvati river which flowed west from the Himalayas. Sarasvati is the wife of Brahma, the creative force of the universe. She is said to have invented Sanskrit, the language of the scriptures and of scholarship, and is especially revered by musicians, artists, writers and students. Her festival is celebrated enthusiastically in colleges and schools as well as in peoples' homes. Plays and music and dance are performed in her honour, and books, pens and musical instruments are laid at her shrines. Some parents choose this auspicious day as their child's first day at school, while others may ask a priest to guide their child's hand in writing letters of the alphabet for the first time.

The 'Great Night of Shiva'

The new moon night of every month is called Shivaratri – 'night of Shiva'. But one night in the year, the fourteenth day of the dark half of Magh, is specially celebrated as Mahashivaratri, the 'Great Night of Shiva'.

The 24-hour period of fasting observed for this festival begins at dawn on the day before the new moon appears. Throughout the night, puja is offered to Shiva in temples and in pandals (open-air tents) specially erected to hold large crowds celebrating the festival. Scriptures are read, *bhajans* are sung in Shiva's honour and the Shiva lingam is ritually bathed with the five *panchagavya* – milk, yogurt, butter, honey and sugar.

The horizontal lines on this Sadhu's forehead indicate that he is a follower of Shiva and the circles are a mark of the Supreme Being.

Puja offerings of grain, leaves, flowers and red kum-kum paste have been made at this shrine to Sarasvati. She is sitting on a lotus flower, a symbol of purity, and is holding the Vedas and prayer beads.

A continuous stream of milk is allowed to flow onto the lingam during the night.

Offerings laid before shrines to Shiva, his wife Parvati and son Ganesh include bel leaves, coconut, fruit, grain, milk and water. A 24-hour fast observed for this festival is broken at dawn the next day.

The Mahashivaratri vow

On festival night, a story is told of a hunter who hid in a bel tree waiting for his prey to pass by. The hunter's view was blocked by the canopy of leaves, so he plucked several, which happened to fall on a Shiva lingam at the base of the tree.

A hind deer came to drink water at a nearby pool, but as the hunter took aim she asked him to spare her life long enough to say good-bye to her children. The hunter was forced to fast as he waited all night and at one point he uttered the name 'Shiva'.

Without realizing it, the hunter had performed the Mahashivaratri vow: he had called on Shiva, offered bel leaves and fasted throughout the night. He was now filled with compassion so when the deer returned in the morning to be killed, the hunter let her go.

THE THREE FORMS OF SHIVA

Shiva's creative power is manifested in the lingam, the form in which he is most often worshipped. In legend, this ancient phallic representation originated when Shiva appeared as a shining column of light before Brahma and Vishnu. They could not find the base or the tip of the light column, thereby acknowledging Shiva as the god without beginning or end.

THE LINGAM

Mahayogi

Shiva Nataraja

In the form of Mahayogi, Shiva is seated high in the Himalayas, deep in meditation. He holds a trident, the symbol of lightning and destructive power. In his knotted hair the face of the river goddess Ganga can sometimes be seen. Around his neck, across his body and in his hair are cobras, ready to attack enemies. His neck is blue from swallowing the poison that threatened to destroy the cosmos.

As Shiva Nataraja, or Lord of the Dance, Shiva symbolizes the eternal rhythm of the universe. The beat of his drum is the source of creation. When it stops, the universe is consumed by fire, before a new rhythm is found for the next creation. His raised foot represents *moksha* (liberation). The other foot rests on a dwarf, symbolizing the triumph of wisdom over ignorance.

Rama Naumi and Hanuman Jayanti

THE RAMAYANA
The *Ramayana* existed as a popular oral folk story before it was written as a Sanskrit text, of which there were several versions. It attained its final form about 2,000 years ago. An epic 24,000 verses in seven books, it is said to have been written by the sage Valmiki. For many Hindus it is the model for the ideal Hindu life.

As an obedient son, Rama accepts his father's decision to exile him from the kingdom. He takes refuge in a forest with his devoted wife, Sita, and loyal brother, Lakshman. As an honourable husband, when Sita is kidnapped Rama searches for her with the help of Lakshman and Hanuman (the monkey general) and shows great courage in rescuing her and destroying Ravana. Later, as a dutiful king, he places his responsibilities of state before his personal happiness and loses Sita, his faithful wife.

Rama Naumi celebrates the birth of Rama, the hero of the *Ramayana*. The festival falls on the ninth day of the bright fortnight of Chaitra. For eight days leading up to it the *Ramayana* is recited by priests and members of the congregation and many fast for various lengths of the time. On Raumi Naumi itself, a typical fast might exclude salt, grain and vegetables, although milk products, such as sweetened yogurt, are drunk, recalling the food given to a new-born child.

Rama and Ravana

In the *Ramayana*, the god Vishnu descended to earth as Rama to subdue and conquer the ten-headed demon king Ravana. Having won the favour of Brahma, Ravana was granted immunity from attack by gods or demons, but he abused his power and mounted violent attacks on the gods.

However, Ravana had been too proud to ask for immunity from mortals, so the gods in consultation decided to send Vishnu in human form to destroy him. Meanwhile, on earth, the ageing and childless King Dasaratha was making offering to heaven that he might be granted a family. His prayer was answered when four sons, including Rama, were born to him, each taking part of Vishnu's nature. This epic tells how Rama, with the support of his family, grew up to vanquish Ravana's evil rule.

Celebration and fasting

The day begins with offerings of fruit and flowers to Rama and prayers dedicated to Vishnu. In northern India, processions focus on a chariot carrying four people dressed as Rama, his wife Sita, brother Lakshman and servant Hanuman.

In some parts of India, public gatherings called *kathas* attract large crowds to listen to readings from the *Ramayana* and

Children at Varanasi watch a tableau depicting characters and events from the Ramayana.

A garlanded statue of Ravana, the demon king who held Sita captive on the island of Lanka.

hear gurus expounding on their meaning. In the temples, an image of the infant Rama is placed in a decorated cradle and covered with a cloth which is lifted at noon, as this is said to be the time of Rama's birth. Worshippers queue to rock the cradle and devotions to Rama continue throughout the day. The day's fasting is broken at midnight with a variety of fruit and nuts.

The monkey god

Hanuman Jayanti, celebrating the birth of the monkey god Hanuman, falls on the full-moon day of Chaitra. Hanuman is a popular folk hero throughout India, honoured for his strength, energy and unwavering devotion to the god Rama.

An unmarried and celibate god, he is a patron of *brahmacharis* (young religious students); because of his power and speed, he is the patron of wrestlers, body-builders and those needing physical stamina.

From early in the morning, devotees gather at Hanuman temples and shrines. There the deity is bathed by priests and smeared with oil and an orange-red paste or powder called sindoora, representing strength and life. Offerings include sweets and fruit, especially bananas.

Pandals are erected where prayers and stories about Hanuman are read aloud and dramas from his life are re-enacted. Often, sporting competitions take place on fields or land nearby. At these events, particularly popular in the states of Uttar Pradesh and Bihar, body-builders and wrestlers, having first sought Hanuman's blessing, compete in displays of strength to honour his bravery and power.

Hanuman, the son of the monkey queen, Anjuna, and the wind god, Vayu, was born at dawn. On seeing the sun rising for the first time, he flew towards it thinking it was a ripe fruit, but was struck down by Indra, the storm god. In anger, Vayu ordered the wind to cease, so to make peace again, Indra promised Hanuman undefeatable strength.

RAMA'S DEVOTED SERVANT

The *Ramayana* tells of Hanuman's strength, courage and devotion to Rama. After Rama's wife, Sita, had been kidnapped, Hanuman searched for many days until he found her imprisoned in the palace garden of Ravana, the demon king of the island of Lanka.

A great army was assembled to release her and in one of the many violent battles that ensued, Rama's brother, Lakshman, was mortally wounded. The only herb powerful enough to cure him grew in the far north, on a remote mountain in the Himalayas.

To save the life of Lakshman, Hanuman flew to this distant mountain, but with so many plants there it was impossible to identify the herb. In desperation, he gathered his strength and pulled the mountain out of the earth, placed it on his back and flew back to the dying Laksham. Along the way, he was wounded but struggled on until he landed on Lanka. The doctor attending Lakshman quickly identified the medicinal herb, plucked it from the mountain and Lakshman's life was saved.

Holi Fires and Festivities

FATHOMING THE FLAMES
When the Holi bonfire is lit, divinations for the success of the coming harvest are made by interpreting the direction of the flames or, once the fire has died down, by examining new barley seeds that were buried in a pot under the fire. Sometimes the fire's embers are taken home and used to rekindle domestic fires while the ashes, it is believed, may be used to provide protection from illness.

KRISHNA AND THE COWGIRLS
Holi is a celebration of the grain harvest in India. It is also a festival of love, which is why the teasing games people play are a reminder of the divine lover, Krishna.

One story tells of a time when Krishna, as a young man, heard the laughter of girls coming from a river. He crept towards them and, seeing that the *gopis* – the girls who tended the cows – were bathing, stole their clothes and laid them out in the branches of a tree beyond their reach. Krishna then teased them before returning their clothes, but each cowgirl fell in love with his beauty.

Krishna's love of life and the tricks he also played on unsuspecting friends and neighbours are recalled in the boisterous Holi celebrations.

Holi is celebrated on the full-moon day in the month of Phalgun, but festivities can last up to five days. The festival takes its name from the demon goddess Holika, who tried to murder the young prince Prahlad.

The story of Holi

Prahlad was the son of King Hiranyaka-sipu who had been given a rare gift by the creator god, Brahma. The king was assured he could not be killed by day or night, inside or outside his house, by human, animal or god. Armed with this gift of immunity from death, the king assumed he was unassailable and forbade worship of any god but himself. His son, however, would honour only Vishnu.

The king ordered serpents to kill Prahlad with their venom, and elephants to push him over a cliff. But Prahlad could not be beaten. The king's sister, Holika, enticed him into a fierce fire, but Vishnu protected his follower and Holika was consumed by the flames. Out of sympathy for Holika, Prahlad named this festival in her memory, which is why bonfires are lit.

Prahlad was still alive and continued to tell his father that Vishnu was present everywhere. Exasperated, the king turned to a pillar. 'Is Vishnu in there?' he demanded, and Prahlad assured him he was. The king kicked the pillar and Vishnu strode out in the form of Narasimha, half-man, half-lion, and tore the king to pieces. Brahma's immunity could not protect him. The king was killed in the evening, so it was neither day nor night, and the creature Naramsimha was not fully human, animal or god.

Paints, powders and bonfires

Holi is celebrated throughout India but is especially important in the north. Houses may be repainted in bright colours in preparation for the festival, and rangoli patterns of coloured powders are often arranged on the ground near the door. Children and adults prepare coloured water and something to squirt it with – a traditional bamboo pistol, a plastic water-pistol or an empty detergent bottle. The water may be tinted with plant juices, in the traditional way, or with shop-bought colours.

Holi lasts for several days in Vrindavan and Mathura, the towns where Krishna spent his childhood. Here, pilgrims stained with coloured water and powder, pass through the Sankhari Khori where Krishna held up Radha and the gopis demanding toll tax.

In the weeks leading up to Holi, sticks of wood, old furniture, hay and cow dung are gathered up and brought by the community to a central location. The bonfire is prepared at the time of the rising moon, and on the eve of the festival, called choti Holi ('small Holi'), it is lit. The following morning everyone, young and old, chases each other, squirting coloured water and playing games. Traditional food for Holi includes the sweet *malpua*, a kind of pancake of milk, sugar and dried fruits; *dahi wada*, lentil patties with a yoghurt sauce; and a preparation of raw jackfruit, a native north Indian fruit similar to breadfruit.

In Bengal, the image of Vishnu is often placed in a decorated swing and offerings of coloured powders are made. In Mathura, the town where Krishna was born, the emphasis is more on the love between Krishna and his consort Radha.

CELEBRATING HOLI

Crowds gather to sing, dance and worship around the huge bonfires that are lit on the eve of Holi. The fires illustrate Vishnu's power – they are believed to purify and cleanse and at Holi they herald the coming of the spring season. Among the puja offerings are grain and coconuts, reminders of the earth's fertility at this time of harvest. The coconuts are cooked in the fire and then, as food that has been blessed by the gods, are shared out among those present.

Hindus celebrate Holi with devotional songs as they follow one of the pilgrimage routes around their village. Holi festivities also include puppet shows, fairs and street theatre.

Holi is one of the liveliest of all Hindu festivals. Thousands of people take to the streets to share in the most boisterous element of the festival – the throwing of coloured powder. Anyone who leaves their house is unlikely to escape.

Ratha Yatra and Raksha Bandhan

UNFINISHED GODS
After Ratha Yatra, the chariot festival, the chariots are dismantled and the wood is distributed to pilgrims and temple kitchens for fuel. Meanwhile, construction work starts once again on the chariots to be used the following year. Every twelve years, the images of Krishna and his brother and sister are newly carved out of hard neem wood, but the lower part of the body and the hands remain incomplete.

This tradition relates to the story of a king of Orissa who prayed for an image of God to appear. The king was told in a dream to search the ocean shore, where he would find a tree trunk on which to carve the image. But, when the trunk was found, it was too hard to carve.

One day, an unknown craftsman arrived at the palace. He agreed to work on the wood on condition that he was not disturbed for fifteen days. After ten days, the king became impatient to glimpse what was happening and opened the door to the workshop. The craftsman had disappeared, leaving the carving unfinished. The king realized that he had been Viswakarma, the divine architect of the heavens and of the palaces of the gods. From that time on, the images of the three deities have been left incomplete.

The most famous Ratha Yatra or chariot festival takes place on the second day in the dark half of Asadha, in the town of Puri in the state of Orissa. Another famous Ratha Yatra is held in Karnataka state but festivities on a smaller scale are widespread in India.

Chariot processions

The date for the major temples to celebrate Ratha Yatra varies according the traditional round of festivals associated with that area. At festival time, an image of the temple deity is taken from its shrine and, in a colourful procession and with great devotion, is paraded through the streets on a *rath* (chariot).

In Puri, at Ratha Yatra, the large wooden images of Krishna, his brother Balaram, and sister Subhadra, are removed from the great temple of Jagganath, the Lord of the Universe. Each deity is placed on an enormous wooden chariot freshly constructed in the style of a temple for the festival. Krishna's chariot is the biggest, with sixteen wheels measuring 2 metres in diameter, and requiring more than 400 men to pull it. Accompanied by a surging crowd, the chariots are pulled all day through the wide main street of the town, on their way from the Temple of Jagganath to their temporary residence in the garden temple of Gundica.

Sibling devotion

The full-moon day of Sravana is the time of Raksha Bandhan. Particularly popular in northern and western India, this is a festival that celebrates the bond between brothers and sisters and strengthens it by the tying of a *rakhi*, or coloured thread. As the sister ties the thread around her brother's wrist, she signifies her love and attachment to him and, in return, he offers her his protection. Raksha Bandhan means 'to bind protection'.

According to legend, the great Vedic god of storms, Indra, led the gods into

Thousands of people in the streets of Puri crowd around the three great chariots carrying Krishna, Balaram and Subhadra.

A rakhi can be a simple cotton or silk thread, often red, or a mixture of several coloured threads plaited together. Sometimes gold or silver thread is woven through; flowers or beads may be stitched on, or a painted Aum symbol or swastika (symbol of good fortune and protection) attached to the threads.

A stall selling a range of coloured rakhis attracts a large crowd in the lead-up to the festival of Raksha Bandhan.

battle against demons, but the demons won control of the heavenly kingdom. To protect Indra from harm in the ongoing battle, his wife tied a silken thread around his wrist. Strengthened by this protective thread, Indra and the gods vanquished the demons and regained their kingdom.

A sister places a *tilak* of vermilion powder or paste on her brother's forehead, and may perform *arti* (the devotional act of offering a sacred flame and accompanying prayers or hymns before the image of a deity) before tying the rakhi onto her brother's right wrist while she recites a mantra to protect him from dangerous or evil influences. She then places a sweet in her brother's mouth, symbolizing the tenderness of her words. In return, her brother blesses her and gives her a present as a sign of his affection. A girl with no brother may tie a rakhi onto a cousin's wrist. If families live far from each other, rakhis are sent by post.

Janmashtami and Ganesh Chaturthi

Ganesha's popularity is reflected in the numerous shrines devoted to him as well as many images of him found in shop windows and on doorways, gateways or road hoardings. His name means 'Lord of all Beings'.

Krishna is the eighth incarnation of the god Vishnu. His birthday is celebrated at the festival of Janmashtami, which falls on the eighth day of the dark fortnight of Sravana.

According to legend, Vishnu was born as Krishna to rid the world of the despotic ruler Kansa. However, Kansa had been forewarned that his sister Devaki would bear a child that would eventually kill him. Every time Devaki gave birth, Kansa ordered that the child be killed.

After Devaki became pregnant for an eighth time, carrying the baby Krishna, she and her husband, Vasudeva, were imprisoned in a dungeon. But, when Krishna was born, the gods intervened, causing the prison guards to fall asleep. The locked doors were divinely opened, allowing Vasudeva to carry his new-born son to safety across the Yamuna river. A baby girl was substituted for Krishna. In the morning, when Kansa tried to murder her, she changed into the goddess Devi and revealed that Krishna was safe.

Birthday celebrations

The moment of Krishna's birth is commemorated at midnight, following a day of fasting, prayer, devotional singing and dancing. Readings are taken from the *Bhagavata Purana*, which tells the story of Krishna's early life. An image of baby Krishna is bathed in a mixture of yogurt, milk, honey and tulasi leaves, which is later distributed as *prashad* (holy food).

After being bathed, Krishna is placed on a decorated swing or cradle while singing fills the temple. As midnight approaches, a special *arti* is offered and, at the stroke of midnight, the temple bells announce Krishna's birth. Worshippers clamour to rock the cradle or push the swing while flowers are showered over the statue. The day's fast is now broken and prashad that has been offered at the shrine is shared out.

Ganesh, the fortune-bringer

The elephant-headed god, Ganesh, remover of obstacles and bringer of fortune, is one of the most popular Hindu deities. Prayers are offered to him before any major undertaking: getting married, buying a house or making a journey.

Ganesh Chaturthi, the festival dedicated to Ganesh, is celebrated throughout India between the fourth and fourteenth

SWEET RICE AND LADDU

Krishna's taste for butter and milk is reflected in festival food and puja offerings such as kahchoris (savoury vegetable and lentil pastries deep fried in ghee), lassi (sweet yoghurt drink) and sweet rice and laddu:

SWEET RICE INGREDIENTS

Half a cup of basmati rice
2 litres whole milk
2 cups of sugar

Simmer the rice in the milk over a low heat for 1 hour, stirring continuously to avoid burning. Add sugar and stir before serving.

LADDU INGREDIENTS

1 cup of gram flour
250 g butter
250 g icing sugar

To make the laddu, cook the flour in the butter over a low heat until it turns golden brown. Fold in the icing sugar and roll into balls 5 cm in diameter and allow to cool.

days in the bright half of Bhadra. The event is particularly important in the state of Maharasthtra, where it is marked by large-scale public celebrations.

A terracotta image of Ganesh is placed in a specially prepared home shrine on the first day of the festival. Puja is offered and a priest performs a ritual said to imbue the statue with life. During the following nine days, the image is worshipped morning and evening with arti, food, incense and devotional songs. Although images are often installed for ten days they can be installed for shorter periods of two, five or seven days and many communities also erect a large image of Ganesh in a public tent or pavilion where daily puja takes place.

After ten days in the shrine, Ganesh is ready to leave and is given a huge and colourful farewell. Statues from homes and temples are paraded through crowded streets, followed by priests, musicians, dancers and singers, to the coast or to a river. People line the shores or river banks and, as the statues are fully immersed in water, they sing a parting song, 'Father Ganesh, come again next year', while final offerings of flowers and coconuts are tossed onto the waters.

Krishna's Childhood Home

Festivals in honour of Krishna are regular events throughout the year in Mathura, the town where Krishna was born, and Vrindavan, the town where he grew up.

In the days preceding Janmashtami, festivities build up as streets and homes are colourfully decorated with mango leaves, or whole banana trees, and the hundreds of temples dedicated to Krishna are dressed in flowers and lights.

At major temples, such as Radha Raman, Banki Behari, Krishna Balarama and Rangaji, dances and dramas are staged depicting events from the Lila, the life-cycle of Krishna. They are performed exclusively by young boys trained to play both male and female parts. Stages are erected in pandals (large open-air tents) for these dance-dramas. Thousands of people sit for long hours absorbed in the stories of the child Krishna.

Day and night, these performances and broadcasts from the temples fill the air with religious music and speech. On the day of Janmashtami, the eighth day of the waning moon, the temples are packed with Krishna devotees, thousands of whom will have travelled long distances to be there.

Musicians and devotees gathered for Janmashtami celebrations near Vrindavan. During the event bhajans, or devotional hymns, will be sung in praise of Krishna and stories told of Krishna's life.

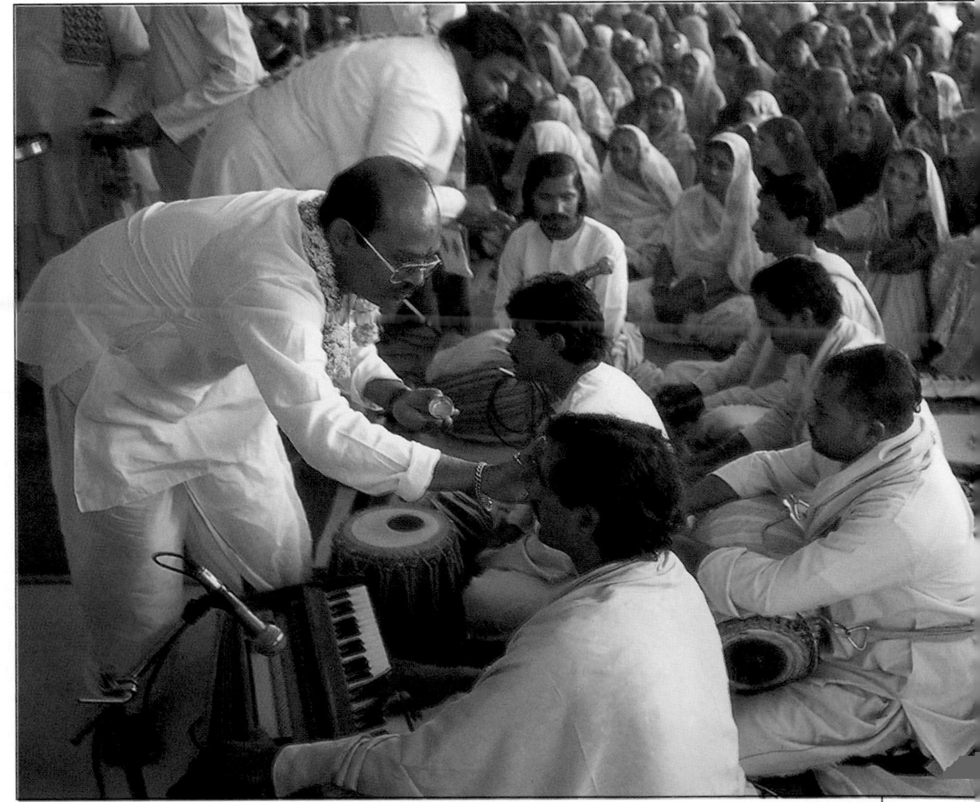

The love between Krishna and Radha symbolizes the divine love between the soul and God.

Durga Puja, Navaratri and Dussehra

Celebrations for Durga Puja or Navaratri begin on the first day of the bright half of Aswin and last for nine nights. Throughout India the festival honours Devi, the female aspect of divine power, who in her various forms can be tender and protective or violent and destructive.

In eastern India, particularly west Bengal, she is honoured in the form of Durga, while in western and northern India different manifestations of Devi are worshipped over the nine nights of Navaratri. The festivities culminate in Dussehra on the tenth day, celebrating the triumph of good over evil, represented by Durga's conquest of the demon Mahishasura, and Rama's destruction of the demon king Ravana.

Durga Puja

Durga is said to descend from the realm of the gods to be present on earth from the sixth to the tenth days of the festival. Images of Durga, the powerful and war-like eight-armed goddess of protection, are made from clay, and then she is

A temple carving of Durga subduing the buffalo demon, Mahishasura, beneath her foot..

A Gujerati Hindu community in Britain perform a stick dance during Navaratri. In India, in Gujerat state, there is a tradition of community dancing around a shrine to Devi during the nine nights of Navaratri. Families and friends meet to take part in joyful garba (hand-clapping) and raf (stick) dances.

dressed in red with a garland and crown traditionally carved from white Indian cork. Special tents – puja mandaps – are erected in areas where the image of Durga is installed, to hold the crowds that gather to worship her.

On Mahalaya, the first day of the festival, hymns and puja are offered to attract Durga's attention, and preparations for the arrival of 'Ma' (Mother), as she is fondly known, continue for the next five days. On the sixth day, her statue is erected in the puja mandaps and a ceremony is held to ritually instil her presence into the image. The goddess is now believed to be present on earth until the tenth day of Aswin.

The sixth day, or Sashthi, is observed by many as a fast day, particularly by mothers who have a special affinity with Durga and pray to 'Ma' for the well-being of their children. The seventh to ninth days of the festival are days of worship and celebration when thousands come to honour Durga before bidding her farewell on the tenth day

The tenth day

Vijayadashmi – 'victorious tenth day' – commemorates Durga's defeat of the demon Mahishasura, who abused the powers granted him by the creator god, Brahma.

Before Durga takes her final leave, her image is symbolically washed by a priest, who captures her reflection in a container of water and she returns to her home with the gods. She is then ceremoniously lifted from her temporary shrine and carried through the streets, attended by singers, dancers and musicians. To farewell cries, the statue is steeped in a river or the sea, with offerings of fruit, flowers and lamps to mark the end of the festival.

NINE ASPECTS OF DEVI

Maya – the source of illusion
Durga – difficult to find
Bhadra – auspicious
Kali – deep blue
Vijaya – full of power
Vaisnavi – energy of Vishnu
Kumuda – giver of enjoyment
Candika – punisher of enemies
Krishna (with a long 'a') – giver of riches

NAVARATRI AND DUSSEHRA

During the nine nights of Navaratri, different aspects of Devi are worshipped and readings are given celebrating her all-encompassing powers.

Among the rituals of Navaratri is the planting of barley grains in a bed of mud near the household shrine to Devi. After daily puja for nine days, the seedlings, which are symbolic of harvest, are pulled up on the tenth day and given to family and friends as a blessing from God.

Some people fast throughout Navaratri, others for shorter periods, and most maintain a vegetarian diet. However, on the eighth day, some communities sacrifice a buffalo, goat or pig, to symbolize Durga's slaying of the demon Mahishasura.

On the tenth day, at the festival of Dussehra, the destruction of the demon king Ravana at the hands of Rama's army is celebrated with the burning of huge effigies of Ravana, his brother Kumbhkarna and son Meghnad. In the *Ramayana*, Rama, in the throes of a fierce battle, prayed to nine different aspects of Devi over nine nights, thereby gaining enough strength finally to defeat Ravana on the 'victorious tenth day'.

In northern India, events from the Ram Lila, the dramatic story of Rama's life, are widely and colourfully re-enacted during Navaratri by professional and amateur performers.

The story reaches its climax with Dusshera, as floats and processions make their way to parks and open grounds where effigies stuffed with fireworks and crackers have been erected. In front of huge crowds, men and small boys dressed as Rama, his brother Lakshman and other *Ramayana* characters restage the final battle. They fire flaming arrows into the effigies, bringing about an explosive and fiery end to the forces of evil.

The Triumph of Light over Darkness

Divali derives from 'Deepavali', meaning a 'row of lamps'. Traditionally the festival lasts five days, but Hindu communities outside India often hold only two days of celebrations. Divali honours Lakshmi, the goddess of wealth and good fortune, and also celebrates the exultant return of Rama and Sita to their kingdom after fourteen years of exile.

Symbolically, Divali reflects the triumph of light over darkness and of good over evil. Coming in the autumn and at harvest time, it is a festival of lights, and for some Hindus it marks the start of the New Year – a period of renewal when houses are cleaned, presents and cards are exchanged and rows of *divas* (clay lamps) are lit to welcome Lakshmi, the bringer of prosperity. For businesses, in particular, this is a traditional time to settle debts and close financial accounts for the year.

Divali is celebrated in a variety of ways throughout India. The rituals that take place on each of the five days and the deities that are honoured vary according to regional traditions.

Wealth and abundance

Divali begins on the thirteenth day of the dark half of Aswin with Dhantrayodashi (meaning 'wealth' and 'thirteenth day'). Lakshmi is worshipped on this day as the

SYMBOLS OF DIVALI

Celebrating the triumph of light over darkness and good over evil, Divali is widely celebrated throughout India and by Hindus worldwide. It is a time to honour Lakshmi the goddess of good fortune and remember the glorious return of Rama and Sita to their kingdom.

SWEETS
Sweets, usually made with a base of ghee or clarified butter, are one of the most popular gifts exchanged between family, friends and neighbours. Small trays of multicoloured sweets are also offered at shrines.

LAKSHMI
Homes and shops are brightly lit to welcome Lakshmi, the goddess of wealth, in the hope that she will bestow abundance. Divali is traditionally the end of the trading year for businesses. Account books are taken to shrines to thank Lakshmi for past trade and to ask for her blessings in the year ahead.

FIREWORKS
As a sign of light conquering darkness, the excitement of Divali is heightened with bonfires, colourful explosions of fireworks and firecrackers, particularly on the third night when the appearance of the new moon marks the beginning of the month of Kartik.

DIVALI CARDS
Since Divali is one of the major Hindu festivals, and for many the start of the New Year, it is a time to resolve differences and affirm bonds of friendship through family reunions, the exchange of cards and gifts and the sharing of festival food.

CLAY LAMPS
Divas, or small clay lamps, filled with ghee or oil are placed in windows, on roofs and around courtyards while rows of divas are also laid before domestic and temple shrines.

goddess of abundance, wealth and generosity. Although people pray to bestow prosperity, the day is also a reminder that wealth should not be abused.

During puja, Lakshmi is ritually washed, dressed, garlanded and offered sweets, fruit, ghee (clarified butter) and flowers. During the festival, the markets in India are full of Divali goods: clay divas, candles, fireworks, *hatri* (small clay structures housing images of Lakshmi) and Divali sweets and savouries. At dusk, candles are lit to welcome Lakshmi and the good fortune that she brings.

The god of death, Yama, is also honoured on the first night, when a diva is placed facing the South, where he rules. Devotions are made to protect the family from premature death and as a reminder that death is part of a natural cycle.

Defeat of the demons

Narak Chaturdashi, which combines the words for hell and fourteenth day, falls on the fourteenth day of the dark half of Aswin. The festival recalls the story of the demon Naraksur, whose battles resulted in the capture and enslavement of 16,000 women. Vishnu heard their prayers for help and came, in the form of Krishna, to defeat Naraksur and liberate the women.

At this time, in West Bengal, it is the goddess Kali that is honoured. The occasion commemorates how the goddess of strength defeated and killed the demon Raktavija. In southern India, it is Narasimha's defeat of the demon king Hiranyakasipu that is celebrated.

Night lights

On Narak Chaturdashi, people rise early to bathe and rub perfumed oils onto their skin. Family and friends then often gather to share a festival breakfast. During the day, puja is offered to Vishnu, Kali or other deities whose triumphs over the forces of evil are being celebrated. In the evening, more divas are lit in windows, on roofs, along pathways and in courtyards.

THE GODDESS LAKSHMI

Lakshmi is the wife of Vishnu who appears as his consort in each of Vishnu's ten incarnations. The two deities are often shown riding Garuda, a giant eagle in the form of a winged man who, as king of the birds, moves with the speed of the wind and light.

In Vishnu's incarnation as Rama, Lakshmi was born from a furrow in a ploughed field as his devoted wife, Sita. When Vishnu appeared as the dwarf Vamana, Lakshmi arose from the waters floating on a lotus flower, a symbol of purity and spiritual strength. When Lakshmi appears alone, she encompasses powerful female energy and is called Lakshmi Mata (Mother Lakshmi).

In the days leading up to Divali, rangoli patterns are drawn near doorways and in courtyards to welcome Lakshmi. Patterns made out of sand, rice, powder or chalk depict deities, religious symbols, animals, trees, birds or geometric designs. Sometimes small footprints are made with rice paste to represent Lakshmi's footprints entering the house

Light, Prosperity and Food

Challenge to the Gods
Bali Pratipada is celebrated at the beginning of Kartik. Pratipada means 'below the opponent's foot', and Bali was a benevolent but ambitious king who is remembered at this time. His rule extended over the heavens, earth and underworld and the gods began to feel that their authority was being challenged.

To curb Bali's power, Vishnu appeared before him in the form of the dwarf Vamana, and asked the king to give him the lands that he could cover in just three strides. Doubting the dwarf could travel very far, Bali agreed. Vamana then changed into a giant and in two strides he submerged the heavens and the earth. On his third stride, Bali offered Vamana his head as a stepping-stone and was forced down into the underworld.

Because Bali accepted his defeat with dignity, Vishnu promised that he would be remembered at Kartik. The prayer that is recited by those who offer devotions to Bali is: 'Let suffering disappear and may Bali's kingdom be restored.'

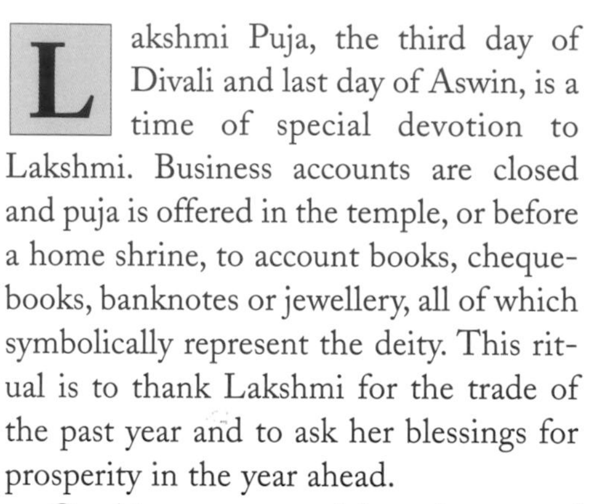

Lakshmi Puja, the third day of Divali and last day of Aswin, is a time of special devotion to Lakshmi. Business accounts are closed and puja is offered in the temple, or before a home shrine, to account books, cheque-books, banknotes or jewellery, all of which symbolically represent the deity. This ritual is to thank Lakshmi for the trade of the past year and to ask her blessings for prosperity in the year ahead.

On this new moon night – the start of a new year for many Hindus – homes, temples and streets shine with divas, candles, lamps and other lights, since it is said that Lakshmi will not enter a dark house. Thousands of divas recall the lamps that were lit to welcome Rama and Sita back to the kingdom of Ayodyha after their long absence. Firecrackers explode in the streets and families share a Divali meal.

Gifts and food

The first day of Kartik marks the start of the new financial year. This fourth day of Divali is also a family day when children receive gifts and husbands traditionally present their wives with a new sari or with gold jewellery. Divali cards and sweets are exchanged during visits to friends or relatives. Many people will try to visit the temple with sweet and savoury food offerings that are built into an *anakoot* or 'hill of grain'. This symbolizes Mount Govardhan, which Krishna lifted with his finger to save the local people and their animals and crops from the fierce floods of Indra, the storm god. When the festival puja has drawn to a close, the food is shared out as *prashad.*

Brothers and Sisters' Day

The second day of Kartik, and final day of Divali, is known as Bhaibij – 'Brothers and Sisters' Day'. It recalls the visit made by the god Yama to his sister Yamuna, goddess of the Yamuna river.

Pleased by this unexpected visit, Yamuna prepared an elaborate meal and, touched by his sister's affection, Yama

A Hindu priest and a group of businessmen in a British temple perform puja over accounts to thank Lakshmi and ask for prosperity in the coming year. The open accounts and cheque books have been marked with a swastika, a symbol of good fortune and protection. Flowers, leaves and fruit have been offered before an image of Lakshmi, and laid on the documents.

DIVALI FOOD

Food is an important part of Divali. Given as offerings at the home shrine or the temple, it is also at the heart of family gatherings and hospitality towards friends and neighbours.

Some dishes, such as barfi or penda, are popular throughout India. Most areas also have their own regional dishes, such as gughara, a sweet Gujerati dish made of coconut, flour, sugar, blackcurrants and cardamom.

Barfi is one of the most popular foods eaten at Hindu festivals and is often included as a puja offering, shared at family celebrations or given as a gift to friends.

Mix together the milk powder and condensed milk until it reaches a crumbling texture. Add the chopped pistachios, pinch of nutmeg and cardamom.

Heat the water and sugar together on a low heat and stir until it turns into thin syrup. Thoroughly mix all the ingredients together. Spread the mixture to a depth of approximately 4 cm onto a baking tray greased with butter or ghee.

Optional: melt 4 pieces of chocolate and then spread onto the mixture and allow to cool, before cutting into pieces.

BARFI INGREDIENTS

- 1 cup of powdered milk
- 1 cup of sugar
- 1 cup of desiccated or grated coconut
- 1 bowl of water
- 1 small tin of condensed milk
- Pistachio nuts
- Pinch of nutmeg
- Pinch of cardamom
- 4 pieces of cooking chocolate (optional)

granted her a wish. She asked him to return each year. Yama replied that it was a pleasure and not a duty to visit her and so he granted her a second wish. Yamuna requested that brothers and sisters who bathe on that day in the Yamuna river be reunited in their next life.

On Bhaibij, brothers visit sisters, female relatives or cousins to affirm family bonds with the exchange of presents and by sharing a meal specially prepared by the women. Also, large crowds gather on the banks of the Yamuna river to bathe in its sacred waters.

A street stall in Vrindavan selling a wide and colourful range of Divali sweets.

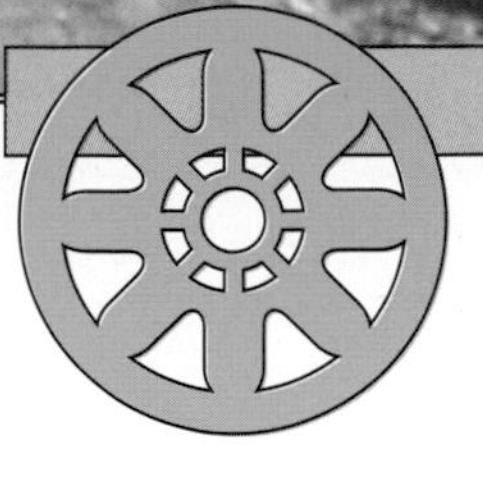

BUDDHIST FESTIVALS

In Buddhist tradition, the title 'Buddha' is given to someone who is rare and extraordinary. A Buddha has woken up to the true nature of all things and has ceased to suffer. Out of compassion and wisdom, a Buddha teaches others so that they too can understand the truth and find release from suffering. Buddha means 'Awakened' or 'Enlightened', and most Buddhists believe that there have been Buddhas in the past and there will continue to be Buddhas in the future.

The founder of Buddhism

The historical Buddha was born Siddhartha Gautama in northern India around the sixth to fifth centuries BC. His father ruled the Sakya people and the Buddha is sometimes given the title 'Sakyamuni', meaning 'sage of the Sakya people'. Raised in the luxury of his father's palace, he was secluded from the realities of the world outside, but in time began to think deeply about sickness, old age and death. Some sources say he was shocked to encounter a sick man, a dying man and a corpse on his first journey outside the palace. He then witnessed the serenity of a wandering ascetic and, at the age of 29, became an ascetic himself to find an answer to the problem of human suffering.

For the next six years, Siddhartha Gautama studied with spiritual teachers and then followed a path of severe austerity, fasting until his body was emaciated. He realized that a life of extremes would not provide the answer to the nature of suffering, and that the truth lay in the 'Middle Way'. Sitting under the bodhi tree, he calmed his mind through meditation and realized the Dharma – the true nature of all things – and so achieved enlightenment.

Sacred languages

'Siddhartha Gautama' and 'Dharma' are from Sanskrit, the common sacred language of ancient India, which is used for many scriptures and scholarly texts of Mahayana Buddhism. The Pali language is found in the scriptures, liturgy and scholarly commentaries of Theravada Buddhism. In Pali, 'Siddhartha Gautama' becomes 'Siddhatha Gotama', and 'Dharma' is 'Dhamma'. This chapter uses mainly Sanskrit terms, with Pali equivalents in parentheses, as appropriate.

Novice Buddhist nuns at Swedagon pagoda in Yangon, Burma.

The Path to Enlightenment

The Buddha gave his first sermon after his enlightenment to a small group of disciples at Sarnath in northern India. Hearing and understanding the Buddha's teachings, these five disciples became enlightened and were the first members of the Sangha (community of monks and nuns). It was at Sarnath that the Buddha first taught the Four Noble Truths and the Eightfold Path, explaining the nature of suffering and the way to end this suffering.

Theravada

The Buddha then travelled and taught in northern India, until his death at the age of 80, by which time he had gathered a large community of disciples. According to tradition, three months after the Buddha's death, 500 Arhats – 'worthy ones' who had achieved enlightenment – gathered to recite what they remembered as the authoritative words of the Buddha. The Buddha's teachings fell into three categories, now called the Tripitaka, or 'Three Baskets'. The traditions and teachings of Buddhism that were established at an early stage are most closely followed by Theravada Buddhists. Theravada means 'Teachings of the Elders'.

Mahayana

By the first century AD, a new kind of literature began to emerge in Indian Buddhism and eventually formed the basis of the Mahayana, or 'Great Vehicle', tradition. These new scriptures claimed to have come directly from the Buddha rather than being commentaries on the Buddha's words. Teachings of scholars were also added to the Mahayana scriptures and certain Buddhist ideas were reinterpreted and adapted in the light of these new scriptures.

Rebirth and release

My life is passing away moment by moment
like water bubbles,
It decays and perishes so quickly;
After death come results of my good and bad
actions
Just like the shadow follows the body.
(Je Tsongkhapa, 'The Foundation of all Excellence', verse 3)

Samsara or 'wandering on' is the endless cycle of death and rebirth. It is said that

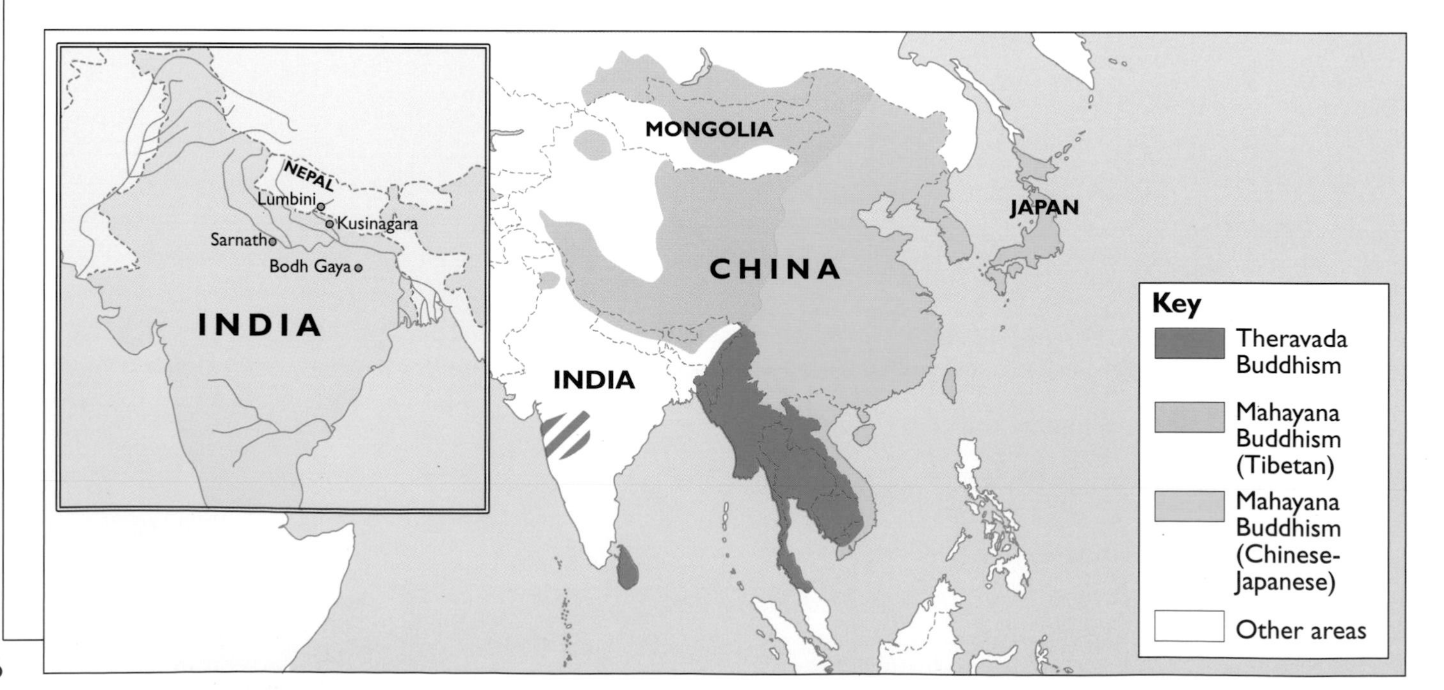

The maps show the spread of Buddhism in Asia. Theravada is also known as Southern Buddhism, Mahayana (Tibetan) as Northern Buddhism, and Mahayana (Chinese-Japanese) as Eastern Buddhism. Four major pilgrimage sites in India and Nepal are associated with the Buddha: his birthplace is Lumbini Grove, he achieved enlightenment at Bodh Gaya, he preached his first sermon at Sarnath and, according to tradition, he died at Kusingara.

Newly ordained monks carrying flower and incense offerings for the Buddha at an ordination ceremony in Sukhotai, Thailand..

we have had innumerable past lives in human and animal form, in heavens and in hells, but human rebirth is precious because it offers the opportunity for spiritual growth and release from samsara.

The movement of beings through rebirth is determined by karma – the law of cause and effect (kamma in Pali). Buddhists believe that there have been and will be immeasurable life cycles, worlds and galaxies, and all are governed by the law of karma. The Buddha likened karma to a seed that will bear fruit in this life and in future lives: every action born out of anger and hatred creates further suffering whereas actions born out of compassion or generosity create happiness and contentment. Merit is built up through positive actions and diminished by negative ones. Since it is the accumulation of karma that determines rebirth, Buddhists try to accumulate positive karma in thought and action.

The goal of the Buddhist path is to achieve nirvana – a final liberation from the laws of karma. Nirvana (nibbana in Pali) literally means 'extinguished', referring to the fires of suffering and craving that finally cease at enlightenment. Nirvana is the state beyond rebirth where there is complete peace. The Buddha described nirvana as 'a place of non-possession and of non-attachment ...the total end of death and decay', but said, ultimately, nirvana transcends any definition.

THE FOUR NOBLE TRUTHS AND THE EIGHTFOLD PATH

The Four Noble Truths are the essential framework upon which Buddhist teachings are based, and to understand them the mind must first be open and at peace.

The First Noble Truth Suffering exists.
The Second Noble Truth There is a reason for suffering.
The Third Noble Truth There is a way to end suffering.
The Fourth Noble Truth The way to end suffering is through the Eightfold Path.

The Buddha compared suffering to an illness that has a cause: once the cause is recognized it can be removed and the illness cured. The cure for the suffering referred to by the Buddha lay in the 'Eightfold Path' or 'Middle Way'. The Path follows a natural progression, each stage building on the preceding one. The Path requires discipline of mind and body and many who decide to embark upon the Path find a teacher to help them understand and practise it.

The Eightfold Path
Right Views Knowing and understanding the Four Noble Truths.
Right Thoughts Letting go of want and desire, and acting with kindness to avoid any hurt.
Right Speech Telling the truth, speaking kindly and wisely.
Right Action Not stealing or cheating.
Right Livelihood Earning a living that does not cause bloodshed or do harm to others.
Right Effort Encouraging and developing positive thought in order to keep to the Path.
Right Mindfulness Being aware of thoughts and actions that affect the world now and will do so in the future.
Right Concentration The peaceful state of mind that arises through correct practice of the Eightfold Path.

A statue from Burma depicting the Buddha's first sermon after his enlightenment. This was given to five companions of the Buddha who had previously practised austerities with him; after hearing and understanding the Buddha's instructions, they also achieved enlightenment.

Devotion, Meditation and Wisdom

THE TRUTH OF THE WORLD
Dharma (Dhamma in Pali) is the underlying nature of all things and the truth of the world. At his enlightenment, the Buddha was awakened to Dharma (the truth) and at the same time he became Dharma itself. Dharma is also the Buddha's teachings on the spiritual path, which are passed on by the Sangha. Thus the Dharma becomes a way of living according to Buddhist teachings to avoid bringing about harm or suffering to others or to oneself. Once the Dharma has been heard and understood in the teachings, it can then be put into practice and, finally, it can be realized through enlightenment.

In Buddhist teachings all things are impermanent: they rise and pass away. Therefore attachments to desires, pain, people or objects are like illusions, since nothing remains the same. Buddhism teaches that suffering and pain are caused by desire and self-centred actions and, to free oneself from this suffering, a person must first of all be aware of it:

Once upon a time there was a traveller lost in a desolate place. Tormented by hunger and thirst, he collapsed and fainted. In his dreams he imagined obtaining delicious foods and feasted on them until his hunger was satisfied. When he awoke, he was still as hungry and thirsty as ever. Because of this, he realized that all things in the world are empty like dreams, and thereafter he tirelessly sought the true awakening of his mind.
(Pratyutpanna-samadhi Sutra)

Meditation

The seventh step of the Eightfold Path teaches that all actions should be performed with mindfulness: being aware of the effect that thoughts and actions will have on others and on yourself. Compassion helps to free the mind from selfish thinking, and actions born of compassion will result in feelings of generosity and tranquillity. Meditation calms the mind so that a peaceful and compassionate state can be cultivated.

There are two basic types of Buddhist meditation: *samatha* (calm meditation) and *vipassana* (insight meditation). In samatha the mind concentrates on a sensation such as breathing, or on an object such as a candle flame, and through Right Effort the mind is calm and focused. This type of meditation lays the foundation for vipassana which opens the mind to analyse all thoughts and feelings. By generating mindfulness to feelings such as anger, desire, pain and frustration, they are allowed to rise and pass away. Gradually, attachments to desires and delusions are weakened and the mind is able to see things as they really are.

Monks collecting food on their daily alms round. Giving to the Sangha and the community at large is an important part of Buddhist practice since it increases compassion for the needs of others. The act of giving also produces merit, improving karma in this life and the next.

The Three Refuges and the Sangha

The expression of commitment to Buddhism is encapsulated in the Three Refuges, which are usually recited at the beginning of an act of devotion:

I take refuge in the Buddha
I take refuge in the Dharma
I take refuge in the Sangha.

'Taking the Refuges' is often accompanied by three bows before a shrine or Buddha image, and then chanting or making offerings. It denotes finding a place of peace and a source of wisdom in a life that is full of demands, suffering and desires. The Buddha, the Dharma (the teachings and path of the Buddha) and the Sangha are also known as the Three Jewels.

The Sangha was formed from the community of monks and nuns that followed the Buddha, and it is their duty to uphold and pass on the Buddha's teachings. In Theravada Buddhism the Sangha includes ordained monks and nuns. In Mahayana Buddhism the Sangha encompasses bodhisattvas and can include scholars, teachers and lay people.

Ordination as a Buddhist monk or nun means submitting to the Vinaya, the monastic rules drawn from the Buddha's teaching. A new monk or nun will enter an ordination tradition or lineage, a line of teachers and disciples often traced back to the Buddha. In the Theravadan tradition, the lineage of female ordination has been broken and women can only take the same precepts as novice monks, though this is gradually changing.

As a commitment to monastic life, a monk or nun will recite the Three Refuges and accept the more than 200 rules of the Vinaya. Their head will be shaved and they will own nothing but their robes and their alms bowl. The Sangha largely rely on lay people for their food, clothes, housing and other essential needs, and in return they offer the precious gift of the Dharma.

Buddhists bowing to show respect to the Three Refuges. Their palms are joined in a gesture known as namaskara.

A statue of Buddha reflected in a lotus pool in the grounds of the ancient Thai capital of Sukhothai.

CHANTING CEREMONY

Performed by monks on behalf of lay people, Paritta is a Thervadan chanting ceremony to offer protection and ward off negative influences. It is common at festivals or celebrations, to mark a family event, shield from illness, grow a good harvest or for general protection.

In the ceremony, the Three Jewels of the Buddha, Dharma and Sangha are represented by monks, the Buddhist scriptures and a relic associated with the Buddha.

The monks are tied to each other by a thread, which is also tied to an image of the Buddha, and pots of water are placed around the area. Sutras (suttas in Pali) are recited, and the thread is cut into short pieces and tied around the necks and wrists of the lay people present.

The water, which is now infused with the blessings from the ceremony, is sprinkled over them. In Mahayana schools, protective chants are called Dharani, a series of words shortened to syllables that create often unintelligible formulas.

Chanting plays an important part in Buddhist practice, and the chanting of monks is particularly effective since through their practice they have a greater understanding of the Dharma. Chanting calms and opens the mind to truth, creates feeling of loving kindness (*metta*) and compassion (*karuna*) and makes merit for those who chant and those who listen.

The Southern Buddhist Calendar

Southern or Theravada Buddhism is the tradition of the majority of people in Thailand, Burma (Myanmar), Cambodia, Laos and Sri Lanka and is practised in parts of India, Bangladesh and Vietnam.

A lunar calendar

The main religious festivals of the Southern Buddhist year are set by the twelve lunar months. However, the New Year is marked by a solar date. Every two or three years, an intercalary month is added between the lunar months of Asalha and Savana to keep in step with the solar calendar. Savana, Potthapada, Assayuja and Kattika are the months of the rains and three of these four months are kept by the Sangha as a period of monastic retreat. Each of the months ends on a full-moon day.

There are various dates that are put forward for the Buddha's birth, varying between c.566 BC and c.486 BC. All sources for the Buddha's life tell that he died at the age of 80, and most Buddhist calendars are dated from his death. In Buddhist tradition, however, it is not regarded as his death but as his final passing into nirvana.

In Buddhist countries, the festivals' calendar includes a variety of celebrations – some directly Buddhist, some containing Buddhist ritual and others that may be linked to the agricultural year, to local folk religion or to regional or national events. Festivals are usually also a holiday when people rest and are reunited with their families. There are often parades and marching bands, with food stalls, street theatre, fortune-telling, acrobats, pantomimes and puppet shows.

UPOSATHA DAYS

The full-moon day, new-moon day and two half-moon days in each lunar month are called *uposatha* days (or *poya* days, in Sri Lanka). In practice, it is the full-moon days that are of most significance since they mark an event in the Buddha's life or in Buddhist history. They are days of special religious observance, particularly in monasteries.

Devout members of the laity will also spend a day and a night at a monastery, meditating, offering food to the monks, talking with the monks or listening to them chanting from the Pali scriptures. Most of the major festivals in the religious calendar fall on the full-moon uposatha days. The lunar cycle may vary slightly from country to country.

A statue of the Buddha being washed during Vesakha celebrations at Wat Chedi in the city of Chiang Mai, Thailand.

CALENDAR OF FESTIVALS FOR SOUTHERN BUDDHISM

The year is based on a lunar cycle but the New Year is marked by a solar date that falls in mid-April. The Pali names for the months have been used here. However, the names vary according to the languages of the countries of Southern Buddhism. The Pali calendar is based on the ancient Indian Sanskrit calendar.

1 NEW YEAR (MID-APRIL AFTER THE SPRING EQUINOX)
Usually lasting three days, this is a time of renewal and reunion. Homes are cleaned, statues of the Buddha are washed and crowds take to the streets for boisterous water festivals.

2 VESAKHA PUJA (FULL-MOON DAY OF VESAKHA)
Known as Buddha Day in the West, this festival celebrates the birth, enlightenment and passing into nirvana of the Buddha.

3 POSON (FULL-MOON DAY OF JETTHA (POSON))
Celebrated in Sri Lanka, the festival recalls the introduction of Buddhism into Sri Lanka by the monk Mahinda, son of the Indian emperor Ashoka, in the third century BC.

4 ASALHA PUJA (FULL-MOON DAY OF ASALHA)
The festival marks the Buddha's first sermon, given in northern India, after he achieved enlightenment. He taught the Four Noble Truths and the Eightfold Path.

5 VASSA (THREE MONTHS USUALLY BEGINNING AT THE END OF ASALHA)
During the three-month period in the rainy season the monks remain in their monasteries. It is a time of retreat and intensified religious observance.

6 PAVARANA (FULL-MOON DAY OF ASSAYUJA)
The festival marks the usual end of Vassa.

7 TAVATIMSA (THE DAY AFTER PAVARANA)
According to tradition, the Buddha journeyed to Heaven during his lifetime to pass his teachings on to his mother. This festival of light recalls his return from Heaven.

8 KATHINA (IN KATTIKA OR MAGGASIRA)
The ceremony in which robes are given to the monks takes place during Kattika if Vassa has ended. If the rains are late, then Kathina is held during the month of Maggasira.

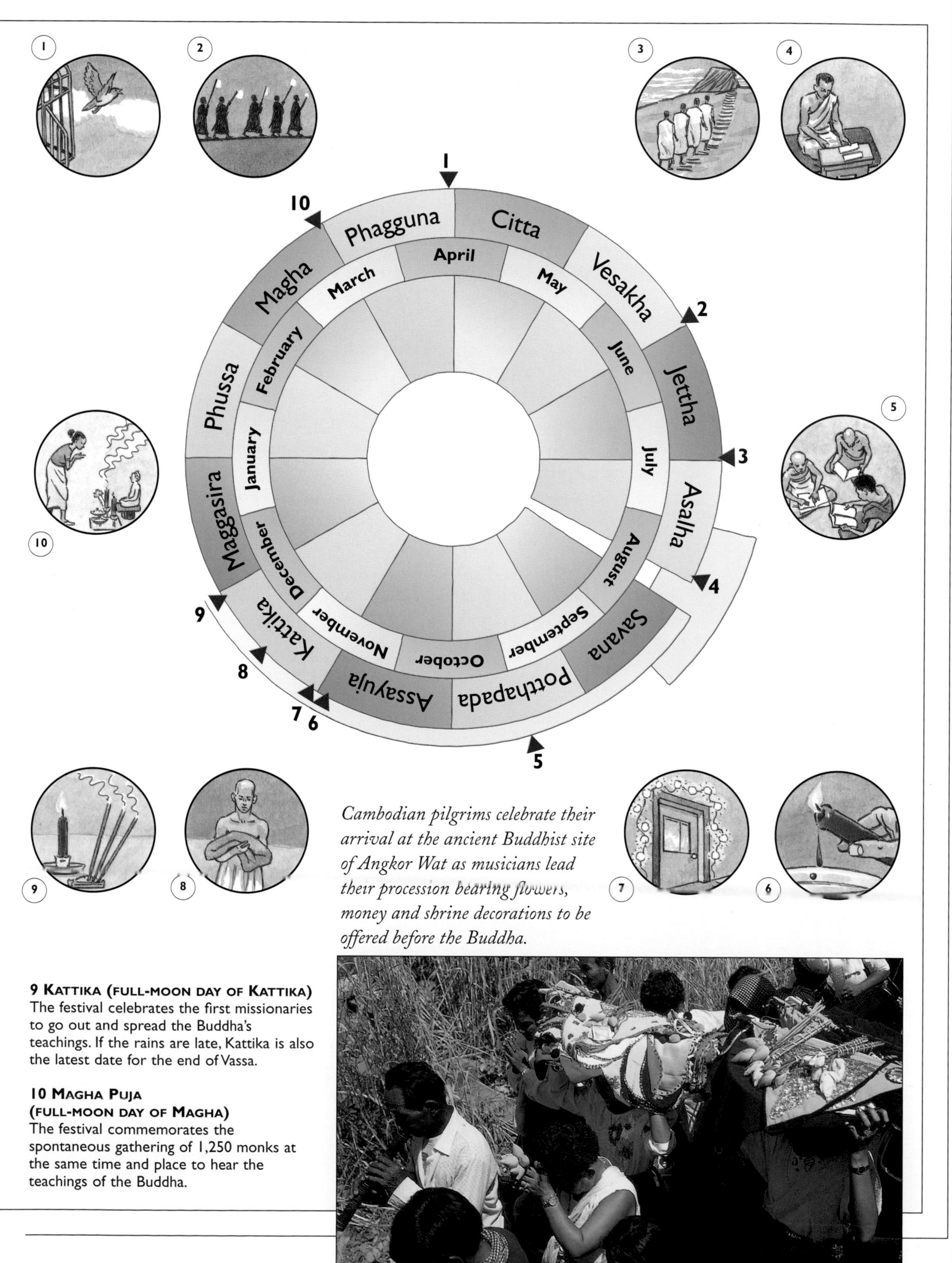

Cambodian pilgrims celebrate their arrival at the ancient Buddhist site of Angkor Wat as musicians lead their procession bearing flowers, money and shrine decorations to be offered before the Buddha.

9 KATTIKA (FULL-MOON DAY OF KATTIKA)
The festival celebrates the first missionaries to go out and spread the Buddha's teachings. If the rains are late, Kattika is also the latest date for the end of Vassa.

10 MAGHA PUJA (FULL-MOON DAY OF MAGHA)
The festival commemorates the spontaneous gathering of 1,250 monks at the same time and place to hear the teachings of the Buddha.

New Year and Vesakha Puja

Water Festivals

New Year water festivals are common in South-East Asia. They are imbued with a carnival atmosphere which has developed out of the original notion of physical and spiritual cleansing. Water festivals range from the gentle throwing of water to boisterous, full-scale water battles.

In Thailand, the three-day festival known as Songkran is regarded as a time of renewal and family reunion. With the last day of the old year falling on 13 April, the next day is regarded as a transition and New Year's Day falls on 15 April. The word Songkran means to 'change place', referring to the changing position of the earth in relation to the sun, following the spring equinox. During Songkran, thousands of people take to the streets with hose-pipes or buckets of water, with the good-natured aim of soaking friends or passers-by. It is not unusual for processions carrying statues of the Buddha to be caught in the crossfire.

The dates of traditional New Year celebrations in Southern Buddhist countries are set by the solar calendar, with festivities lasting three days between 13 and 15 April. In Sri Lanka this is a time of harvesting and thanksgiving. In Burma, Thailand, Cambodia and Laos it marks the end of the dry period and heralds the coming of summer. New Year was not originally a Buddhist festival, but Buddhist rituals have become associated with celebrations marking the beginning of the year.

A fresh start

In the days before New Year, houses are thoroughly cleaned of the past year's dirt and dust. This not only marks a fresh start but also symbolically prevents misfortune being carried forward. In temples and shrines, statues of the Buddha are washed with scented water. As a sign of respect water is ceremoniously poured onto the hands of monks, parents and elderly relatives. Offerings may also be made to monks and presents given to relatives. These activities combine to accumulate merit for the future and cleanse away misdeeds of the past.

Buddhists in Cambodia, Laos and Thailand build stupas out of sand in temple grounds or on river banks. Then, on New Year's Day, the sand is levelled off to form a new floor or is swept away by the river, just as negative actions should be cleared away. It is a time for showing sympathy for living creatures by releasing fish, turtles or caged birds. As this is a dry period, fish are often trapped in low-level rivers and so rescuing them is an act of compassion.

In Sri Lanka, New Year's Day always falls on 14 April but the exact start is set at a time deemed auspicious according to astrological readings. In the hours leading up to this, families cook outside and many people rest at home since it is deemed unlucky to work during the *punyakalaya*, the few hours between the end of the old year and the beginning of the new.

As an act of compassion to living creatures, a captive eel is released into a river during the festival of Vesakha Puja.

Vesakha Puja

The festival of Vesakha Puja, also known as Wesak Puja, falls on the full-moon day of the month of Vesakha. A major event, it celebrates the birth of Buddha as Prince Siddhatha, his enlightenment under the bodhi tree and his passing into nirvana at death. Many Buddhists regard it as the most important festival of the religious year. In the West it is called Buddha Day and is widely celebrated by a range of traditions.

Temples are the focal point of the festival; people gather to pay homage to the Buddha with flowers, incense, lamps and food. Vesakha Puja is a time to focus the mind on Buddhist precepts and to accumulate merit by means such as alms-giving, showing compassion to captive animals and listening to the chants or teachings of the monks. It is at festival time, in particular, that the laity have the opportunity for increased religious observance.

Houses and temples are decorated with flowers and lit with lanterns, candles or strings of light – a symbol of the Buddha's enlightenment. In the evening, crowds hold torch-lit processions in the temples and surrounding streets.

In Thailand, Cambodia and Laos, monks lead the laity three times around the stupa or temple shrine-hall, in honour of the Three Jewels (the Buddha, Dharma and Sangha). Then the community gathers to listen to a sermon on the Buddha, sometimes lasting the whole night. In Burma, bodhi trees are garlanded with flowers and sprinkled with scented water.

Sri Lankans celebrate the Buddha's life with lively street theatre, pantomines and displays of light and art. At major street junctions in most large Sri Lankan towns, *pandala* are erected using high scaffolding and Buddha images or scenes from Buddhist stories are created using flashing light bulbs. Families and friends set up *dansala*, or alms huts, in the streets, offering free food to passers-by or preparing pots of food to feed stray animals.

FOOD OFFERINGS

Visitors to the temple on festival days are likely to include food among their offerings to the Buddha and the Sangha. Just as the festivals reflect a variety of local colour and tradition, so do the foods cooked at festival time. Rice is one of the staple foods offered as alms, but a variety of sweet and savoury dishes may also be prepared. Although vegetarianism is not compulsory, vegetarian food is more common on festival days since the lay community will try to follow the Five Precepts of Buddhism. The act of giving (dana) to the monks or the wider community is central to Buddhist practice since it cultivates sensitivity to the needs of others.

Chiang Mai in northern Thailand is famous for its water festival. For several days the streets are thronged with people taking part in the Songkran celebrations.

SRI LANKAN KIRIBAT

INGREDIENTS

1 cup rice
2½ cups of water
1 cup coconut milk
1 whole peeled garlic
pinch of salt

Chilli paste:
1 onion
1 chilli pepper
juice of fresh lime
pinch of salt

Kiribat or milk rice is eaten on special occasions, such as New Year, Vesakaha Puja or birthdays.

1. Boil the rice with more water than usual so that it is slightly overcooked and sticky (1 measure of rice to 2½ measures of water).
2. Prepare coconut milk either from desiccated coconut and hot water or from coconut milk powder.
3. Cover the cooked rice with the coconut milk, add a pinch of salt and a whole peeled garlic clove and bring to the boil again.
4. Turn off the heat and allow the rice to set. The result should be a very sticky, glutinous rice that can be pressed into a bowl to give it a round shape when turned upside down onto a plate.
5. Kiribat is eaten warm, not hot or cold, and always with a hot chilli paste.

To make the chilli paste, cut one onion into very thin slices and mash with chilli pieces (not powder), salt and lime juice, using a pestle and mortar. As this paste is very hot you only need a pea-sized amount (or less) with every mouthful.

Asalha Puja

ORDINATION
There is an increase in the number of monks ordained in the weeks leading up to Asalha. Many temporary ordinations of young men also take place as they enter monasteries for three months to develop Buddhist practice. The tradition in the Theravadan countries of South-East Asia is for young men to join the Sangha at least once (usually during Vassa) as a preparation for adulthood. Some men return later in life to take on temporary ordination, and for men of senior years doing so is considered a means of building merit that will affect their next life.

Asalha Puja falls on the full-moon day of the month of Asalha. The festival recalls the time that the Buddha renounced his life of wealth and luxury and began his journey to understanding why suffering exists and how to end it. When the Buddha achieved enlightenment, he gave his first sermon to five disciples in an animal park at Sarnath in northern India. He taught the Four Noble Truths and the Eightfold Path. His first sermon became known as the 'Setting in Motion of the Wheel of Dharma', meaning that the Buddha's teachings on the true nature of all things had now begun.

THE FIVE PRECEPTS

I undertake the rule of training of refraining from:
Harming living beings
Taking what is not given
Misuse of the senses
False speech
Self-intoxicaton due to alcoholic drink or drugs.

The Five Precepts constitute an ethical code or 'rules of training'. By accepting them, an individual is making a commitment to live by Buddhist teachings. The promise to abide by the Five Precepts can be made privately by chanting them to oneself, or – more traditionally – they are chanted by a monk and then repeated by the individual.

Since it is often difficult for the average lay person to abide by the Five Precepts all the time, on festival and other uposatha days people make a special effort to chant the Precepts and live by them. Members of the lay community who want to follow Buddhist practice more strictly can stay overnight at the monastery during festivals or in the period of Vassa, and take on Eight Precepts for a limited time.

Those who wish to commit themselves to a strict ethical code on a long-term basis but without becoming fully ordained members of the Sangha can permanently undertake the Eight Precepts or the novice's Ten Precepts.

A time for reflection

Asalha Puja is a day for focusing on the Buddha's teaching, when many people visit monasteries to make offerings and listen to sermons or teachings by the monks. The day often ends with candle-lit processions three times around the stupa or shrine hall to honour the Three Jewels.

The festival marks the beginning of Vassa, the three-month period of rains and a time of retreat, when monks remain in their monasteries to focus on study and meditation. The tradition began when the Buddha's disciples ceased their wanderings during the rainy season to take refuge in shelters that they built themselves or were provided by followers.

Overall it is a quieter and more reflective period in lay society. Some people intensify their religious practice by observing the uposatha days at their local monasteries, and any public or family celebrations such as marriage are often postponed until Vassa has ended.

Procession of the Sacred Tooth

Esala Perahera is a Sri Lankan festival celebrated during the month of Asalha (Esala in Sri Lanka). Huge, colourful processions (perahera) are organized on the streets of Kandy and the highlight is the procession of the Sacred Tooth, a relic of the Buddha. On the festival's tenth night – the night of the full moon – more than a hundred richly decorated elephants parade through the streets in a sea of drummers, whip-crackers, torch-bearers and other performers to the accompaniment of exploding fireworks.

The festival honours the Buddha and invokes blessings for health, rain and successful crops. The main elephant in the procession – the Dalada Maligawa Tusker – carries on its back a replica of the ornate golden relic casket of the Sacred Tooth. The Tooth is believed to have been smuggled onto the island in the hair of an

An ornately caparisoned elephant makes its way through the streets of Kandy as part of the Esala Perahera procession.

Indian princess in the fourth century AD, and has always been treated with the utmost reverence.

The elephant that previously carried the Sacred Tooth, called Raja Tusker, was much loved by the Sri Lankan people. When the animal died, his body was preserved in a side-building in the Dalada Maligawa complex where the Sacred Tooth is housed.

Sri Lanka's first Buddhists

The festival of Poson celebrates the bringing of Buddhism to Sri Lanka in the third century BC by the monk Mahinda, the son of the Indian emperor Ashoka. It takes place on the full-moon day of the month of Jettha, which Sri Lankans call Poson.

On that day, thousands of Buddhists climb the 1,840 stone steps of Mihintale rock where Mahinda is believed to have introduced Buddhist teachings to King Devanampiyatissa. The rock is pitted with sixty-eight caves, or cells, built by the king to house Mahinda and a community of Buddhist monks. At the spot below the peak where the king and the monk first met, stands Ambastala Stupa which holds the relics of Mahinda himself. In his lifetime, Mahinda asked his father, Emperor Ashoka, to send relics of the Buddha as a constant reminder of the Dharma for the people of Sri Lanka. Along with the relics that Mahinda's sister brought to the island was a bodhi sapling. The tree was planted in the royal Mahamega garden and it still grows there today.

Although Mihintale is the main site of pilgrimage at Poson, the festival is celebrated throughout the island. Many people visit temples and offer alms to the Sangha and the poor. All over Sri Lanka, Buddhist teachings and especially the arrival of Buddhism are celebrated in songs, dramas and parades.

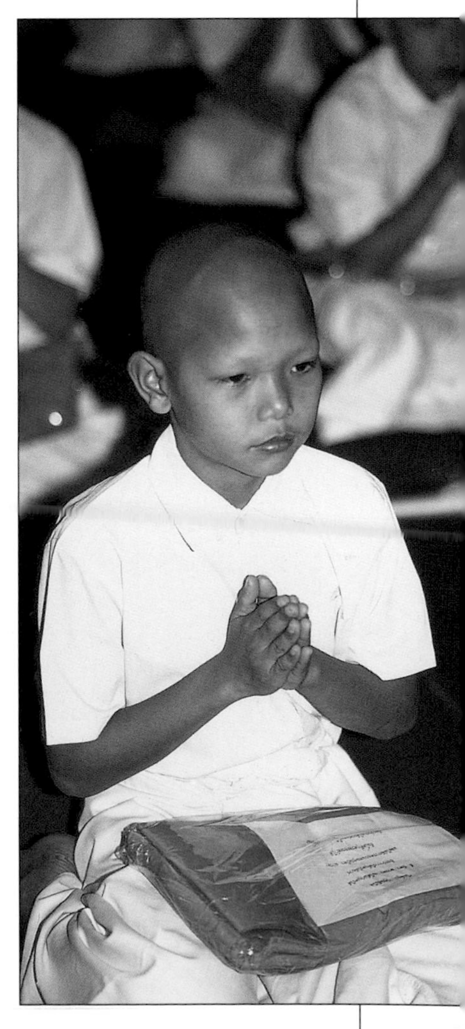

At the beginning of Vassa, a young boy accepts temporary ordination in a Burmese monastery.

Pavarana, Tavatimsa and Kathina

UNITY OF THE SANGHA
According to the Vinaya (code of monastic rules), the Sangha must take part in Pavarana in preparation for the Kathina festival. The monks are invited to point out each other's faults or weaknesses in a ceremony that is not open to the public. As a way of maintaining the monastic rules and unity of the Sangha, the monks have to be open to criticism from both their junior and senior colleagues. This is seen as a way for the monks to help each other refine their Buddhist practice.

Pavarana marks the end of Vassa, the period of monastic retreat, and usually falls on the full-moon day of Assayuja. On this day of meditation and chanting, the monks perform a ceremony in which wax from a burning candle drips into a container of water, infusing the water with the merit accumulated by the monks from their earlier period of intense study and meditation. They sprinkle this water on the lay people gathered at the monastery. This ceremony is also performed on occasions such as funerals, when people may wish to transfer merit to their dead relatives.

Festival of light

In South-East Asia, Tavatimsa is a festival of light that marks the Buddha's return from Heaven. According to tradition, the Buddha ascended to the Tavatimsa Heaven during the period of Vassa and passed on teachings to his mother, before returning to earth. Tavatimsa Heaven, or the 'Heaven of Thirty-Three Gods', is one of the Heavens into which, Buddhists believe, it is possible to be reborn.

The festival takes place on the day following Pavarana. Lights are hung in houses, on driveways and in temples. Lighted candles placed in small decorated rafts made of leaves are sent floating down rivers. The light symbolizes the illumination of enlightenment that the Buddha brought back to earth after being in the Tavatimsa Heaven, and signifies a new beginning after the period of Vassa.

Robe-giving ceremony

Kathina takes place during the month after Vassa. The ceremonial presentation of robes at Kathina honours the role of the Sangha within the Buddhist community. The act of giving (*dana*) is central to this festival, reflecting the interdepen-

dency of the Sangha and the lay community. Through acts of generosity, both individuals and the community experience a sense of well-being and contentment which in itself creates merit. The laity offer gifts to meet the practical needs of the monks and, in return, the monks offer the gift of the Dharma.

The Kathina offerings are usually organized by a communal group from a street, village or local club. These people buy sufficient pieces of cloth to make one robe and donate other essential items.

Dressed for the festival and often accompanied by musicians, community members make their way in a procession to the monastery to present their gifts. Following the rules set down in the Vinaya, the cloth must be a gift to the Sangha as a whole and not intended for any particular individual. The cloth is taken away to be dyed and made into a robe that same day. A monk is then nominated to receive the finished robe.

The pieces of the cloth recall the patches of rags that the early Buddhist monks had to collect wherever they could find them, as they travelled from village to village. Committed to a life of simplicity, they dyed these worn patches and sewed them by hand into robes.

Joss sticks are lit as part of daily puja as well as at festival times.

GATHERING OF THE 'WORTHY ONES'

Magha Puja, on the full-moon day of Magha, commemorates the spontaneous, large gathering of Arhats to honour the Buddha. Arhat, meaning 'worthy', refers to someone whose spiritual training is complete: the person has experienced nirvana in his or her lifetime and will not be reborn into another life.

According to tradition, when the Buddha arrived at the city of Rajagaha in northern India, 1,250 Arahats, guided by the Dharma and without advance planning, assembled at Wat Veruvana to hear him speak. It is said that this happened in the first year after his enlightenment. The Buddha summarized his teachings in 423 verses called Dhammapada, or 'Verses on Dhamma':
Not to do any evil, to cultivate good, to purify one's mind – this is the teaching of the Buddhas. Forebearing patience is the highest authority, Nibbana is supreme say the Buddhas. (Dhammapada, verses 183–4).

During the day, Buddhists visit the temple to offer alms, perform puja (acts of devotion) and listen to the monks chanting or delivering sermons. In the evening, lay people and monks join in a candlelit procession around the temple three times in honour of the Three Jewels.

On behalf of the community, representatives of a village offer cloth to the abbot of their local monastery during Kathina celebrations

The Eastern Buddhist Calendar

Eastern Buddhism is found largely in China, Japan, Vietnam and Korea. Many Buddhists in these countries may also have a close relationship with other major religious traditions. For example, Buddhism may be practised alongside Taoism in China, or Shinto in Japan, and it is not unusual for festivals to be celebrated with equal commitment by both traditions. Some festivals are commonly shared, such as New Year or the Buddhist festival of Ullambana (O-Bon in Japan), which is also known as the Hungry Ghost festival in Taoism.

The year follows a lunar calendar that begins in January–February each year. A lunar year has twelve moons that each lasts $29\frac{1}{2}$ days. However, to keep full days in each moon, some lunar months are 30 days' long and others last 29 days. On average, each lunar year falls short of the solar year by 10, 11 or 12 days, and so an intercalary month is added every two or three years to reconcile the lunar and solar calendars.

A New Year banquet prepared by a family from Hong Kong to share with their friends and neighbours. The food itself and the names of each dish are symbolically associated with the wish for good fortune, health, wealth and prosperity in the year ahead.

CALENDAR FOR FESTIVALS OF EASTERN BUDDHISM

The lunar calendar was introduced into Japan from China and Korea in the sixth century AD. It continued to be used there until 1872, when the Gregorian calendar was officially adopted for business and daily life. Religious festivals were gradually set on solar dates, particularly in large cities and in eastern Japan. Lunar dates are kept for some religious ceremonies in small communities and in western Japan. For example, the festival of O-Bon might be celebrated on 13–15 August or on the 13th–15th days of the seventh lunar month.

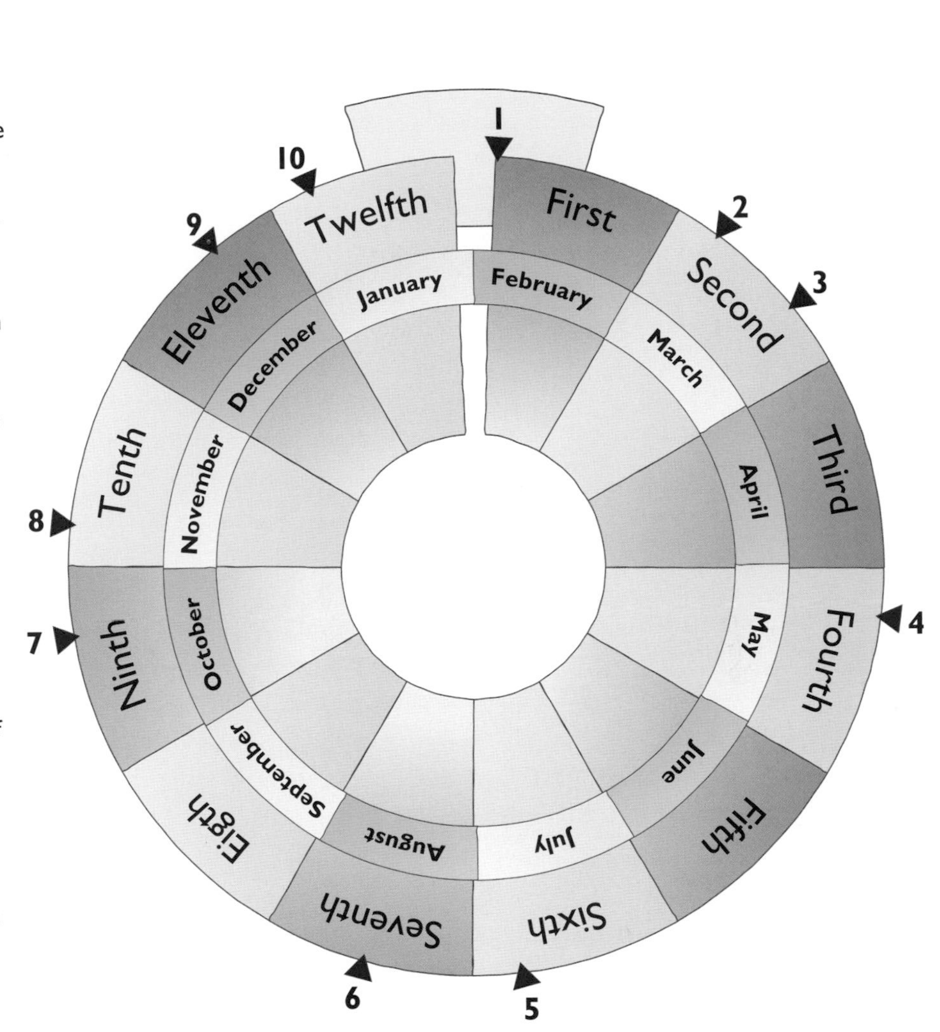

1 NEW YEAR (1ST DAY OF THE FIRST LUNAR MONTH)
Families travel long distances to celebrate together, houses are thoroughly cleaned and offerings are made before domestic shrines and in temples. This day is also the Birthday of Maitreya Buddha, who is regarded as the future Buddha (called Mi-lo-Fo in China).

2 DEATH OF SAKYAMUNI BUDDHA
The final passing of the Buddha into nirvana at death (parinirvana) is commemorated on the 8th day of the second month, and in Japan on 15 February.

3 BIRTHDAY OF KUAN YIN (19TH DAY OF SECOND MONTH)
Honoured as the Bodhisattva of Compassion who has been reincarnated in this world many times, Kuan Yin (Kwannon in Japan and Korea) is the female form of the bodhisattiva. Avolokitesvara is the male form.

4 BIRTH OF SAKYAMUNI BUDDHA
The Buddha's birthday is celebrated on the 8th day of the fourth month and in Japan on 8 April.

5 ENLIGHTENMENT OF KUAN YIN
Falls on the 19th day of the 6th month.

6 ULLAMBANA (THE HUNGRY GHOSTS FESTIVAL)
Families visit graves to honour their ancestors and to ease the suffering of unsettled spirits. The festival falls on the 15th day of the seventh month in the lunar calendar, except in Japan, where it is is remembered on the 13–15 August and is known as O-Bon.

7 DEATH OF KUAN YIN
Commemoration on the 19th day of the ninth lunar month.

8 ANNIVERSARY OF THE DEATH OF BODHIDHARMA
The death of the Indian monk who founded the Ch'an (Meditation) school of Buddhism in China is commemorated on the 5th day of the tenth month. The focus of this practice is on deep insight and enlightenment through meditation. In Japan this is known as Zen.

9 BIRTHDAY OF AMITABHA BUDDHA (THE BUDDHA OF INFINITE LIGHT)
Known in Japanese as Amida, and in Chinese as A-mi-t'o, this festival falls on the 17th day of the eleventh month. According to the Pure Land Sutras, those who faithfully hear and meditate upon the name of Amitabha Buddha will be guided at death to the Pure Land.

10 ENLIGHTENMENT OF SAKYAMUNI BUDDHA
The Buddha's enlightenment under a bodhi tree at Bodh Gaya is celebrated on the 8th day of the twelfth month and on 8 December in Japan.

Members of a Chinese opera company on a visit to Manchester, UK, make their way to the stage to perform before a large crowd gathered in the city centre to celebrate Chinese New Year.

New Year Celebrations

The Festival of Tet
In Vietnam, the seven-day festival of Tet marks both the New Year holiday and the beginning of spring. This is the most important week of the year, and determines the fortunes of the coming twelve months. In rituals combining Buddhism, Taoism and indigenous folk religion, houses are cleaned, debts paid, new clothes purchased and miniature orange or peach trees in bloom exchanged. As the New Year food is prepared, including *banh chung* (lard and bean filled steamed rice cakes), noodle soup and spring rolls, offerings are regularly made to the family ancestors at the household shrine.

In China, Buddhists celebrate the New Year along with other Chinese, in rituals that combine Buddhist practice and Taoist tradition. A very important element is the symbolic cleansing away of mistakes or misdeeds of the past year, together with the accumulation of positive merit to carry into the coming year.

Throughout China, at this most auspicious time of year, people are on the move to rejoin their families. Houses are thoroughly cleaned and devotions are made to Buddhas and bodhisattvas in home shrines and in temples. All through the New Year period, fresh flowers, food, incense, candles and money are offered during temple visits.

Vegetarianism
One distinctive influence of Buddhism on Chinese New Year celebrations is the consumption of vegetarian food. It is believed that having an animal killed for food at this time would carry negative karma into the coming year.

There are also many symbolic rituals associated with the New Year for optimizing the good fortune that this period brings. For example, sharp knives are safely put away lest they cut through the potential luck that is now prevalent. Also, small orange trees, which produce miniature oranges, are purchased because an abundance of fruit represents wealth and prosperity ahead.

Japanese New Year
The final day of the old year in Japan is called omisoka. This is a time for family and friends to reunite in one of the biggest festivals of the Japanese calendar. In the days leading up to omisoka, the past is physically and symbolically

Accompanied by the explosions of fireworks to frighten away unluckly spirits, a 'lion' dances its way through the streets to bestow the good fortune of New Year on shops and restaurants in Guangxi, China.

swept away during a period of thorough house-cleaning known as *susu-hari*, or 'soot-sweeping'.

By New Year's Eve, preparations are complete as families and relatives share buckwheat noodles called *toshikoshi*, or 'year's crossing', in the hope that their lives and fortunes will be as long as these noodles. At the approach of midnight, Buddhist temple bells ring out 108 times. Each peal of the bell must die down before it can be rung again and it can take nearly an hour to complete the tolls. Human beings are believed to have 108 passions that must be overcome to achieve enlightenment. Each toll of the bell is meant to drive away one of these passions.

The New Year begins the three-day festival of O Shogatsu. Before the sun has risen, Buddhists and Shintos flock to temples to pray for a prosperous and healthy year ahead. This practice is rooted in the Shinto tradition of being present at the Shinto shrine before dawn in order to honour guardian spirits as dawn breaks. The *hatsu-mairi*, or first visit, should be made as early as possible to invoke New Year blessings, although any time up to 7 January is permitted.

Celebrations of the Buddha's lifetime

The Buddha's birth, enlightenment and passing into nirvana at death are commemorated on the 8th day of, respectively, the fourth, twelfth and second lunar months. In Japan these dates fall on 8 April, 8 December and 15 February. All three occasions are times to honour the Buddha, but the Buddha's birth in particular is a day for great celebration.

Special bowls of food are prepared for the Buddha as well as incense, candles and flower offerings. Flowers have a particular association with the birth of the Buddha. It is said that he was born in a flower grove at Lumbini and flowers sprang up as he walked his first seven steps in the four cardinal directions. According to the stories, the baby was then bathed with water sent down by the gods, so statues of the Buddha as a child are bathed in scented water or tea. Throughout the day and night, people visit the temple to offer alms, and to meditate or listen to the chanting and teaching of the monks.

In China it is an occasion for showing compassion and accumulating merit by freeing captive animals, especially birds. The streets around temples are often lined with stalls selling caged birds waiting to be freed. In Korea, the temples and courtyards are illuminated with paper lanterns while devotions to the Buddha continue into the night.

JAPANESE FLOWER FESTIVAL

In Japan the Buddha's birth is called Hana Matsuri, or 'Flower Festival'. It derives from a pre-Buddhist festival in which wild mountain flowers were gathered to summon sprits to protect the rice fields.

The Buddha's birth is recreated by setting up a *hanamido*, or flower hall, in the temple grounds. Adorned with flowers, this shrine represents the flower grove in Lumbini where the Buddha was born. A statue of the Buddha as a child is placed in a bowl of water in the middle of the flower hall and visitors pour *amacha*, sweet hydrangea tea, over the Buddha. The hydrangea tea symbolizes the pure water poured by dragons onto the Buddha at birth. Prepared from dried and boiled hydrangea leaves, the tea is distributed at the temple and taken home to share with the family, since it is believed that it has protective powers. In the past, spells written in amacha ink were hung upside-down outside the gate to ward off snakes or dangerous animals.

In celebration of the Buddha's birth, sweet hydrangea tea is poured over a statue of the Buddha that has been placed in a flower hall, or hanamido, in the courtyard of a Japanese temple.

Kuan Yin, Ullambana and O-Bon

DIVINATION AND KUAN YIN'S GUIDANCE
At festival times in China and Japan, and on occasions when important decisions have to be made, Kuan Yin's help is often sought through divination. A number is chosen at random linked to a poem or reading that offers guidance. Traditionally, sticks of wood are shaken in a cylindrical container that is open at one end. The first stick to fall out will have the divination number written on it. The individual then hands this number in at the divination stall and receives a reading in return. In some Chinese temples, a myna bird is released and the reading that it lands on is the chosen reading. In Japan, nowadays, the divination is performed by a machine. The important factor, whatever the divination process, is random selection.

Three festivals celebrate Kuan Yin, the Heavenly Bodhisattva of Compassion. They fall on the 19th day of the second, sixth and ninth months. The name Kuan Yin means the 'Regarder of Cries', and is based on the Sanskrit name Avolokitesvara, meaning 'The Lord who Looks Down'.

Kuan Yin is depicted in male or female form and appears in many guises, as a monk or a nun, a sage or a teacher of another faith. Kuan Yin can mysteriously appear as a vision to help at a particluar time and then disappears once she has eased the suffering of those who have called on her. Kuan Yin (called Kwannon in Japan) is a figure of deep personal devotion and one of the most popular of the Heavenly bodhisattvas, who are destined to become Buddhas but delay their final release from samsara until all beings are saved. (In Northern Buddhism the line of Dalai Lamas of Tibet are considered manifestations of Avolokitesvara.)

A woman prepares to throw divination sticks before a shrine to Kuan Yin at the 'Temple of 10,000 Buddhas' in Hong Kong. As the wooden container is gently shaken, the sticks edge forward and a reading is taken from the first stick to fall. The readings that are given as a result of the divination are intended to offer guidance to those who seek her help.

Kuan Yin is regarded as the protector of those who are caught in storms since she can control the elements. She also helps women who want to bear children, and students who are to sit examinations. Prayers are offered to Kuan Yin by the sick and she is associated with sudden appearances and miraculous cures. At festival times, extra-special devotions are offered to her including food, incense, flowers and donations for the printing of devotional books.

Ancestors and spirits

The Ullambana festival, which falls on the 15th day of the seventh month, is dedicated to honouring ancestors and easing the suffering of unsettled spirits. The literal meaning of Ullambana is 'to hang upside down', and implies terrible suffering.

During the festival, families visit cemeteries to clean graves, lay flowers and make offerings of food and incense. Sometimes they may share a meal at the graveside to bring together symbolically the worlds of the living and the dead. In China, this festival focuses on the restless spirits of the dead that were not given proper funeral rites and is commonly known as Chung Yuan – 'The Hungry Ghosts Festival'. It is believed that the gates of Hell are opened on the first day of the seventh month to release the troubled spirits, who can cause accidents and bring misfortune. Buddhist and Taoist monks perform chanting ceremonies in temples and travel to areas that may be associated with an accident or natural disaster where the suffering spirits are likely to roam.

Respect for ancestors

In Japan, the Ullambana festival is known as O-Bon. It lasts for three days, from 13 to 15 August, and is widely celebrated by both Buddhists and Shintos. O-Bon reflects deep respect for ancestors and the belief that they can still have a powerful effect on the world of the living. *Ohaka mairi*, the ritual of visiting graves and lighting the family lanterns, is a central feature of O-Bon.

To ensure the well-being of the ancestors, dirt and dust are swept from the graves, flowers and incense are offered and candle-lit lanterns are hung at the graveside. Each lantern has a *kamon*, or family crest, that will enable the spirits of the dead to recognize their way home. Fireworks add to the festive atmosphere of the gatherings of family and friends and, as the evening draws on, the lanterns set the cemeteries aglow. When the noise and candles have finally burned out, the lanterns are taken down and brought home again.

Spirit shrines

Preparations are also made in the home to receive the ancestors back on the first day of O-Bon (or Hatsubon, as the festival is called if the family member has died in the previous year). Spirit shrines laden with fruit and vegetables are set up in front of the family Buddhist shrine, and a monk is invited in to recite sutras, thereby transferring merit to the dead. To help guide the spirits back, paths are cleared and a *mukae-bi*, or 'welcoming flame', is lit outside the house, or a bonfire may be lit to illuminate the area.

Many people follow a vegetarian diet during O-Bon or share the favourite food of their dead relatives. As the festival draws to a close, the *okuri-bi*, or 'farewell fire', is lit for the spirits and small lanterns are released to float down rivers or be carried out to sea.

TRADITIONAL DANCES

In the cool of the evening during O-Bon, a dance called the *bon-odori* is held in local parks or other open-air spaces or in the temples.

The venues are illuminated with coloured lanterns. Dressed in light cotton summer kimonos, the dancers move in a wide circle around the drummer or musicians at the centre. Each area has its own bon-odori, which incorporates movements representing local features such as rivers or mountains, or local occupations such as mining or farming. It is thought that these dances are pre-Buddhist and were incorporated into the O-Bon festival.

Women and children wearing yukata (summer kimono) dance in a circle during an evening bon odori held in a neighbourhood park.

The Northern Buddhist Calendar

Northern Buddhism is found in Tibet, Mongolia, parts of China and the Himalayan regions of Nepal, Bhutan and India. There are also small pockets of Northern Buddhists in the Russian republics of Tuva, Buryatia and Kalmykia.

The festival year follows the Tibetan lunar calendar of twelve lunar months, with New Year falling on the first day of the first lunar month. Before the Tibetan calendar was systemized in AD 1027, the flowering of the apricot tree marked the beginning of the New Year. Now, the celebrations are fixed to the new moon of the first month. In the Tibetan calendar, every month begins with a new moon and the full moon falls on the fifteenth day. Every three years, an intercalary month is added to realign with the solar calendar.

A father and son celebrate Tibetan New Year close to Bodnath Stupa in the Kathmandu Valley, Nepal.

Suppression and resurgence

Tibet has traditionally had a very rich and widely celebrated festival calendar. However, after the suppression of Tibetan Buddhism and the flight of its leader, the Dalai Lama, following the Chinese invasion of Tibet, such public celebrations were forbidden. In the early 1980s some religious freedom was restored and Tibetan festivals are again celebrated, albeit on a smaller scale. Today, Tibetan Buddhist tradition is being maintained and is being spread by the wide-ranging Tibetan community in exile in northern India, Nepal, Europe and North America.

The spread of Tibetan Buddhism

Buddhism was introduced into Tibet from India in the middle of the seventh century AD, and became established late in the eighth century under the influence of the Indian teacher Padmasambhava. Later, Tibetan Buddhism was brought to the Himalayan kingdoms of Bhutan, Ladakh and Sikkim, the last two of which are now part of India.

The Sherpa people of north-east Nepal are a Tibetan people. Since the Chinese invasion of Tibet, large numbers of Tibetan refugees have settled in Nepal and other Himalayan regions. In the sixteenth century, Tibetan Buddhism became established in Mongolia, having first been introduced much earlier into the Mongolian Empire. It was through the Mongols that Tibetan Buddhism reached the Asiatic nomadic peoples in areas that are now part of Russia.

THE TIBETAN CALENDAR

The following list includes the major festivals of the Tibetan year. Most of these are also celebrated in other Northern Buddhist regions, though possibly under a different name. Each country or region also has its own special festivals, for example, to mark the beginning of spring or the end of the harvest; to bestow healthy livestock; or to honour the founder of a sect or local deity associated with a monastery.

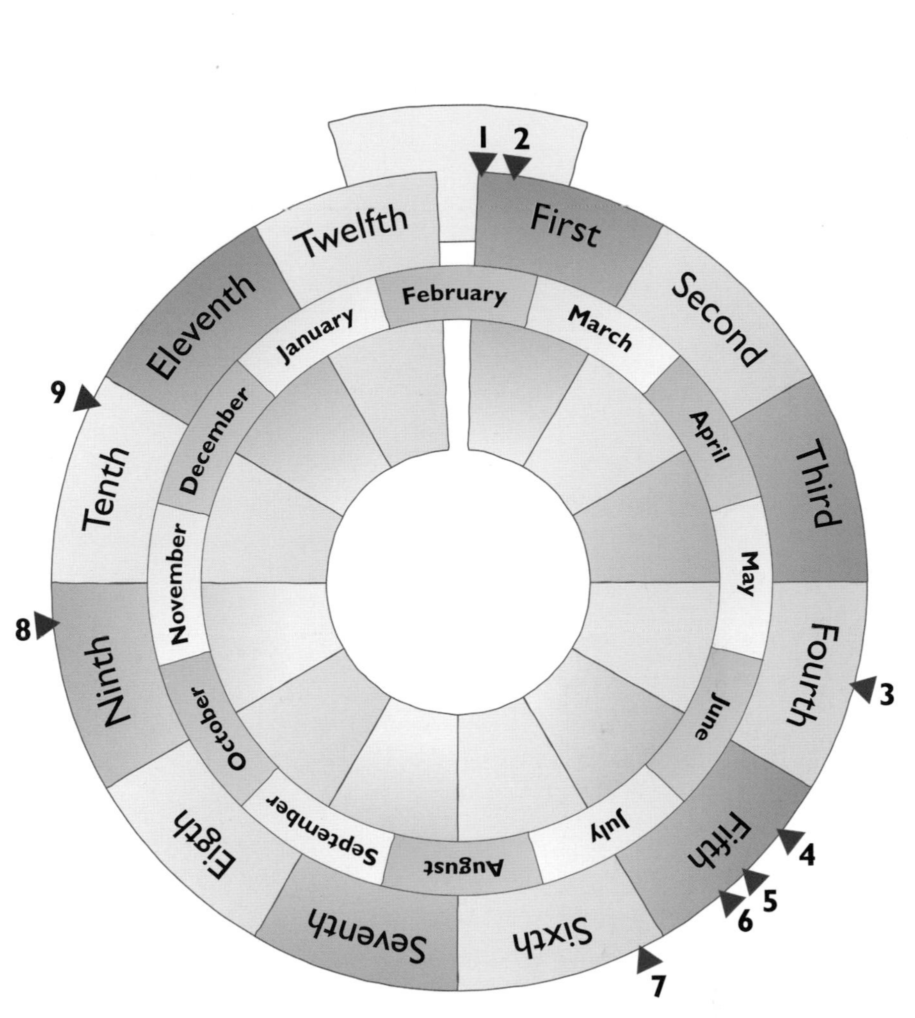

1 LOSAR (TIBETAN NEW YEAR FESTIVAL)
The Tibetan year begins in mid-to-late-February. Preparations for the New Year begin several weeks before, as houses are cleaned, and food and special entertainments are prepared. The festival period that begins at New Year lasts for several weeks into the first lunar month.

2 MONLAM CHEMNO
The 'Great Prayer Festival' of Monlam Chemno, which honours the teachings of the Buddha, begins on the 4th day of the first lunar month. The main ceremonies take place at the Jokhang Monastery in Lhasa where lamas (teachers), monks and pilgrims gather for lectures and debates. The 15th day of Monlam Chemno is the occasion of the 'Butter Sculpture Festival', in which huge sculptures made out of butter are displayed in the monasteries.

3 SAKADAWA
The Buddha's Birth, Enlightenment and Passing into Nirvana falls on the 15th day of the fourth lunar month. After two weeks of fasting and prayer, this is a day of celebration. People visit monasteries to see extensive displays of colourful Buddhist paintings and watch lamas performing traditional masked dancing.

4 GURU RINPOCHE'S BIRTHDAY
The festival, held on the 10th day of the fifth lunar month, commemorates the Indian teacher Padmasambhava who established Buddhist teachings in Tibet in the eighth century AD.

5 INCENSE OFFERING DAY
On the 15th day of the fifth Tibetan month, prayer flags are raised on hilltops and incense is burned on bonfires to commemorate the completion of the building of the Samye monastery. The spirits and ghosts that had prevented building work for many years were finally appeased when Guru Rinpoche performed the purification rite of burning juniper incense.

6 THE DALAI LAMA'S BIRTHDAY
Held on 6 July, it rivals Incense Offering Day in its popularity. Incense is burned on hilltop bonfires and in temples and monasteries, and prayers are offered for the long life of the Dalai Lama.

7 CHOKOR DUCHEN
Commemorates the Buddha's first sermon after his enlightenment, on the 4th day of the sixth lunar month. Families listen to and meditate on the Buddha's teachings at home or in temples.

8 LHABAB DUCHEN
A day and night of strict fasting and prayer on the 22nd day of the ninth month marks the descent of the Buddha from Heaven after passing the teachings on to his mother.

9 NGACHO CHENMO
The 25th day of the tenth lunar month is a festival of lights, commemorating Je Tsongkhapa, founder of the Gelug school of Tibetan Buddhism.

British monks belonging to the New Kadampa tradition of Tibetan Buddhism offer devotions before a shrine to the Buddha in Yorkshire, UK.

Gutor, Losar and Monlam Chemno

The Dalai Lama
In 1950 Chinese communist forces invaded Tibet. Nine years later, following an uprising against Chinese rule, the Dalai Lama, who is the spiritual and temporal head of Tibetan Buddhism, was forced to flee Tibet. He was offered exile in Dharamsala in northern India. In the years that followed, thousands more monks and other Tibetans have sought exile in Dharamsala. This has become an administrative centre for the Dalai Lama and a leading centre for the study and practice of Tibetan Buddhism.

An example of the way that Tibetan Buddhism is being influenced by its increasingly global spread is the celebration of the Dalai Lama's birthday on 6 July. Unlike the other festivals of Northern Buddhism, this event is fixed to the Western calendar and is celebrated in Tibet and widely beyond.

Losar, the Tibetan New Year, is the most spectacular festival of the Tibetan calendar. The celebrations last for the whole of Choturdawa, the first month. The period of preparation for the New Year is called Gutor. Losar, the New Year festival, is followed by Monlam Chemno (Great Prayer Festival), culminating in the Butter Sculpture Festival.

Preparations for the New Year festival commence at the beginning of the twelfth month. People begin to gather festival food and they ensure that costumes and entertainments are ready for the Losar festivities. Barley seedlings are grown at home in small pots and then placed in front of shrines to the Buddha as an offering for a successful harvest. In the middle of the month, households prepare doughnuts fried in butter, which are modelled into a wide variety of shapes including ears of corn and flowers.

Before the New Year

The festival of Gutor takes place in the final three days leading up to the New Year, as the negative aspects of the past are symbolically cleared away. On the 29th day, the houses are thoroughly cleaned and all dirt is swept away. New rugs are then laid on the floor or paintings are hung up. Eight auspicious symbols are painted with flour on the central wall of the kitchen and a swastika – an ancient

Young performers in a Tibetan opera that is being staged alongside puppet shows and traditional dances to entertain pilgrims gathered for Losar festivities.

Tibetan monks lead a procession around the Bodnath stupa to celebrate Losar. Bodnath has become an important centre of religious practice for the many Tibetans seeking refuge in Nepal.

symbol of early Buddhism that is believed to bring good fortune – is painted with lime on the front door.

In the evening, flour dumplings called *gutu* are shared among the family and costumed monks visit the home. As the monks chant and perform special rituals, members of the family light firecrackers or torches and go through the house shouting loudly to frighten away any unlucky spirits.

On the 30th day, elaborate piles of grains, which the monks have arranged inside their monasteries as offerings, are brought into public spaces and are burned to dispel negative forces of the past year and purify the coming year. That evening, food offerings including wheat dough, fruit and butter are laid before Buddha statues.

New Year's Day

On New Year's Day, everyone rises early to offer devotion to the Buddha and to share in the first ritual meal of the New Year. Families do go out to visit teachers or high lamas at monasteries and temples, but otherwise they remain at home for the first day of Losar. On the second day, they begin their visits to relatives and friends. In every community, there is a great celebration with fireworks, masked dances, performances of Tibetan opera and wrestling, horseracing or archery displays.

The Great Prayer Festival

Monlam Chemno, the Great Prayer Festival, honours the teachings of Sakyamuni Buddha. It takes place at Jokhang Monastery in Lhasa from the 4th day of the first lunar month. Thousands of monks, lamas and pilgrims come to participate or listen to the debates, lectures and prayers. Visiting pilgrims offer alms, including butter and lamps, to the monastery. The joyous spirit that began with Losar continues through Monlam Chemno with puppet shows, dances or Tibetan opera based on Buddhist stories.

BARLEY, BUTTER AND GINSENG

As New Year approaches, every household or community prepares a *droso chemar* – a container filled with a mixture of barley grains, roasted barley flour and wild ginseng.

This is adorned with upright ears of barley or multicoloured strips of butter. Sometimes a coloured butter scultpure of a sheep's head is added.

Droso chemar represents the wish for a good harvest, prosperity and healthy livestock, and the contents are eaten early on New Year's morning. The most senior member of the group offers the container to everyone present, who takes some grains, then tosses a few into the air as an offering to Heaven and eats the remainder.

The celebrations continue with a variety of grain and butter dishes washed down with barley beer and hot pear soup.

The period of Monlam Chemno culminates in the Butter Sculpture Festival, which falls on the 15th day of the first lunar month. Day and night, pilgrims view the huge ornate butter sculptures, surrounded by butter lamps, that are built in and around the monasteries.

The teaching and prayer associated with Monlam Chemno continues in Jokhang Monastery until the 25th day of the first lunar month, when the monastery performs a ceremony to greet Maitreya, the future Buddha.

TIBETAN NEW YEAR DOUGHNUTS

Mix together the flour, cheese, honey and salt. If the mixture is too sticky, add more flour to create a doughy consistency. Roll the mixture into small flour-coated balls and fry slowly until golden brown.

INGREDIENTS

½ cup of barley flour (if barley flour is unavailable, wheat flour can be substituted)
1 cup grated cheese
4 tablespoons honey
pinch of salt
butter for frying

Sakadawa, Incense-Burning Day, and the two Duchen

THE 'PRECIOUS TEACHER'
Guru Rinpoche, meaning 'Precious Teacher', is the name given to Padmasambhava, the Indian teacher who established Tibetan Buddhism. His birthday, on the 10th day of the fifth lunar month, is celebrated by all Tibetans. The event is characterized by temple and monastery visits to make offerings of food and candles, meditate and listen to the monks chanting. It is also a time of celebration marked by feasts, dancing and storytelling.

The day has special significance for followers of the Nying-ma tradition, who offer elaborate prayers for Guru Rinpoche that last almost the whole day. The Nying-ma, one of the four main schools of Tibetan Buddhism, traces its roots back to Guru Rinpoche.

The Sakadawa festival, on the 15th day of the fourth month, commemorates the Buddha's birth, his enlightenment and his passing into nirvana. Because of the sanctity of that particular day, the entire fourth month is considered auspicious and carries the name Sakadawa.

The 1st to the 15th days of Sakadawa are a time of fasting and prayer for all Tibetans. Ordinary activities are reduced to make more time for visiting temples and monasteries, making offerings, and sponsoring meals at monasteries or inviting groups of monks or nuns – sometimes as many as twenty or thirty – into the home to be fed. During such visits, the monks may recite the entire teachings of the Buddha, translated into Tibetan as the 108 volumes of the *bKa"gyur*. All the monks present take part in the recitation, so if there are many of them it may be finished in a day. If there are few, it can take up to eight or nine days to complete.

Fasting and prayer

During these fifteen days people abstain from eating certain foods, particularly meat, and some observe a kind of fasting called Nyumgne. This involves alternate days of compete fasting on the one day and eating only one meal on the next. Sakadawa is also a popular time for retreats. Groups of ten or so people may gather together, invite two monks or nuns to join them and for ten days they will all fast and pray together.

On the fifteenth day, the day of Sakadawa, monasteries and temples are full as people make offerings of candles and food listen to the chanting, watch the monks perform traditional masked dances and view the displays of Buddhist paintings. The fast is broken, and the day is celebrated with a vegetarian feast.

Incense-Burning Day

One of the liveliest and most popular festivals of the year, the Incense Offering Day to All the Deities in the World, falls on the 15th day of the fifth month. It commemorates the successful completion of the Samye Monastery in Lhasa after Guru Rinpoche, the great teacher of Tibetan Buddhism, had subdued the spirits and ghosts hindering its construction.

Bonfires are lit on hilltops surrounding the valleys, and lumps of pure incense are burned as offerings to all the deities and spirits. Throughout the morning, scented smoke billows up above the valleys. The area around the fires is adorned with prayer flags of blue, white, red, green and yellow, symbolizing sky, cloud, fire, water and earth. In the afternoon, people return to the valleys and gather in parks for open-air celebrations that include picnics, singing, dancing and storytelling.

Teachings and contemplation

On the 4th day of the sixth lunar month, Chokor Duchen celebrates the Buddha's first sermon after his enlightenment. The day is set aside for remembering the teachings of the Buddha. The name Chokor means 'turning the Dharma Wheel', signifying that this day is for perpetuating the traditional teachings of the Buddha as handed down through many generations.

Consequently, the principal activity on this day is to congregate together and hear the teachings expounded by learned monks. The monasteries organize large gatherings, where lectures given throughout the day are accompanied by fasting. Similar but smaller gatherings take place in people's homes. The day is not so much for festivities as for serious contemplation of the Dharma – the truth of the Buddha's teachings.

A solemn occasion

The festival of Lhabab Duchen remembers the Buddha's descent to earth from Heaven after passing on the teachings to his mother. It falls on the 22nd day of the ninth lunar month, and the main observance is rigorous fasting which begins on the day before, when people rise at 4.30 in the morning and fast until noon.

After a midday meal, they fast totally for 36 hours, until dawn the following day. This kind of fasting is quite common among Tibetans and can include even drinking water, although the sick and the weak are not required to follow the fast so strictly. During the fast period, processions and prayer recitals are held, filling the time with religious observance. Lhabab Duchen can be a demanding and intensive time, and there is no feasting associated with the day.

MONGOLIAN OVOO

Ovoo are shrines found throughout the Mongolian landscape, and are often used as the only recognizable points for navigation across the open steppes.

They are made of stones piled on top of each other and marked with Buddhist prayer flags, scraps of paper bearing inscribed petitions, crutches or splints to mark a healed limb, photographs of deceased relatives or other offerings left by passers-by.

The ovoo reflect Buddhist and shamanistic traditions. They designate a place where a Buddhist sage may have taught or where a birth or significant historical event may have occurred, or a point on the landscape where a powerful spirit is believed to reside. Ovoo festivals vary according to each site and its history. Many people gather at an ovoo to celebrate the end of winter and to pray for rains, successful hunting or healthy livestock. After sutras have been recited by Buddhist monks, and offerings made at the ovoo, the community celebrates with feasting and demonstrations of horse-riding and archery skills.

Monks recite sutras next to an ovoo that has been erected to mark the boundaries of a sacred site in Arhangai, Mongolia.

SIKH FESTIVALS

The Sikh faith began in the fifteenth century AD in the Punjab region, which now straddles the border between India and Pakistan. Guru Nanak, born into a Hindu family in a society divided between Hinduism and Islam, reacted against what he saw as the formalism of both faiths. He taught personal devotion to a formless and unknowable God – Waheguru, or 'wonderful teacher'. Travelling around India, he attracted many disciples (Sikh means 'disciple' in Punjabi) who developed their own religious practice, and constituted distinctive communities, laying great stress on equality and service to others.

The Sikh faith teaches the importance of being fit and active in defence of the weak or the oppressed. Here, at the celebration of Guru Nanak's birthday, Khalsa members parade through the streets with Sikh flags.

Following the Gurus

Guru Nanak, the first Sikh Guru, was succeeded by nine other human Gurus until, in 1708, the collection of Sikh writings was instituted as the Guru for all time to come. Sikhs revere their scripture – the Guru Granth Sahib – as they would a living teacher.

Sikhs worldwide and celebration

There are 15 million Sikhs worldwide. Most of them live in India, mainly in the Punjab. But Sikhs have migrated to many parts of the world, and there are sizeable communities in the UK, the United States and Canada, and smaller ones in East Africa, Europe, Malaysia, Indonesia, Australia and New Zealand. There are also small communities of converts, especially in the United States.

Sikh festivals are known as *gurpurb* – 'Guru's remembrance day'. They are all celebrated in similar ways, but there are variations in the readings and hymns. Two essential features of any Sikh festival are the reading of the scriptures and the provision of food. In the 48 hours leading up to a festival, the Guru Granth Sahib is read aloud from beginning to end, using a relay of readers. At the end of the service, a small portion of Karah Parshad, a sweet food, is given to all the worshippers, and throughout the festival free meals are served to all comers, religious or not. In India, some *gurdwaras* (temples) may need to provide meals for thousands of visitors at festival time.

Pilgrms crossing the lake at Amritsar to visit the Golden Temple, the Harimandir, where the Guru Granth Sahib is kept.

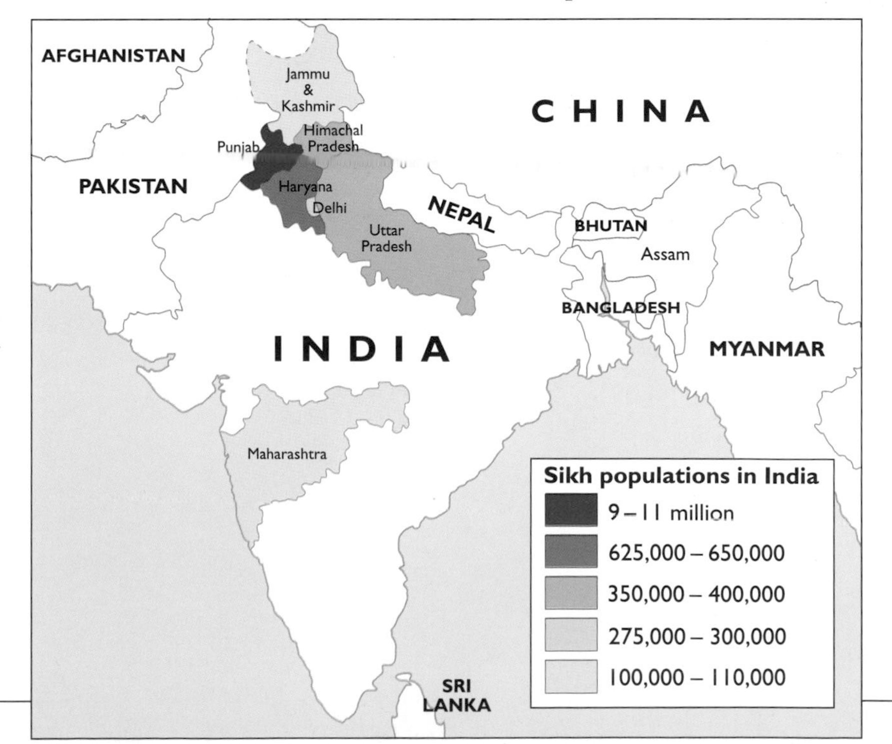

Sikh populations were once more widely spread within India, but the disturbances at independence and partition in 1947, and tensions with the Indian government more recently, have given rise to increasing migration to the Punjab.

Teaching and Worship

Guru Nanak, who first taught the Sikh faith, was born in 1469 at Tawalpindi, in the Punjab area of what is now Pakistan. At his birth, it was predicted that he would praise God and would teach many others to praise God.

Numerous stories are told of Nanak's abilities as a child. As a young man working for a local Muslim governor, he impressed all who knew him with his wisdom and ability. One day, Nanak's clothes were found on the river bank where he had been meditating, and it was feared that he had been drowned. After three days, Nanak returned, but did not speak for a day. His first words were, 'There is neither Hindu nor Muslim, so whose path shall I follow? I shall follow God's path. God is neither Hindu nor Muslim and the path I follow is God's.'

Nanak left his job with the governor and began a life of travelling and teaching. He became known as 'Guru Nanak', and taught the indefinable mystery of God and the irrelevance of external rituals. He stood out against the Hindu caste system of the time, insisting that all his followers were equal, and all should share whatever work had to be done. They became known as Sikhs (disciples) and established communities in many parts of India.

As they arrive at the gurdwara for the festival celebrations, Sikhs bring some food or money as a contribution to the langar, the communal meal being prepared. They may spend some time working in the kitchen or serving the meal, as well as in prayer.

The Gurus

Rather than choosing one of his sons as his successor, Guru Nanak underlined the principles of equality that he had been teaching by choosing as the next leader a man called Lehna who had been particularly devoted to him. Guru Nanak renamed him Angad, 'part of me'.

In all, there were nine successors to Guru Nanak, each one nominated by his predecessor. Guru Gobind Singh, the last of the nine, died in 1708. He declared that the collection of hymns and poems written by several of the Gurus and by other devout people should, from that time on, be the Guru for the Sikhs. This book is now known as the Guru Granth Sahib, and Sikhs look to it for guidance and inspiration in their lives, just as earlier Sikhs looked to their human Gurus. The dates of birth, death, and guruship of these Gurus are known as *gurpurbs* and celebrated as minor or major festivals.

The gurdwara

A Sikh temple is known as a gurdwara – 'door of the Guru'. It functions as both community centre and place of worship, but its central role is as the home of the Guru Granth Sahib, the scripture treated as a living Guru. Where possible, and especially in India, the gurdwara is open all day for prayer at any time. There are also regular services, often twice a day in India, or in other countries on a day that is convenient; in Europe and North America this is often a Sunday.

The congregation sits cross-legged on the floor. There is no priesthood in Sikhism. Anyone may preach a sermon

When the Guru Granth Sahib is open, at least one Sikh always sits by it, as an attendant sits by a living Guru.

and read the scripture, although a *granthi* (reader) may be employed to help the congregation.

Following the example of Guru Nanak, hymn singing is a very important part of Sikh worship. The hymns in the Guru Granth Sahib each have their traditional tune, which may be sung by a group of musicians or by the whole congregation. Singing is regarded as calming the mind and feeding the soul.

BEING A SIKH

All Sikh men wear five signs of their faith. Each of these begins with the letter 'K' in Punjabi, so they are known as 'the five K's'. They signify that the wearer is a full member of the Khalsa, the brotherhood founded at the festival of Baisakhi. The five K's are:

KESH: uncut hair. Devout Sikhs never cut their hair or their beard.

KANGA: a comb to keep the hair in place.

KARA: a steel bangle, a complete circle symbolizing one God and one truth without beginning or end. The steel symbolizes strength.

KIRPAN: a small sword or dagger, reminding the Sikh of the need to fight against oppression in any form.

KACCHERA: short trousers or breeches, dating from a time when men usually wore robes. The breeches signify readiness to ride into battle.

Nearly all Sikhs also wear a turban. This is not one of the five K's, but is worn to keep the hair tidy, and to resemble Guru Gobind Singh as closely as possible. It is a visible sign of commitment to the Sikh faith.

Sikhs are encouraged to refrain from all drugs (except medicine), including tobacco and alcohol, and many do not eat meat.

The concept of *sewa* (service) is central to Sikhism. Many Sikhs are involved in service of various sorts to all members of the community in which they live. Humble or unpleasant work undertaken for others is one of the highest ideals.

COMMITMENT TO THE FAITH

The Baisakhi gathering of 1699 laid the foundations of Sikhism as it exists today, and many Sikh rituals and beliefs, while they are practised and remembered throughout the year, have a special importance at Baisakhi.

NISHAN SAHIB
The Sikh flag, Nishan Sahib, stands outside each gurdwara and in many Sikh homes. At Baisakhi the pole is washed and the flag renewed with songs, hymns and rejoicing.

KARAH PARSHAD
A mixture of flour, semolina, sugar and butter is cooked and stirred with a khanda while special prayers are said. At the end of every Sikh ceremony a small portion is distributed to every worshipper, symbolizing the sweetness of God.

GURU GOBIND SINGH
Guru Gobind Singh, the last human Guru and founder of the Khalsa, told the Sikhs, 'Be like me'. His resistance to persecution and injustice is an inspiration to Sikhs.

AMRIT
Water and sugar is stirred with a Khanda, the traditional Sikh sword, to make amrit. At Baisakhi each person joining the Khalsa drinks some amrit and their eyes and hair are sprinkled with it.

VEGETARIAN FOOD
At every Sikh festival, food is provided free of charge to all comers, whether they are Sikhs or not. The food is always vegetarian so that all may eat it whatever their beliefs.

Times and Seasons

The original Sikh calendar, still used by some Sikhs, was based on a Hindu lunar calendar similar to that on page 87. Three major festivals, Baisakhi, Divali and Hola Mohalla (Holi) have the same dates and variants of the same names as Hindu festivals. However, many Sikhs felt it was unsuitable to use a Hindu calendar rather than one based on their own faith.

Nanakshahi, a reformed calendar, was introduced in 1999, the tercentenary of the founding of the Khalsa. This is based on a solar year, and converts directly and easily into western dates. The years of the Nanakshahi calendar are counted from the birth of Guru Nanak in 1469.

AKHAND PATH
All Sikh festivals are celebrated with a continuous reading of the Guru Granth Sahib by a team of readers, each one reading for two or three hours. The complete reading takes around 48 hours and finishes on the day of the festival, when everyone gathers for the last five pages.

Hola Mohalla is specially celebrated at Anandpur in India, with street processions and displays of skill.

THE SIKH CALENDAR

The calendar shown is the Nanakshahi calendar. The dates of festivals based on the lunar calendar may differ by as much as 15 days.

1 HOLA MOHALLA (CHET 1)
Celebration, especially in Anandpur, dated according to the lunar calendar, featuring games and martial arts competitions.

2 DEATH OF GURU HARGOBIND (CHET 6)

3 BAISAKHI (VAISAKH 1)
Commemoration of the founding of the Khalsa. Initiation into the Khalsa takes place at this time.

4 DEATH OF GURU ANGAD ; DEATH OF GURU HAR KRISHAN (VAISAKH 3)

5 BIRTH OF GURU ANGAD ; BIRTH OF GURU TEGH BAHADUR (VAISAKH 5)

6 BIRTH OF GURU ARJAN (VAISAKH 19)

7 BIRTH OF GURU AMAR DAS (JETH 9)

8 MARTYRDOM OF GURU ARJAN (HARH 2)
Guru Arjan was the first Sikh martyr, who was tortured to death by fire. Refreshing drinks are offered to passers-by to commemorate the event.

9 BIRTH OF GURU HARGOBIND (HARH 21)

10 BIRTH OF GURU HAR KRISHAN (SAWAN 8)

11 INSTALLATION OF THE GURU GRANTH SAHIB IN THE GOLDEN TEMPLE (BHADON 17)
Guru Arjan, having ordered the collection and collation of hymns, installed the work in the Golden Temple at Amritsar.

12 DEATHS OF GURU AMAR AND GURU RAM DAS (ASU 2)

13 DEATH OF GURU NANAK (ASU 8)

14 BIRTH OF GURU RAM DAS (ASU 25)

15 DIVALI (ENDS ON KATIK 2)
Four-day festival, still calculated on a lunar calendar. A celebration of the release from prison of the sixth guru, Guru Hargobind, and the 52 fellow-prisoners who held on to his tasselled cloak.

16 INSTALLATION OF THE GURU GRANTH SAHIB AS ETERNAL GURU; DEATH OF GURU HAR RAI (KATIK 6)

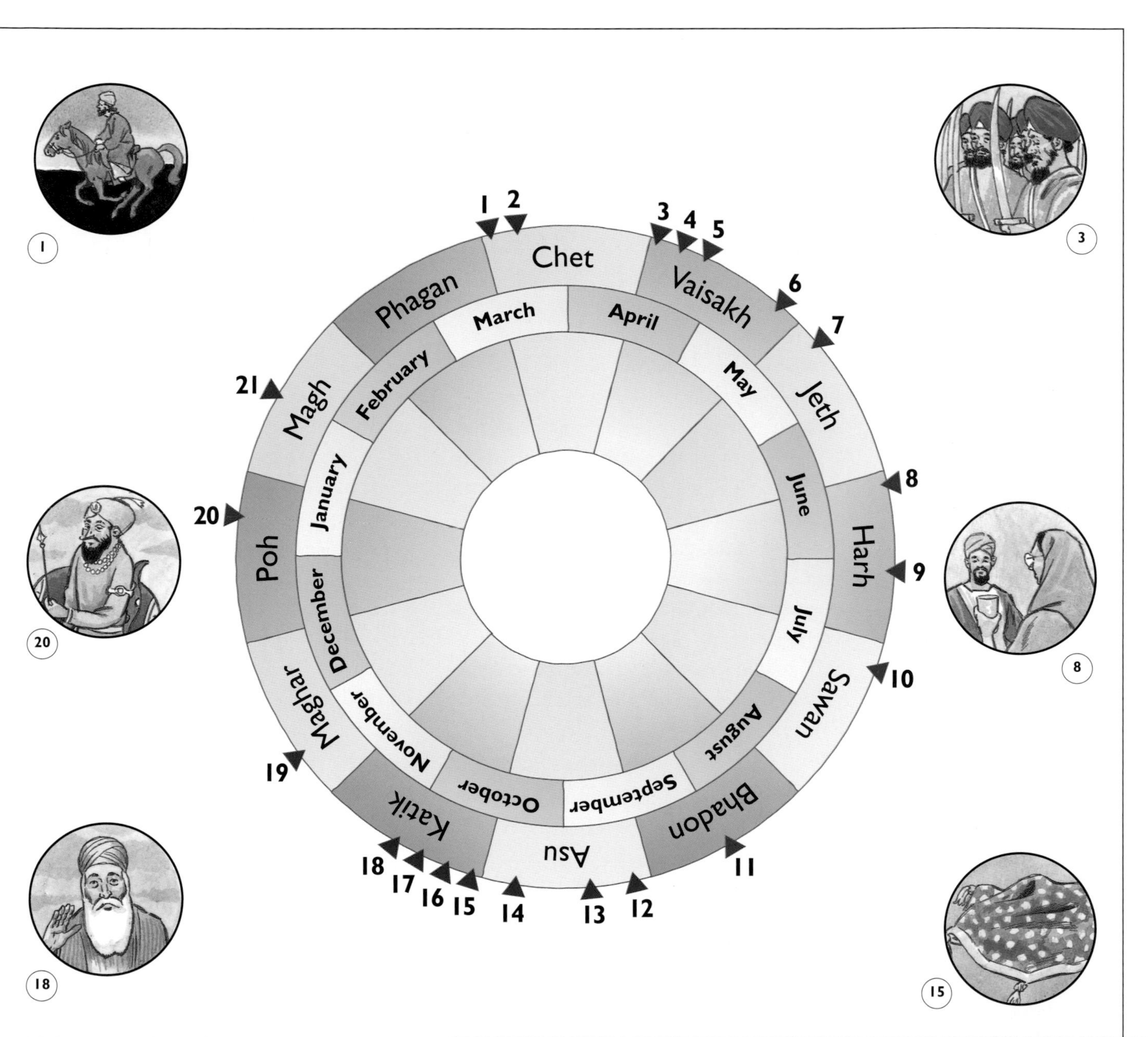

17 Death of Guru Gobind Singh (Katik 7)

18 Birth of Guru Nanak (full moon of Katik)
This date, calculated according to the lunar calendar, has not been fixed in the new calendar. Although historical research suggests that Guru Nanak was in fact born on Vaisakh 1, the traditional date has not been changed.

19 Martyrdom of Guru Tegh Bahadur (Maghar 11)

20 Birth of Guru Gobind Singh (Poh 23)
The last human Guru, who initiated the Khalsa and instituted the Guru Granth Sahib as the Guru for the Sikhs for all time to come.

21 Birth of Guru Har Rai (Magh 19)

Baisakhi

In 1699, at Anandpur, the Sikh leader, Guru Gobind Rai, asked for a volunteer who was willing to give up even his life to defend the Sikh faith, which was under threat. The Guru took the brave man into his tent, and came out alone, his sword dripping with blood. Four more volunteers followed in turn, each prepared to lay down his life. Then Guru Gobind drew back the door of the tent and revealed the five men, dressed in saffron robes, turbans on their heads and swords in their hands.
These men were now called the Panj Pyare – the Five Beloved – because of their dedication. To show that Sikhs would no more be afraid to stand up for their faith, Guru Gobind declared that all Sikh men would take the name Singh, meaning 'lion', and all women the name Kaur, or 'princess'. The Guru is now known as Guru Gobind Singh, and the brotherhood of Sikhs, which began with the Five Beloved, is the Khalsa.

Hola Mohalla, Divali and Gurpurbs

The birth of Guru Nanak, the founder and first Guru of Sikhism, has traditionally been celebrated on the full moon day of the lunar month of Katik. This practice has continued under the new calendar, although many now think that it is not the true date of his birth. Stories of his birth and childhood indicate that this was no ordinary baby. It is said that he did not cry at all when he was born, but smiled with extraordinary sweetness. It was prophesied that he would praise God and teach others to do so, and from a very early age he showed a wisdom that astonished his teachers and his family.

Celebrations of Guru Nanak's birth often last three days, culminating in a major celebration on the full-moon day. Processions led by men representing the Five Beloved, and carrying the Guru Granth Sahib on a platform, go through the streets with musicians and singers. As at Divali, homes, shops and streets are lit with lamps, and the Golden Temple in Amritsar is lit with coloured lights. On the final day, gurdwaras open very early, and families may spend the whole day there, praying, singing, helping to prepare the food in the langar and eating together.

Khalsa Initiation

Any Sikh – man or woman – sufficiently committed may join the Khalsa. The ceremony is performed during the Baisakhi festival. Five Khalsa Sikhs, representing the Five Beloved, attend, wearing the five K's, and candidates are initiated in groups of five. Water with sugar is stirred with a Khanda, while the Guru Granth Sahib is read or sung. Then each candidate kneels and is sprinkled with *amrit* (sweet water), while declaring, 'The Khalsa belongs to God, and to God alone belongs the Victory.'

Martyrdom

Guru Arjan was the fifth Guru of Sikhism, and a great preacher and leader. He collated and composed the hymns of the Guru Granth Sahib, built the Golden Temple at Amritsar and attracted many new converts to the faith.

When Arjan became Guru in 1581, the emperor at the time, Akbar, was tolerant, even friendly, towards the Sikhs. But when he died, his son Jehangir became Emperor, and Guru Arjan offended him by giving food and shelter to his brother and rival. Arjan was summoned to present himself before Jehangir, and, knowing that he faced likely execution, appointed his son Hargobind as the next Guru.

Jehangir berated Arjan for helping his enemy, ordered him to change the words of the Guru Granth Sahib and to pay a huge fine. Arjan refused, so he was tortured to death with red-hot sand and boiling water. Throughout, he remained miraculously calm, saying only, 'The heated cauldron has become cold' and 'God is the strength of the strengthless.'

In memory of the manner of Guru Arjan's execution, Sikhs hold a procession and prayers, giving out drinks of fruit juice or *sharbat*, a sweetened milk drink, and inviting passers-by to be refreshed 'in the Guru's name'.

Religious freedom

After the death of his father, Guru Hargobind continued to build up the numerical and military strength of the Sikh community. Soon, he too was perceived as a threat by Emperor Jehangir, who imprisoned him, together with a

Guru Nanak's birthday is celebrated in Anandpur with a procession led by five Sikhs (the Panj Pyare) accompanying the Guru Granth Sahib.

number of Hindu rulers, in the fort of Gwalior. After widespread opposition, however, Jehangir was persuaded to order Guru Hargobind's release.

Guru Hargobind refused to leave the fort unless his fellow-prisoners were also set free. Jehangir's officials arrived at what they thought was a face-saving compromise. They said that he could be accompanied by as many of the Hindu rulers as could hold on to him as he passed through the narrow exit passage from the fort, thinking that this would mean that only one or two others could leave. But Guru Hargobind ordered a cloak to be made with a large number of long tassels, and left the fort with fifty-two of his fellow-prisoners holding on to his garments.

On his return to Amritsar, the people lighted lamps in welcome. Today, Divali commemorates that event and is celebrated with lamps and fireworks, as a festival of religious freedom. Sikhs all over the world light oil lamps in their homes, shops and offices, and the Golden Temple is lit with thousands of coloured lights.

This Sikh print shows scenes from the life of Guru Arjan. The top left picture shows him compiling the Guru Granth Sahib; the bottom left shows his death by torture.

HOLA MOHALLA

Hola Mohalla developed from the Hindu festival of Holi, which was celebrated by many Sikhs.

Guru Gobind Singh, the founder of the Khalsa, wanted to give the festival a more distinctively Sikh emphasis, so, in 1700, he held a great fair at Anandpur, in the Punjab, with sports, games and martial arts. He took the feminine word 'Holi' and transformed it into the masculine 'Hola Mohalla'.

The festival is still celebrated today. It lasts for three days in the year and brings thousands of people to Anandpur. Tribute is paid to Guru Gobind Singh's bravery, and hymns are sung. But the real highlight is the martial arts competitions, including archery, horse-riding and sword fighting featuring the Nihangs – Sikhs who live a military and dedicated lifestyle and wear distinctive tall turbans.

Many gurdwaras around the world hold celebrations and athletics competitions on a smaller scale, along with sermons delivered on the theme of protecting the weak and standing up for justice.

A display of swordsmanship celebrating Hola Mohalla in Anandpur.

TAOIST FESTIVALS

Taoism takes its name from the Chinese word for road or pathway. The Tao is the moral way to live in accordance with ancient traditions and values, but the Tao is also the origin of all things, described as the 'Origin of the One'. The Tao is the creative cosmic force that is manifest in the natural order of the universe.

By the second century AD, various traditions of indigenous Chinese folk religion had fused to form the 'religion of the Tao'. By the sixth or seventh century, the Tao had taken on three main forms: the Tao as the absolute source of all existence; the Tao as a teacher of the Way, personified by the sage Lao Tzu; and the Tao as the written word that appears in the classic text, the *Tao Te Ching*.

Modern times

Although Buddhism and Confucianism were widely practised in China, Taoism functioned as the main expression of religion at a local level until the Communist takeover in 1949. The Cultural Revolution (1966–76), a dramatic attack on all that was traditional in China, almost destroyed Taoism, but in recent years it has undergone a steady but impressive recovery.

Taoism at a popular level continues to combine a mixture of Taoist elements, such as divination, the quest for immortality, exorcism and worship of protective deities, with the belief in salvationary figures from the Buddhist tradition such as the bodhisattva Kuan Yin. Taoist rites are followed to mark birth, marriage or death, and Taoist rituals performed to calm the 'hungry ghosts' or restless spirits, or to rebalance the forces of heaven and earth and maintain harmony in the community and the world at large.

Taoist monks have also been returning to their traditional centres of study, such as the sacred mountains or the great Taoist colleges. Here the esoteric and meditational practices of Taoist tradition are taught, and the ancient scriptures studied. The sacred mountains of Taoism are the backbone of the faith, and the re-establishment of the thousands of temple sites upon them is a slow process but one that is vital to the recovery of Taoism.

The Tao-
The Origin of Life

Although the core of Taoist teaching is that all life comes from the Tao, many Taoists also believe in a vast pantheon of deities who exercise influence over every aspect of life.

Most Chinese communities, particularly rural ones, will have a temple to the local god, a shrine to the town god and domestic shrines to the earth god. In addition, there is likely to be an ancestor shrine in the home to venerate grandparents and parents. Alongside photographs of the ancestors, there may sometimes be a small statue of Kuan Yin, a figure from Buddhist tradition regarded as a goddess of Mercy, and a statue of a favourite Taoist deity such as Kuan Ti, the god of wealth, or Lu Tung Pin, the god of health.

During the upheavals of the Cultural Revolution in China more than nine-tenths of the statues and paintings in temples and shrines were destroyed and many of the deities associated with the old, imperial system were not replaced. As temples continue to be repaired and new shrines appear, it is deities associated with family, health and prosperity that are particularly honoured.

Yin and Yang

If the Tao is the origin of all life, yin and yang are the two cosmic forces that shape and balance life. They are in a continual struggle to overcome each other. But, since yang contains the seed of yin and yin contains the seed of yang, they will always be in a state of flux and it is this dynamic tension that produces life.

Yin is female, cool and fluid, the force seen in the moon and in rain, floods and cold. Yang is masculine, heavy and hot, the force that is seen in the sun and in fire, droughts and heat.

The best example of the rise and fall of yin and yang is in the change of seasons. Yin rises as the cool of winter approaches, reaching its peak in the winter cold. Then yin recedes as spring arrives, and yang begins its ascendancy, to peak in the burning heat of summer.

Yin and yang are not gods, nor are they considered divine powers. They are purely natural forces created out of the emptiness that existed at the beginning of time.

A page from the yearly Chinese almanac showing the Kitchen God and his wife, and listing the 'Joints and Breaths' of the year.

THE ENERGY OF LIFE
Ch'i is the life-giving breath or energy that animates all life. It is constantly moving and changing, gathering and dispersing in the cycle of the seasons, in the landscape and in every living being. It is the energy that courses through the earth and through our bodies. The sites where it circulates freely and smoothly produce positive energy. When ch'i is blocked or dispersed, negative energy is allowed to settle and decay. Taoism teaches that each person has within him- or herself all the ch'i that he or she will ever have. The quest for immortality, an ancient tradition of Taoism, is a way of preserving this ch'i. Ensuring the smooth flow of ch'i and balancing yin and yang are central to Chinese medicine and are at the core of all diagnoses and prescriptions.

Taoists lighting candles in the courtyard of a temple in Xian.

Times and Seasons

The Chinese festival year follows a lunar calendar of twelve moons, each moon lasting just over $29\frac{1}{2}$ days. To create months that end with full days, six 'small months' are allocated 29 days each, and six 'large months' 30 days each, making a total of 354 days. Occasionally the length of the year changes, so there may be seven 'small months', making 353 days in the year, or seven 'large months', making 355 days in the year. Overall, the Chinese lunar year is short of the solar year by between ten and twelve days, so an intercalary month is added to the lunar calendar about every three years.

The agricultural year

The solar calendar is traditionally used by farmers to guide them through the agricultural year. This is divided into twenty-four phases known as the 'Twenty Four Joints and Breaths' of the year, each phase lasting just over two weeks. The dates of the phases vary slightly each year. The first phase – Li Ch'un (Beginning of Spring) – starts around 5 February and the final phase –Ta Han (Great Cold) – starts around 21 January.

THE CHINESE ALMANAC

The T'ung Shu is the yearly Chinese almanac, listing astrological and astronomical data for every day of the year. Using its detailed tables, many Chinese people consult the alamanac to determine auspicious days to marry, open a business, begin a journey, move house or make personal decisions.

The first reference to a yearly calendar dates back more than 4,000 years, to the time when Emperor Yao commanded his astronomers to calculate a calendar that listed the timing of the seasons so that his people would know when to sow and when to reap. Soon the calendar began to include auspicious dates for dealing with matters of state and was used for calculating the astrological fortunes of the emperor. However, the earliest example of personal fortune-telling does not appear until the first century BC.

Taoist nuns take part in a procession alongside musicians, acrobats and local people to celebrate the opening of a new temple dedicated to a town god in Shaanxi province.

THE TAOIST CALENDAR AND FESTIVALS

Major festivals such as Chinese New Year or Ch'ing Ming are celebrated widely in China, but there are also hundreds of smaller festivals associated with local deities, heroes, historical events or sacred sites.

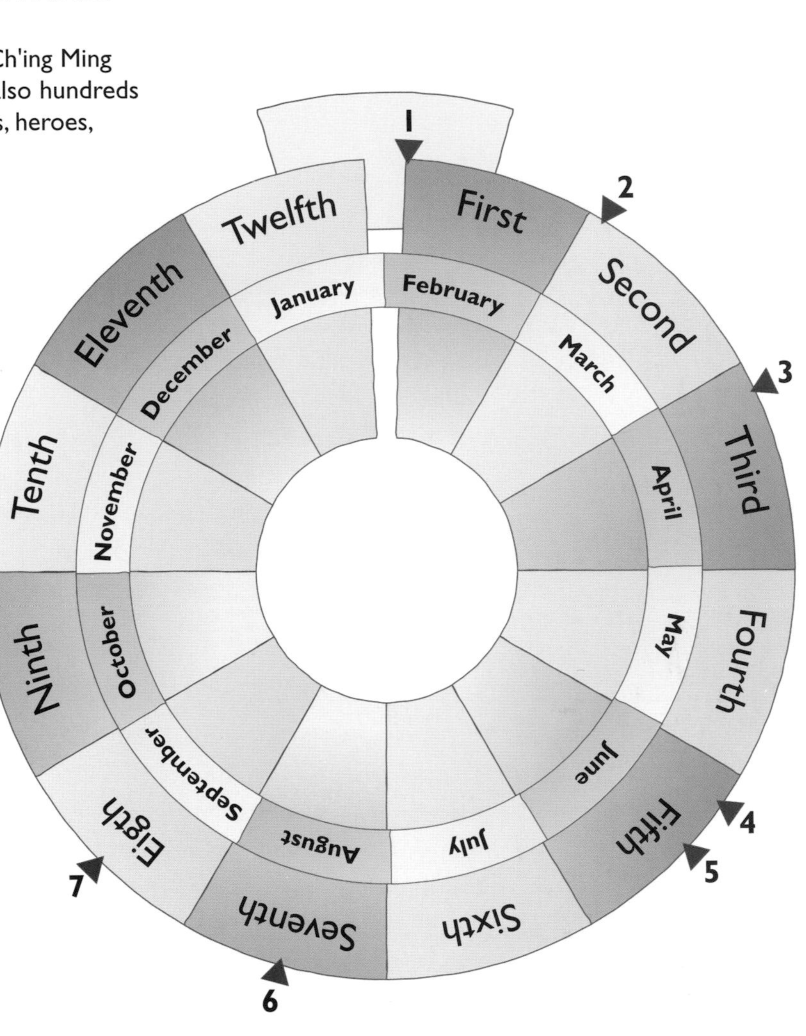

1 NEW YEAR (1ST DAY OF THE FIRST LUNAR MONTH)
At the most important festival on the Chinese calendar, misfortune or mistakes of the past are symbolically swept away and preparations made to welcome the good fortune that the New Year brings. Protective charms are hung in the house, firecrackers are let off to frighten away evil spirits, divinatory readings are made in the temples, elaborate festival food is shared and gifts are exchanged.

2 BIRTHDAY OF T'U TI KUNG, THE EARTH GOD (2ND DAY OF THE SECOND LUNAR MONTH)
Small shrines to the Earth God – the guardian spirit who protects every home, shop, village or field – are widespread in Chinese communities. His shrine is renewed with lucky red paper, candles, incense and food offerings.

3 CH'ING MING (4 OR 5 APRIL)
Family visits are made to graves to clean them and lay offerings of flowers, incense and food. Afterwards, the family usually sit down to share a meal at the graveside.

4 DRAGON BOAT FESTIVAL (5TH DAY OF THE FIFTH LUNAR MONTH)
Races are held between long, decorated canoe-shaped boats with dragon-headed prows. Popular in southern and central China, the festival commemorates the suicide of an honest court official of the third century BC.

5 BIRTHDAY OF KUAN TI (13TH DAY OF THE FIFTH LUNAR MONTH)
Special offerings are laid before the shrine to the god of war found in many homes. A figure of loyalty, courage and strength, he is also the patron of restaurants, merchants and business.

6 HUNGRY GHOSTS FESTIVAL (15TH DAY OF THE SEVENTH LUNAR MONTH)
The festival placates the restless spirits of the 'hungry ghosts' – those who died without proper funeral rites – in order to prevent them causing trouble among the living.

7 MID-AUTUMN FESTIVAL/ MOON FESTIVAL (15TH DAY OF THE EIGHTH LUNAR MONTH)
The beauty of the full autumn moon is celebrated with incense and lantern processions. Traditionally, it is also a time for weddings arrangements and engagement announcements.

HEAVENLY STEMS AND EARTHLY BRANCHES

Chinese time is traditionally calculated in cycles of 60 years, which is due to the interaction of astrological features known as Heavenly Stems and Earthly Branches.

There are ten Heavenly Stems and twelve Earthly Branches. Every year, a Stem pairs up with a Branch, starting with the first of each in the first year of the cycle, and so on repeatedly to make sixty different combinations over 60 years. The cycle then starts over again.

The Chinese name for each year is taken from these combinations. For example, year 2005 will be Yi Yu – Yi is the Heavenly Stem, and Yu the Earthly Branch.

New Year, Ch'ing Ming, the Dragon Boat Festival

New Year, the major festival of the Chinese year, is a period of renewal and family reunion. The final days of the old year are given over to intense preparation, as houses are cleaned in the belief that disappointments and mistakes are swept away along with the dirt and dust of the past. These days are also the time to settle debts, resolve arguments or return favours, to avoid carrying any misfortune into the coming year.

The Kitchen God

On the 23rd day of the twelfth month, paper images of the Kitchen God are taken down and ceremoniously burned to release his spirit. It is believed that the Kitchen God has been guarding the family, observing their strengths and weaknesses, and now it is time for him to report to the Jade Emperor in Heaven. Before burning the Kitchen God, incense is offered to him and his lips are smeared with honey, sugar or sweet wine so that his report on the family will be sweet. The Kitchen God is due to return to the family on New Year's Eve, when new images are hung on the walls and he begins his watch once again.

The celebration meal that the family share at home on the last night of the year is usually vegetarian and includes food that has a symbolic significance such as 'eight treasures pudding', a pastry made of sticky rice filled with nuts, raisins and dates. The 'treasures' are said to bestow happiness, health, wealth and longevity on the family.

Good fortune and symbolic gifts

As New Year's Day arrives, firecrackers are let off to frighten away evil spirits that may be wandering at this time of the year. Traditionally, no one should cook or work on these early days of the year, and knives are put away to avoid cutting into the good fortune that is prevalent. Everyone tries to avoid using unlucky words, such as 'sickness', 'loss' or 'death', since these are bad omens, and even words that have a similar pronunciation are avoided.

As part of the New Year's gift-giving, children receive packets of 'lucky money' in red envelopes with pictures of a peach tree or a pine tree (symbols of long life),

THE MID-AUTUMN FESTIVAL
The Mid-Autumn Festival, celebrating the beauty and luminosity of the mid-autumn moon, was traditionally associated with women because of the moon's strong yin qualities. A table placed outdoors was laid with round fruit such as apples, pomegranates, peaches, and offerings of 'moon' cakes, tea, wine and 'spirit money'.

Nowadays this tradition is less common although the festival is still widely celebrated with a family meal, often followed by a visit to a park at dusk when ornate lanterns and candles are lit and incense is burned to greet the full moon.

A dragon dances and weaves its way through the crowds gathered to celebrate New Year in Manchester, UK. To the clamour of fireworks, drums and cymbals, the powerful dragon traditionally frightens away evil spirits and bestows good fortune.

a carp (symbol of success) or with the Chinese characters for good luck and prosperity.

Ancestors and heroes

Ch'ing Ming is one of the twenty-four 'Joints and Breaths' that measure the solar year. The name means 'clear and bright', and the festival marks the annual cleaning and visiting of family graves when inscriptions are repainted, and fresh offerings of food, incense and candles are laid to honour the ancestors. It can be a festive occasion as the family sits down to share a picnic at the graveside, before leaving behind small paper offerings under a stone to show that the grave has been tended.

The Dragon Month

The fifth month of the Chinese year is traditionally associated with the dragon, and the 'double fifth' – the fifth day of the fifth month – is a particularly powerful day. Dragon Boat races are the feature of this festival – races between long, swift boats carved with the colourful head and tail of a dragon.

The event recalls the story of Ch'u Yuen, a heroic official who drowned himself to draw attention to the corrupt government. As the fish rose to eat his body, the local villagers took to their boats, throwing rice onto the water to lure them away. The rice that the fishermen threw is remembered in the most popular festival food, steamed rice dumplings – balls of glutinous rice containing peanuts, beans, cooked meats or preserved eggs, all wrapped up in bamboo leaves and tied with raffia.

The Hungry Ghosts Festival

It is said that the gates of the underworld are opened during the seventh month to allow the restless spirits of the dead to wander the earth.

They are the 'hungry ghosts', the disembodied spirits of those who were not given proper burial rights; who received none of the usual offerings of food or paper clothing, houses, cars or 'spirit' money that are traditionally burned at a funeral to provide the dead with the means to survive in the next world. Because the hungry ghosts were not shown this respect, they are resentful and dangerous. The Hungry Ghosts Festival is dedicated to them, to calm their anger and enable them to return peacefully to the underworld for another year.

At a Hungry Ghosts Festival in Hong Kong, a huge paper effigy of Tai Si Wong is present to oversee the proceedings and report back to the Jade Emperor. After the paper offerings to the dead are burnt, he is set alight, thereby releasing him for his journey to Heaven.

ZOROASTRIAN FESTIVALS

The Zoroastrian religion is named after the Prophet Zarathustra (known in the West as 'Zoroaster'). Zarathrustra lived in Persia (Iran) sometime between 1400 and 1200 BC, and is held to be the first to develop a 'prophetic' religion, based on the revelation of divine truths.

Originally, his teachings were memorized by priests and handed down orally in the Avestan language. Many centuries later, they were written down, using a specially invented alphabet. The scriptures, called 'the Avesta', contain seventeen hymns, or Gathas, said to have been composed by Zarathustra, plus a collection of later hymns, prayers and liturgies.

Zoroastrianism became the state religion of the Persian Empire in the sixth century BC. Its influence was curtailed when Persia was conquered by Alexander the Great, and later, in the seventh century AD by the Arabs, who were Muslims.

A Zoroastrian priest in a fire temple in Isfahan, Persia.

In the ninth century, oppression of the Zoroastrian community led to many followers taking refuge in India. Today there are fewer than half a million Zoroastrians worldwide. Most live in India, where they are called Parsees (meaning 'Persians').

Good versus evil

Zoroastrianism focuses on the cosmic struggle between the forces of good and evil. Ahura Mazda, the supreme, eternal God and creator of life, battles against Angra Mainyu, the destructive force. Every act of human greed, hatred or evil weakens Ahura Mazda, but if human beings work for good, Ahura Mazda is strengthened in his fight.

Through correct action and ritual, Zoroastrians believe they can help tip the balance in this cosmic, dualistic struggle. In practice, this means action to benefit the community at large, such as involvement in medical, educational and civic organizations. Zoroastrians believe that, after death, a person's soul is taken to the Bridge of Judgement where their good and bad deeds are assessed. If bad deeds outweigh the good, the soul is led to a place of torment; if good deeds prevail, it is led to paradise.

No Ruz

No Ruz, or New Year's Day, is the major festival of the Zoroastrian year. It celebrates the creation of fire – a symbol of righteousness – and looks forward to the final triumph of good over evil. On the Fasli calendar – one of three Zorastrian calendars – No Ruz is held on 21 March. On the ancient Qadimi and Shahanshahi calendars, the festival takes place in July and August, respectively.

Preparations begin days ahead, with houses being cleaned and new clothes made. During the last five days of the old year, the 'Feast of all Souls' is celebrated, with recitals of hymns by Zarasthrustra to welcome the souls of the dead.

SEVEN SEASONAL CELEBRATIONS

Gahambar or 'proper season' is the term for six of the seven obligatory festivals instituted by Zarathrustra to honour Ahura Mazda and the Amesha Spentas ('Holy Immortals'). A seventh festival – No Ruz – marks the beginning of the New Year. The Amesha Spentas dwell in and protect the 'seven creations of the world'.

Festivals and the 'seven creations'

1 MAIDHYOIZAREMAYA
(Mid-spring) Sky
2 MAIDHYOISHEMA
(Mid-summer) Water
3 PAITISHAHYA
(Bringing in corn) Earth
4 AYATHRIMA
(Homecoming of the herds) Plants
5 MAIDHYAIRYA
(Mid-winter) Cattle
6 HAMASPATHMAEDAYA
(All Souls) Humans
7 NO RUZ
(New Day) Fire

No Ruz is a joyous occasion, marked by visits to fire temples to pray for the well-being of the family and community, and by festival meals, exchanging presents and calling on relatives and friends.

The New Year table

The family table is covered with a clean white tablecloth, and various foods and symbolic objects are placed upon it. These include a copy of the Gathas, a lit lamp, painted eggs for productivity, fish swimming in a bowl, to represent life, a silver coin for wealth, sprouting beans or wheat, representing prosperity, and sweets and rosewater for happiness.

The food consists of seven types that, in Persian, start with the letter 's' and seven others that begin with 'sh'. They include wine, sugar, milk, syrup, honey, sweetmeats and sweets. They symbolize the 'seven creations' of Zoroastrianism and welcome the arrival of spring.

When family and friends exchange greetings on No Ruz, they say 'May you be with us at the ceremony and may you be righteous.' Before sharing the meal, guests are invited to smile into a mirror laid on the table, so that their smile may continue throughout the year. They are then asked to look at the silver coin, to be blessed with prosperity in the year ahead.

THE THREE ZOROASTRIAN CALENDARS

The ancient Iranian calendar had twelve months of 30 days each. In the third century AD, five days were added to the end of each year. The calender continued to undergo various reforms to stabilize it according to the seasons. There are now three Zoroastrian calendars in use:

Fasli ('seaonal') 365 days in the year, with a day added every every fourth year.

Shahanshahi (or Shenshai) 360 days, based on the old religious calendar, and adjusted from time to time by adding an extra month.

Qadimi ('ancient') adopted in the eighteenth century by those who believed the Irani calendar represented a more ancient tradition. The Qadimi is one month ahead of the Shahanshahi.

SHINTO FESTIVALS

Shinto, or the 'Way of the Kami', is the indigenous folk religion of Japan. *Kami* are the sacred and mysterious powers found throughout heaven and earth. They may be the spirits in mountains, in animals, trees or oceans, or spirits that are patrons to fishermen, farmers or other groups. They may be the guardians or founding spirits of a village, a family or the nation as whole. To Japanese people, kami are close to everyday life and they worship them at *jinja,* or shrines.

Many festivals celebrate seasonal changes and the agricultural cycle. For instance, the festival 'Autumn Moon Viewing', traditionally held on the 15th day of the eighth month in the lunar calendar, celebrates the beauty and clarity of the full moon. Between the end of April and late June, 'Rice Planting' festivals take place to invoke the kami of the rice plant. Even though nowadays rice planting is largely mechanized, many of the offering rituals have survived.

Four festivals – New Year, O Bon, spring equinox and autumn equinox – honour the ancestors, whose peace and well-being are believed directly to affect the fortunes and health of the family and the community. Originally, New Year was a festival to welcome ancestors back home, but now the emphasis is on collective visiting of major shrines and temples.

A well beneath a tori gate in the grounds of a Shinto temple.

The Japanese year is traditionally divided into four seasons: spring, summer, autumn and winter. Even before the introduction of the Gregorian calendar in 1872, farmers kept in harmony with the seasons by using a solar dating system, the *nijushi sekki*, alongside the lunar calendar. The year was made up of twenty-four periods of 15 or 16 days each. The first day of each period has a name describing its season. For example, Risshun, or 'becoming spring', is regarded as the first day of spring.

Celebrating the New Year

In Shintoism, each year is treated as a distinct unit, and all debts should be settled and all duties performed before starting afresh in the new year. The coming of the new year is when the kami are revitalized, making it the most auspicious time to seek their blessing.

The 25–28 December is the time for *mochi-tsuki*, the traditional pounding of rice to make *mochi* (rice cakes). Some of these are put aside as offerings before the household shrine and the rest, which symbolically contain rice kami, are eaten over the New Year.

The last day of the year is called *omisoka*. By then, people will have cleaned their houses, made any final arrangements and prepared their *osechi ryori*: nests of boxes containing food such as fish and sliced vegetables in sweet vinegar, that will be eaten during *Oshogatsu*, the first three days of the New Year.

At omisoka a pine decoration (*kadomatsu*) is hung on both sides of the entrance to the home to welcome good fortune, and a *shimenawa* (a straw rope laced with strips of paper) is hung above the front entrance to prevent evil spirits entering. Millions of people travel to Shinto temples and shrines during Oshogatsu to make the important first visit of the year, praying for health and prosperity for themselves and their families in the months ahead.

Dolls and flowers

Hina Matsuri – 'Doll Festival' – takes place on 3 March. Elaborately dressed dolls are displayed at home on a special tiered platform. Originally, simple straw or paper dolls were placed near babies to ward off disease, and on the third day of the third lunar month they were floated downstream to carry away illness. Hina Matsuri is now known as 'Girls' Day', and is a time to pray for the protection, health and happiness of young girls.

On 8 April, Hana Matsuri – 'Flower Festival' – celebrates the birth of the Buddha. The occasion also recalls a time when wild mountain flowers were gathered to protect the kami of the rice fields.

Honouring the ancestors

Higan is a time when visits are made to family graves to clear burial plots and lay offerings of flowers, food and incense. It takes place in the seven-day period surrounding the spring equinox, which falls on 20 or 21 March, and again at the time of the autumn equinox, occurring on 23 or 24 September.

In spring, in southern Japan, Higan coincides with the cherry blossom trees coming into bloom. Renowned for its fragility and beauty, the cherry blossom is a symbol of purity and simplicity, and its flowering season, from March to early May, brings thousands of people outdoors to picnic under the trees.

O-BON FESTIVAL

Dedicated to the ancestors, O-Bon lasts from 13 to 15 August. At this time, it is believed, the spirits of the ancestors return to the family home, where they are welcomed and venerated. Fires are lit to guide the spirits back, lanterns are hung, food and flower offerings are laid before ancestor shrines and memorial services are held to honour them. As the festival draws to a close, the fires are rekindled to bid them farewell, until their return the following year. A fuller description of O-Bon is given on pages 122-3

One of the elaborately decorated floats that are pulled through the streets of Kyoto during Gion Matsuri, a festival inaugurated in AD 869 to combat an epidemic that had threatened this ancient capital.

Jain Festivals

Jain means 'follower of the Jina' or 'spiritual victor' – someone whose soul has overcome desires and broken its attachment to the physical world. Jina is the name given by Jains to the twenty-four *tirthankaras*: great teachers who showed that it is possible for ordinary people to overcome physical constraints so that their soul can attain a pure state free from rebirth. The word tirthankara means 'bridge-maker', indicating the role as guide and example for those who wish to achieve the same goal.

Journey to enlightenment

Jains believe that every living being has an eternal soul that passes from one life to the next. The soul is bound by karma – matter that attaches itself to the soul through greed, passion, deceit or hatred. Only when the soul breaks free of these karmic ties, does it attain true knowledge and freedom. The spiritual journey to free the soul from suffering is not governed by a deity, divine force or activity: each individual is responsible for his or her own journey to enlightenment, using the guidance provided by the Jinas.

Offering Puja at the feet of a Jain statue.

Jain history begins with the great teacher Mahavira, who lived from 599 to 527 BC. Jains believe, however, that the universe is eternal and time passes in cycles each lasting millions of years. In each cycle there is a time of ascent, when human behaviour and all life progress; and a time of descent, when knowledge and behaviour are in decline. Mahavira was the last of the twenty-four Tirthankaras, who lived in the current cycle, which is regarded as being in a period of decline.

Following the death of Mahavira, two main groups arose within the Jain tradition. They were divided over issues of scripture, the role of women, clothing and monastic practice. The Digambaras maintained that someone who has truly renounced all worldly attachments should go naked. The Shvetambaras said that Mahavira's teaching did not demand this, and the wearing of a simple white garment would be sufficient to indicate worldly renunciation. All Jains, however, share a commitment to the practice of *ahimsa* – non-violence – as a means of separating the soul not only from acts of injury to anything that has life, but from feelings of aggression or harm. The practice of ahimsa is central to the soul's journey to final liberation.

Timing of the Festivals

The Jain religious year follows the months of the ancient Indian Sanskrit calendar used by Hindus. Each month is made up of 30 *tithis*, or lunar days, which are equivalent to approximately 29^{1}2 solar days. A dark fortnight, or *krsnapaksha*, in every month begins with the appearance of the full moon and is followed by a bright half, or *suklapaksha*, which starts with the new moon.

The principal Jain festivals are linked to major events in the lives of the Tirthankaras, particularly Rshabha, the first Tirthankara, Parshva, the twenty-third, and Mahavira, the twenty-fourth and final Tirthankara. There are also a number of fast days in each month. The most prominent of these falls on the third day of the bright half of the month of Vaisakha and commemorates the first occasion that Rshabha was given alms. The most important festival for most Jains, however, is Paryushana – a period of retreat, study and reflection – which occurs in the month of Bhadrapad (August–September).

MEDITATION AND CONFESSION

The Paryushana festival stems from the tradition that monks and nuns remain in one place during the rainy season, which normally lasts about four months, and a minimum of seventy days.

Paryushana must begin by the fifth day of the bright half of Bhadrapad. It is celebrated for eight days by the lay members of the Shvetambaras, but ten days by lay members of the Digambaras.

The rains' retreat gives members of the lay community the opportunity to renew their faith, listen to readings and commentaries on scriptures and practise austerities alongside the monastic community.

In addition to fasting and study, this is a time for individuals to concentrate on their spiritual development, using a form of meditation called *pratikramana*, which means 'turning back'. Part of this practice is a reflection on past transgressions, leading up to Samvatsari, the final day of the festival, when lay people confess their misdeeds both to each other and to the monastic community.

A lay woman offers early morning puja before a statue of a Tirthankara at a Jain temple in Khajuraho. This act of worship helps to focus the mind on detachment from the material world and thereby reduce the ties of karma.

BAHA'I FESTIVALS

The Baha'i faith originated in the mid-nineteenth century in what is today Iran. It is based on the belief that the man born as Mirza Husayn Ali in 1817 was the prophet sent by God to the present age. He is now known as Baha'u'llah, the 'Glory of God'. He was preceded, and his prophethood foretold, by a man known as the Bab – according to Shi'a tradition, a gate through whom God communicates with humanity. After great persecution of himself and his followers, the Bab was executed by firing squad in 1850. One of his closest followers was Mirza Husayn Ali, from a wealthy Persian Muslim family, whom he named Baha'u'llah, 'Glory of God'. Baha'u'llah was a prolific writer and his writings are regarded as revelation from God. After his death in 1892 his son, 'Abdu'l Baha, was appointed interpreter of his father's writings.

The faith and its followers

Baha'is believe in One God, creator of all, who has revealed himself through different prophets at different times. To Baha'is, the sacred texts of Krishna, Moses, Buddha, Jesus and Muhammad were appropriate for their respective times, with each set of revelations superseded by the next, as humanity, which is held to be essentially good, continues to develop socially and religiously.

Today there are some 5 million Baha'is, distributed over every continent of the world. In Iran the faith has been strongly persecuted, and although Baha'is of Iranian origin are still numerous, most of the faithful today are from outside Iran, and traditions and practices depend on the local context.

Entrance to the tomb of Baha'u'llah in Haifa, Israel.

After the Bab's execution Baha'u'llah was put in prison, where he had a mystical experience which showed him that he was the prophet foretold by the Bab. Even after his release, Baha'u'llah told no one of his experience until 1863. He was then living in exile in Baghdad and was summoned to appear before the Ottoman authorities in Constantinople. Before setting off, he spent twelve days in a large garden near his house, where many Babis (followers of the Bab) gathered round him. There, he declared his prophethood to a few of his closest associates.

Baha'is commemorate the twelve days as the festival of Ridvan, especially the first day, when Baha'u'llah arrived in the garden, the ninth, when his family joined him, and the twelfth, when he left for Constantinople. There, Baha'u'llah was held under house arrest until, in 1868, he and his family were exiled to the remote and bleak city of Acre, in present-day Israel. Here Baha'u'llah continued his writing and the Baha'i faith began to spread around the world. Baha'is celebrate 'Abdu'l Baha's life and works on the 'Day of the Covenant', (4 Qawl) believing that both father and son ascended to heaven when they died.

FEASTING AND FASTING

Baha'i's follow a calendar introduced by the Bab, with nineteen months of nineteen days each, making a total of 361 days. Most of the festivals are related to the lives of the Bab, Baha'u'llah and 'Abdu'l Baha. Baha'i years are counted from the date of the Bab's declaration. On major festival days Baha'is do no work, but celebrate across the world in different ways.

Naw-Ruz is a very ancient Persian festival, and some traditions, such as growing green shoots on a plate, are still practised by Iranian Baha'is. It is celebrated at the spring equinox, bringing the fasting period of 'Ala to an end with feasting and rejoicing.

During the month of 'Ala, adult Baha'is refrain from food and drink in daylight hours. The intercalary days are a time for giving gifts and for hospitality and celebration.

During Ridvan each Baha'i assembly elects an administrative body for that year. On the first day of every month each local assembly meets, often in a member's home, for the 'Nineteen-day Feast'. This is an evening of prayer and devotional readings, with a democratic discussion of assembly business and also a social gathering with food and games.

BAHA'I NINETEEN-MONTH CALENDAR

1 NAW-RUZ – New Year's Day (1 BAHA)

2 RIDVAN (13 JALAL–5 JAMAL)

3 ANNIVERSARY OF THE DECLARATION OF THE BAB (7 'AZAMAT)

4 ASCENSION OF BAHA'U'LLAH (13 'AZAMAT)

5 ANNIVERSARY OF THE MARTYRDOM OF THE BAB (16 RAHMAT)

6 ANNIVERSARY OF THE BIRTH OF THE BAB (5 'ILM)

7 BIRTHDAY OF BAHA'U'LLAH (12 QUDRAT)

8 INTERCALARY DAYS

9 FAST OF 'ALA

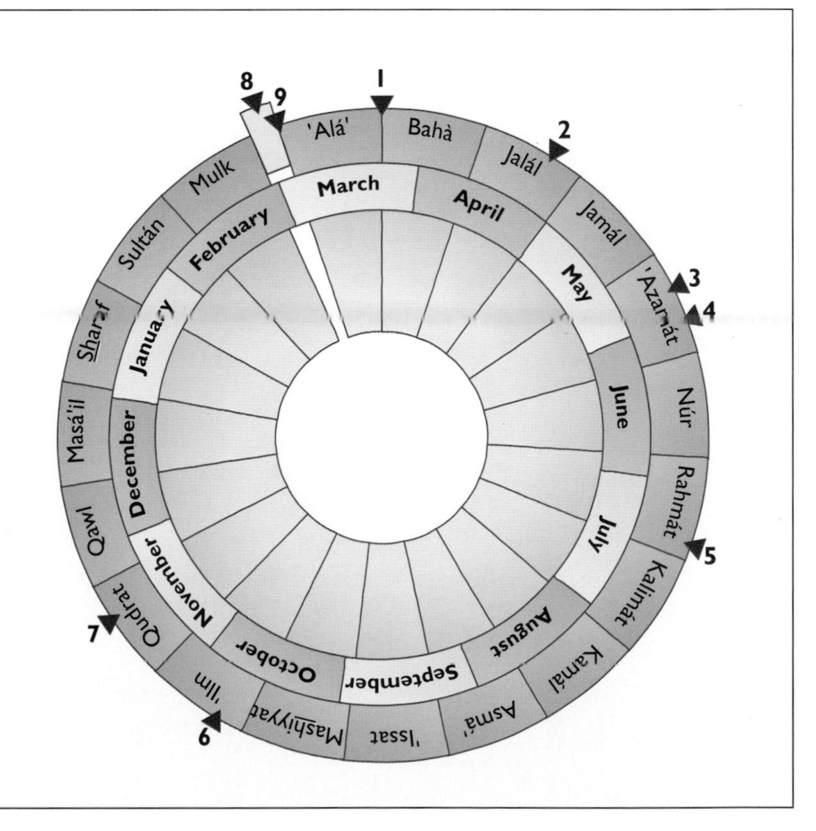

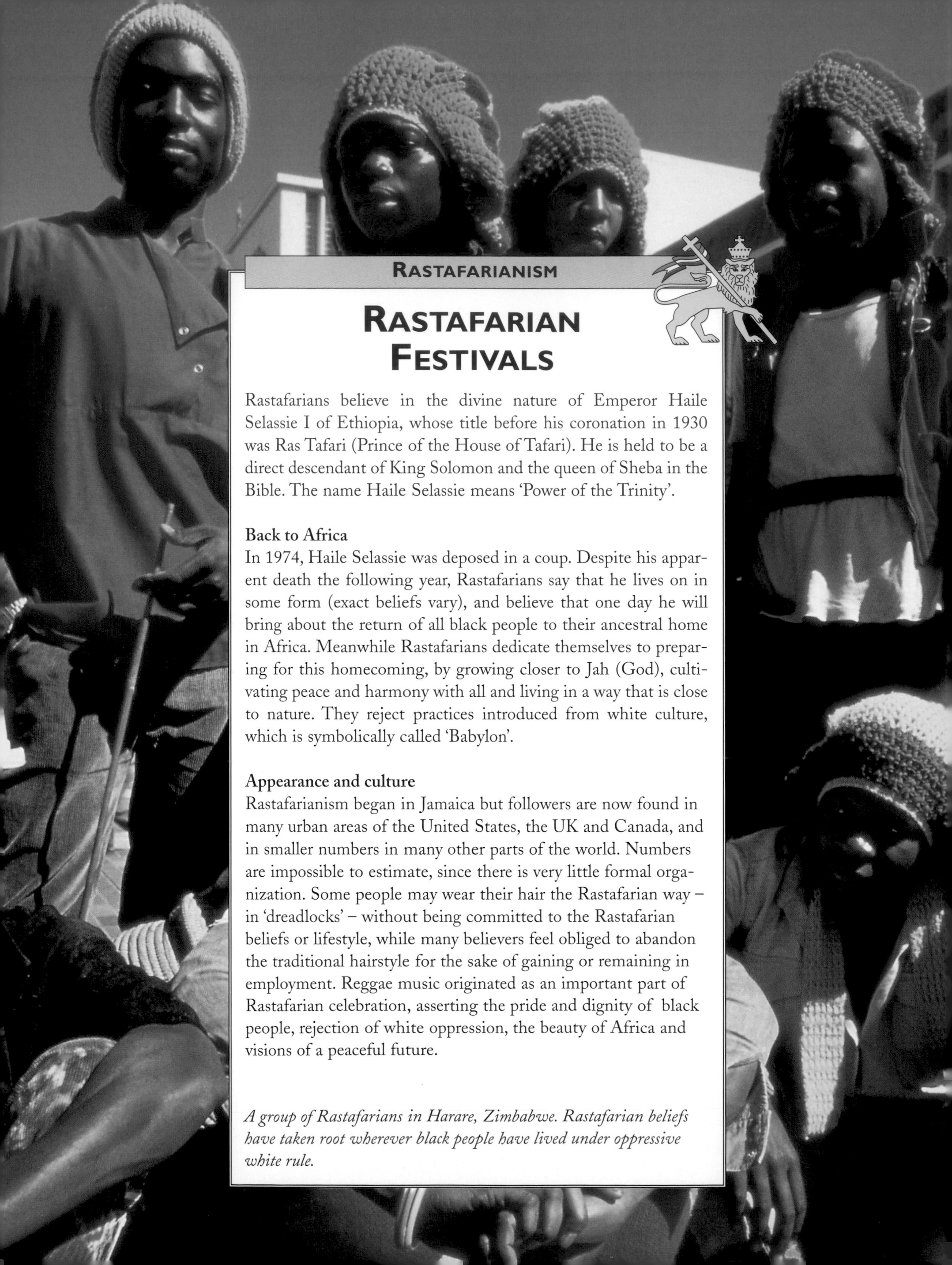

RASTAFARIAN FESTIVALS

Rastafarians believe in the divine nature of Emperor Haile Selassie I of Ethiopia, whose title before his coronation in 1930 was Ras Tafari (Prince of the House of Tafari). He is held to be a direct descendant of King Solomon and the queen of Sheba in the Bible. The name Haile Selassie means 'Power of the Trinity'.

Back to Africa

In 1974, Haile Selassie was deposed in a coup. Despite his apparent death the following year, Rastafarians say that he lives on in some form (exact beliefs vary), and believe that one day he will bring about the return of all black people to their ancestral home in Africa. Meanwhile Rastafarians dedicate themselves to preparing for this homecoming, by growing closer to Jah (God), cultivating peace and harmony with all and living in a way that is close to nature. They reject practices introduced from white culture, which is symbolically called 'Babylon'.

Appearance and culture

Rastafarianism began in Jamaica but followers are now found in many urban areas of the United States, the UK and Canada, and in smaller numbers in many other parts of the world. Numbers are impossible to estimate, since there is very little formal organization. Some people may wear their hair the Rastafarian way – in 'dreadlocks' – without being committed to the Rastafarian beliefs or lifestyle, while many believers feel obliged to abandon the traditional hairstyle for the sake of gaining or remaining in employment. Reggae music originated as an important part of Rastafarian celebration, asserting the pride and dignity of black people, rejection of white oppression, the beauty of Africa and visions of a peaceful future.

A group of Rastafarians in Harare, Zimbabwe. Rastafarian beliefs have taken root wherever black people have lived under oppressive white rule.

Most local Rastafarian groups meet once a week for prayer and study, and sometimes hold a larger, monthly meeting with prayers and psalms, which continues into the night with singing, chanting and drumming.

A Nyabingi ceremony brings together believers from a wider area, and often lasts for several days. There is chanting, drumming, singing, praying and dancing as well as the sharing of vegetarian food and the smoking of Ganja (marijuana).

Some of the occasions for a Nyabingi are based on the Julian calendar used by the Ethiopian Orthodox Church, with which the Rastafarian faith has strong links. Hence, Ethiopian New Year is celebrated on 11 September, and Christmas Day on 7 January. Other occasions, including Haile Selassie's birthday (23 July) and the anniversaries of his coronation (2 November), are specifically Rastafarian. Influential prophets and teachers may also be commemorated, but there is no official festival calendar.

Rastafarian teaching from the Bible. Rastafarians lay great stress on individual bible study and interpretation.

Symbolism

Rastafarians have a specialized form of language that helps them express some of their beliefs and assert their distinctiveness from the cultures around them. When speaking in the first person among themselves, and sometimes not only among themselves, they use the form 'I and I'. This expresses the unity between all people of goodwill, and between human beings and Jah (God). Reinforcing this symbolism, many other words are changed to include the syllable 'I'. A Nyabingi, for example, is sometimes known as an 'Issemble' (adapted from 'assemble').

The Rastafarian colours are red, gold and green. Red symbolizes the blood of martyrs and others killed as a result of oppression by whites; gold represents the wealth of Ethiopia and green stands for its vegetation.

Rastafarian men often grow their hair long and twist it into dreadlocks. They wash their hair in pure water but do not comb it. Not only is long hair a symbol of black pride, it also obeys a verse in the Bible (Leviticus 21:5) that forbids the cutting of hair.

THE HOLY PIBY

Rastafarians use the same scriptures as Jews and Christians, but their interpretations are different. Some use the King James English version of the Bible, but treat it with caution because it was translated by white people. Most use the Holy Piby, a version held to be a translation from Amharic (the language of Ethiopia).

THE HOLY HERB

The use of Ganja, a form of marijuana, is an essential part of religious life for Rastafarians. While they forbid the taking of other drugs, including coffee, they believe that the 'herbs' mentioned in the Bible refer to the sacramental use of Ganja. They do not use Ganja recreationally, but it is used in all major celebrations, to enhance feelings of peace and community, aid meditation and inspire religious visions.

Festivals in the Future

Festivals tend to be one of the most long-lasting of all features of religion, and their centrality, proved over time, is the bedrock of most faiths. But, increasingly, they are being celebrated for reasons that have little or nothing to do with their original purpose. For example, the Christian population of Japan is less than 3 per cent, yet Christmas in Japan is a huge event – popular, widespread and commercially lucrative. For many it is a winter festival that offers an opportunity for shopping, food, friends and enjoyment.

In Britain, schools now regularly 'celebrate' Chinese New Year and Divali. For some schools this reflects the ethnic and religious mix of the school, but in most cases these festivals have become part of the festival calendar of the school, valued for their classroom usefulness, colour, vibrancy and accessibility. At the same time, arts festivals, gastronomic festivals, street festivals and many other events are increasing in number, drawing together people who have similar interests and enjoyments.

While all the faiths still have their major festivals, many lesser festivals have died out over the centuries. For example, in Britain, Whitsun used to be an important festival and was the reason for a public holiday. 'Whit walks' were popular as were 'Whit fairs', especially in the north of England. But, over the past fifty years or so, this festival has become much less significant for people. Meanwhile many new festivals are being created. Only time will tell whether they find their place in popular culture – the determining factor in whether they are successful. Unless we need them in some way, they will not take root.

International weeks concerned with issues as diverse as mountains, refugees, women and children also try to build upon the tradition of festivals, and, increasingly, international organizations have sought to create festivals and celebrations. These can usefully focus attention on important matters, but often fall into the trap of preaching rather than entertaining. One thing that all the great religious festivals have in common is that they are primarily entertaining.

However, some of the newer festivals whose emphasis is on entertainment would seem to be there primarily to get people to spend money. Father's Day, Grandmother's Day and so on are largely commercial ventures, although they may grow in importance in a culture where families are fragmenting. So is it commercialism or family need that is driving these new festivals? It is hard to know at present.

In the Middle Ages an average Christian country, such as Italy, would have had as many as a hundred holy days, or holidays. Nowadays, in most cultures, far fewer festivals are celebrated, but the shorter working week gives people more free time for recreation of other kinds. Perhaps the rise of newer festivals is a sign that, in an increasingly flexible pattern of shift work, there is the need today, more than any time in the past few hundred years, to set aside some fixed time for celebration, fasting and feasting, and for partying and reflection.

Moreover, the desire to celebrate would appear to be growing. More and more people are taking an interest in the stories, rituals, foods, clothes and theatre associated with festivals, some of which have crossed over boundaries of culture and religion to become part of the worldwide range of entertainment. As a result, the original reason behind them may be forgotten. But even if different communities give these great, ancient festivals a new meaning that has little to do with the original one, they will probably function in much the same way – providing a time for reflection and thought as well as fun.

In 2001, members of eleven faiths gathered alongside the World Wildlife Find for Nature in the Kathmandu Valley, Nepal. They celebrated a wide range of environmental projects that were developed and run by faith communities worldwide.

Glossary of Festival Terms

Since festivals are predominantly religious, glossary entries are keyed to the relevant religion(s) as follows: [B] = Buddhism; [C] = Christianity; [H] = Hinduism; [I] = Islam; [Ja] = Jainism; [Ju] = Judaism; [R] = Rastafariansim; [S] =Sikhism; [Sh] = Shintoism; [T] =Taoism; [gen.] = general.

ahimsa [H, Ja] the principle of non-violence.
Akhand path [S] a continuous reading of the Guru Granth Sahib.
Allah [I] the Arabic word for God.
amrit [S] sweetened water used for initiation into the Khalsa.
Apostle [C] one of the original followers of Jesus appointed to preach his message.
Ark [Ju] in a synagogue, the cupboard or curtained alcove where the Torah scrolls are kept. In biblical times, the stone tablets of the Law were carried in a special Ark or chest with carrying poles.
arti (H) light offered to a deity or deities during puja, using a special lamp, accompanied by prayers.
ascension [C] Jesus' return to heaven forty days after his resurrection.
Ashkenazi [Ju] the tradition of Judaism that developed in northern Europe.
atman [H] the personal, individual spirit or soul.
Aum (H) the sacred syllable, according to scriptures the first sound out of which the rest of the universe was created.
avatar [H] one of the incarnations of a god, especially Vishnu.

bhakti [H] loving devotion to a particular deity.
bodhisattva [B] a being destined to become a Buddha; a bodhisattva compassionately helps others while maturing their own wisdom.
Brahman [H] the energy that sustains the universe, the world-soul.
brahmin [H] a member of the highest caste, often a priest or teacher.

canon [gen.] a collection of texts that by agreement comprises the authentic scriptures.
crucifixion [C] usually, the death of Jesus by being nailed to a cross; the standard Roman method of execution.

denomination [C] a division of Christianity.
dhamma see dharma.
dharma [B, H] the natural, unchanging laws that sustain the universe; in Hinduism, law or social duty; in Buddhism, the teachings and the truth of the world.
diva [H] a small lamp, usually made of clay, with a wick, which burns oil or ghee.

enlightenment [B] the state of being aware of, or awakened to, the true nature of existence and the realization of the way to end suffering.
Exodus [Ju, C] the release of the Hebrew people from captivity in Egypt and their journey to the Promised Land, as described the book of Exodus in the Bible.
exorcism [gen.] the casting out or laying to rest of ghosts or evil spirits.

five Ks [S] the five signs of faith worn by Sikh men: kesh, uncut hair; kanga, a comb; kara, a steel bangle; kirpan, a small sword or dagger; kacchera, short trousers or breeches.

Gospel [C] one of the four accounts of the life of Jesus in the New Testament.
Granthi [S] one who has studied the Sikh scriptures and faith.
Gregorian [gen.] the calendar introduced by Pope Gregory XIII in 1582, now adopted as the standard calendar in the western world.
gurdwara [S] the Sikh place of worship.
Gurpurb [S] a festival commemorating the birth or death of one of the Sikh gurus
guru [B, H, S] a religious teacher.
Guru Granth Sahib [S] the Sikh holy book, regarded as a living guru.

Hadith [I] the words of the Prophet Muhammad, care fully recorded and used as a guide to Muslim life.
Hajj [I] pilgrimage to Makkah.
Hijrah [I] the migration of Muslims from Makkah to found the first Islamic state in Medina in AD 622.

imam [I] the leader and teacher of a Muslim community.
incarnation [C, H, B, Ja, S] taking on a body of flesh: in Christianity, the earthly life of God as Jesus; in Hinduism, the earthly lives of Vishnu; in several faiths, one of the many lives of an individual.

Jah [R] the Rastafarian word for God.
Jina [Ja] conqueror, the title given by Jains to twenty-four great teachers.

Julian [gen.] the calendar first introduced by Julius Caesar, precursor of the Gregorian calendar; still used by a few religious groups.

Ka'ba [I] the House of God in Makkah, a cube-shaped structure, the centre of Muslim prayer.
kami [Sh] spirits found in the natural world, in sacred objects or in symbols; or divine beings.
kamma see **karma**.
karma [B, H, Ja] the accumulated effects of actions in this and previous lives; the law of cause and effect.
Khalsa [S] the community of committed Sikhs dedicated to upholding their faith and defending the weak.

laity [gen.] ordinary members of a religious community; believers who have not been ordained as a monks, nuns or priests.
layman/laywoman a member of the laity.
lama [B] in Tibetan Buddhism, a religious teacher.
langar [S] the free meal offered to all comers when Sikhs meet for worship.
lingam (H) phallic representation of the god Shiva, the form in which he is most often worshipped.

Mahayana [B] 'Great Vehicle', the northern and eastern traditions of Buddhism.
mantra [B, H, Ja] words that are repeated as worship or meditation.
menorah [Ju] a lamp-stand or candelabrum. The traditional symbol of Judaism is a seven-branched menorah recalling the one in the Temple of Jerusalem. At the festival of Hanukah a nine-branched menorah is lit.
Mishnah [Ju] a second-century AD compilation of judgements and discussions by rabbis to help interpret the Torah.
moksha [H, Ja] release from the cycle of rebirth.
mosque [I] Muslim house of worship.

nibbana see **nirvana**.
nirvana [B] final release from the law of karma; a state of supreme peace and liberation from suffering.
Nyabingi [R] Rastafarian meeting for chanting and prayer.

Om see **Aum**.
Orthodox [C, Ju] in Christianity, the churches that arose in the eastern Roman Empire; in Judaism, the tradition that upholds a strict and literal interpretation of the Jewish law.

pantheon [gen.] several gods within one faith or belief system.
prashad (H) food offerings sanctified at the temple or shrine and then offered to devotees present.
prophet [Ju, C, I] a man or woman who acts as a messenger from God, either in words or actions.
puja [B, H, Ja] the act of worship or devotion.

Qur'an [I] the Muslim holy book, containing the revelations given to the Prophet Muhammad.

rabbi [Ju] Hebrew for 'teacher'. A rabbi leads the worship and study in a synagogue.
rakhi [H] a ribbon or thread tied round the wrist as a token of protection.
rangoli [H] patterns made at festival times with coloured powder, rice or sand.
reincarnation [H, B, Ja, S] being reborn in a different body or form.
relic [gen.] part of the body or belongings of a holy person, revered by the faithful.
resurrection [C] rising from death, especially Jesus' rise from death, celebrated at the Easter festival.

Sabbath [Ju] English version of the Hebrew word Shabbat – see **Shabbat**.
samsara [H, Ja] the endless cycle of death and rebirth.
Sangha [B] the community of Buddhist monks and nuns.
Sephardi [Ju] the tradition of Judaism that developed in countries bordering the Mediterranean.
sewa [S] the principle of humble service to others.
Shabbat [Ju] the seventh day of the week, set aside for celebration and relaxation, when no work is done.
shahada [I] testimony summarizing the central belief of Islam.
shari'ah [I] the system of Muslim civil and criminal law.
Shema [Ju] the first and most important words of the Ten Commandments, enjoining wholehearted worship of the one God; named after the first word, shema – 'hear' in Hebrew.
Shi'a [I] the smaller of the two main divisions of Islam, named after the 'partisans' of Muhammad's son-in-law Ali.
Shivite [H] a worshipper of the god Shiva.
stupa [B] a bell-shaped structure usually associated with a temple, which contains relics.
sukkah [Ju] a temporary shelter made for the festival of Sukkot.
sunnah [I] the actions of the Prophet Muhammad, carefully recorded and used as a guide to Muslim life.

Sunni [I] the largest division of Islam.
sutra [B] a piece of teaching said to have been delivered by the historical Buddha; often named after its place of delivery, the person to whom it was addressed or its subject matter.
sutta see **sutra**.
synagogue [Ju] Jewish house of prayer, study and community.

Talmud [Ju] a sixth-century AD compilation of judgements and discussions by rabbis to help interpret the Torah.
Tao [T] the creative cosmic force that is manifest in the natural order of the universe.
testament [C] 'witness'. Christians divide the Bible into two parts, the Old Testament (the witness of the Jewish prophets) and the New Testament (the witnesses to the life of Jesus).
Theravada [B] 'Teachings of the Elders', the southern tradition of Buddhism, found in Sri Lanka and South East Asia.
tirthankara [Ja] 'bridge-maker', title given to those who have achieved freedom from rebirth and taught a way for others to follow.
Torah [Ju] the Law. The word is used for God's everlasting law, for the particular laws as given to Moses on Mount Sinai and for the first five books of the Hebrew Bible, which contain these laws.
Tripitaka [B] 'Three Baskets', the three groups of Theravada Buddhist texts.

ummah [I] the worldwide community of all Muslims.
uposatha [B] day of special religious observance regulated by phases of the moon.
Vaishnavite [H] a devotee of Vishnu in one of his forms, often that of Krishna.
Veda [H, Ja] the most ancient Sanskrit scriptures.
Vinaya [B] one of three divisions of Buddhist texts relating to the formation of the Sangha and its code of conduct.

zakat [I] welfare tax paid as a proportion of wealth by all Muslims.
zodiac [gen.] the path apparently taken by the sun against the background of the fixed stars as the year progresses; divisions in this path into different 'signs', used to track the passage of the year.

FURTHER READING AND WEB SITES

Smart , Ninian , The World's Religions 2nd Ed 1998, Cambridge University Press; ISBN: 0521637481
Zaehner , R.C. (Editor), The Hutchinson Encyclopedia of Living Faiths revised edition 1997, Helicon; ISBN: 1859862187
The New Penguin Handbook of Living Religions 2nd Ed 2000, Penguin Books; ISBN: 0140514805
Bowker , John (Editor), The Concise Oxford Dictionary of World Religions abridged and updated edition, 2000, Oxford Paperbacks; ISBN: 0192800949
Hinnells, John R. (Editor), The Penguin Dictionary of Religions, Penguin, 1984; ISBN 0140511067
Breuilly, O'Brien and Palmer, Religions of the World, Macdonald Young Books, 1997
Weller, Paul, (Editor), Religions in the UK: A Multi-Faith Dictionary 2nd Ed 1997, The Multi-Faith Centre at the University of Derby; ISBN 0901437689

SOME USEFUL WEBSITES

Baha'i:
http://newbounty.new-era.net/bahaivision
Buddhism
http://www.buddhanet.org
Christianity
http://www.oca.org *(Website of the Orthodox Church in America)*
http://www.catholic.org
Hinduism
http://www.hindunet.org
Islam
http://www.islam.org
Judaism
http://virtualjerusalem.com
Rastafarian
since web information changes rapidly, we recommend using a search engine
Sikhism
http://www.sikhseek.com
Several faiths:
http://home.about.com/religion *(follow links to information about a particular faith)*
http://www.holidays.net *(information about many different religious and other festivals)*
http://www.bbc.co.uk/worldservice/people/features/world_religions

Index